MANAGEMENT SCIENCE

*A Bayesian
Introduction*

PRENTICE-HALL INTERNATIONAL, INC., *London*
PRENTICE-HALL OF AUSTRALIA, PTY. LTD., *Sydney*
PRENTICE-HALL OF CANADA, LTD., *Toronto*
PRENTICE-HALL OF INDIA PRIVATE LTD., *New Delhi*
PRENTICE-HALL OF JAPAN, INC., *Tokyo*

PRENTICE-HALL INTERNATIONAL SERIES IN MANAGEMENT

PRENTICE-HALL, INC.

PRENTICE-HALL INTERNATIONAL, INC., UNITED KINGDOM AND EIRE

PRENTICE-HALL OF CANADA, LTD., CANADA

J. H. DE BUSSY, LTD., HOLLAND AND FLEMISH-SPEAKING BELGIUM

DUNOD PRESS, FRANCE

MARUZEN COMPANY, LTD., FAR EAST

HERRERO HERMANOS, SUCS., SPAIN AND LATIN AMERICA

R. OLDENBOURG VERLAG, GERMANY

ULRICO HOEPLI EDITORS, ITALY

MANAGEMENT SCIENCE

A Bayesian Introduction

WILLIAM T. MORRIS

Professor of Industrial Engineering
The Ohio State University

PRENTICE-HALL, INC.
Englewood Cliffs, N. J.

Current Printing (last digit):

10 9 8 7 6 5 4 3 2 1

Library of Congress Catalog Card Number 68-20860
Printed in the United States of America

Preface

This book has two objectives: first, to present a balanced view of management science as a discipline and as a profession, and, secondly, to examine the possibilities for using Bayesian logic as an integrating structure to illuminate a fundamental unity among some of the diverse ideas in management science. The book suggests that bringing science to the support of management involves analysis and experiment, deduction and inference, modeling existing systems and designing new ones. Management science relies not only on mathematics but also on the findings of the behavioral sciences. It calls for both withdrawal into the abstractions of the laboratory and immersion in the pressures and complexities of managerial and organizational affairs.

The reader needs a basic knowledge of probability theory and will be helped by knowing some elementary calculus. A few exercises are directed to those who have also studied statistics.

My greatest intellectual debt is to the work of Robert Schlaifer whose books have brought about a virtual revolution in our thinking about management problems. I am indebted also to the graduate students whom I had the privilege of joining in research on applications of Bayesian ideas. My chairman, Dr. David F. Baker, arranged generous support for the research, writing, and testing involved in this effort. Miss Lynn Bowen and Mrs. Yvonne Kohli have cheerfully and skillfully done the typing.

W. T. M.

vii

Contents

Part III

Professional Problems of Management Science   185

I

The Basic Logic
of
Learning
and
Decision

1

Management and Science

Introduction

One basic problem of the profession of management is making reasonable decisions in the face of uncertainty or incomplete knowledge as to the consequences of one's actions. Establishing an inventory policy, funding a research project, launching a new project—all involve greater or lesser residues of uncertainty even after the reasonably available information has been considered. Meeting uncertainty is a pervasive problem which appears in many areas of human affairs including, of course, science. How to reduce uncertainty, how much to reduce it before acting, and what actions are reasonable in the face of uncertainty are the basic issues to be examined in this book. Do science and management answer questions in similar or quite different ways? What can be expected if one undertakes to use the approaches to these problems which are characteristic of science in the context of the ongoing affairs with which managers must cope?

To understand these problems it is helpful to have an overview, a conceptual structure, or a model with which to organize our ideas about that diverse, complex, sometimes subtle, always changing activity called *management*. Of the many ways of conceptualizing management, this book chooses one which aims at making particularly clear its relation to science and to the structure of a discipline which is coming to be called *management*

3

science. Care is needed in doing this, for we are on tricky ground. A considerable history of confusion surrounds various efforts to associate the notion of management with that of science. It may be best at the very outset to attempt some small clarification of the issues which have plagued both those who claimed that management was a science and those who denied that it ever could be.

References to *science* have, in the past, often been references to physics, in some ways the most successful of the sciences. Questions as to whether management was a science or whether it would become one, could often be understood as questions about similarities between management and physics. On the surface, the two activities are quite dissimilar. Physics is thought of as characterized by general laws of wide applicability producing highly reliable predictions, by carefully controlled laboratory experiments yielding very precise measurements, and by a pervading atmosphere of objectivity and impersonality. In short, classical physics is thought to have pretty thoroughly eliminated uncertainty about those phenomena which it has investigated.

Management, on the other hand, is often thought of as an activity in which experiments are difficult to control, most interesting aspects cannot be measured precisely, general laws are completely lacking, each management problem is viewed as unique, and the intuitive or "judgmental" application of subjective experience is the rule. Management is indeed an activity pervaded by high uncertainty and apparently in no interesting way like physics. This difficulty has arisen whenever some management phenomenon has been measured with precision, perhaps with a stop watch, and some attempt made at expressing the phenomenon in mathematical terms. Then management began in some small way to look like physics, and people were tempted to think that in some large way management could be like physics. Managers themselves have been justifiably impatient with any such proposal since it was so obviously out of touch with what they took to be the real nature of their work. In their impatience, however, they often succumbed to the temptation of asserting that science could in no useful way be related to management and that management must forever remain an art in which experience counts for nearly everything. Only rather recently has the heat of these discussions given way to what appears to be a somewhat clearer understanding of the underlying relation between science and management and of the ways in which this relationship can be enhanced.

Management as a Learning Process

The most useful overview or model of management is one which regards it as a learning process. This model, in its simplest terms, conceives of management as a process involving such steps as

1. Recognizing and conceptualizing a management decision problem, using both past experience and available data.

2. Making and implementing the decision.

3. Learning from the results of the decision how it should be modified and adding these results to the reservoir of experience on which future decisions may draw.

The process is thus one of deciding, acting, and learning from the resulting experience how to act more effectively in the future. It pictures management as a dynamic process and suggests that one may regard management as the mechanism by which organizational learning takes place. Similarly, one may think of management as the adaptive mechanism by which the firm continually readjusts itself, seeking an effective relationship with its environment.

It is not difficult, however, to picture science, too, as essentially a learning process. The names for the steps may differ but, as will be shown, the process is essentially the same. In a first model of scientific work, the scientist may be thought of as raising hypotheses based on his past experience and available knowledge, designing experiments to test these hypotheses, and assimilating the results of the experiments into his body of knowledge, to become a basis for the design of future experiments. One cannot help but notice, however, that the scientist is likely to be very explicit and public about these steps, whereas the manager is likely to leave much of their detail implicit in his thinking and to be content to have the process remain privately intuitive and perhaps even subconscious.

This leads, however to the basic hypotheses which will be the focus of attention.

1. The learning or adaptive process of science and of management can, however implicit or explicit, however intuitive or deliberate, be usefully regarded as involving essentially the same steps.

2. In at least some management situations, the effectiveness of the learning process can be enhanced by efforts to make it more like the explicit, deliberate, reasonable process of science.

3. The objective of management science is to improve and seek to optimize the process by which an organization learns or adapts.

The reader is urged to exercise the traditional caution of the conservative scientist and regard these statements as tentative hypotheses. The present task is to make them operational and explore the possible grounds for their confirmation.

A Model of Management

The first necessary step is to enrich our model of the management process. In doing this, be careful to note that no one is supposed to produce a description of the activities of every manager, nor a description of every management situation in exhaustive detail. One seeks only a model which is useful, in the sense that if management is thought of "as if" it were like the model, one is led toward insights which result ultimately in improvements in the actual management process.

A first enrichment of this model of the management process appears in Fig. 1-1. The process begins with a stimulus which suggests to the manager that

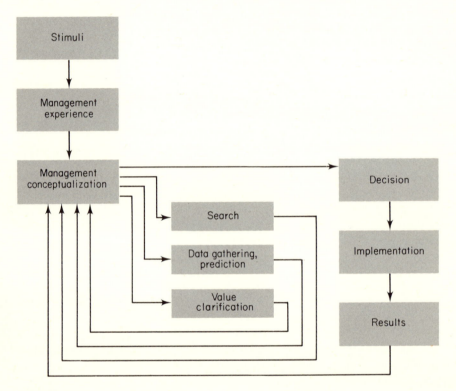

FIGURE 1-1

a decision situation is at hand: A machine has broken down; someone has resigned; a competitor has just launched a new product; last week's production report has just come in; the Federal Reserve Board has raised the discount rate—some such event serves as a stimulus to decision. Drawing both on his implicit past experience and the explicit experience in the firm's "data bank," a first conceptualization of the decision emerges in the manager's mind. Indeed, a *decision* means a conceptualization of a choice situation. This first conceptualization may be characterized by clarity and low uncertainty, particularly if the choice problem is a routine or familiar one. In such cases, the manager is ready to act without further delay.

Alternatively, the initial conceptualization may be characterized by confusion, doubts, missing information—in short, it may be characterized by high uncertainty. The manager may thus be dissatisfied with his conceptualization and unwilling to rely upon it as a basis for decision and action. Then we suppose he undertakes some program for reducing his uncertainty. Being uncertain that he is considering all of the reasonably available courses of action, the manager may undertake a program of search for additional alternatives. If he does so, and additional actions are discovered, these become part of his modified conceptualization of the decision problem. The crucial question here is how long to go on searching for additional actions before initiating some other response to the decision situation. Of course, after responding in some other way, the manager may later return to search again.

For any course of action under consideration, uncertainty about its consequences may prompt the gathering of additional data in order to yield better predictions of the results. Here again, the crucial question is how much additional data to gather before responding in some other way. Here of course, is the analog of the scientist's problem of how many times to replicate his experiment. The manager may alternate between searching for additional actions and gathering data on those discovered, terminating the search-prediction process when he has discovered an action which is, in some sense, "satisfactory" to him.

A third response to his conceptualization may be *value clarification*. Although there is a tendency to assume that a manager's objectives or goals are perfectly clear and operationally defined, this is, it would appear, seldom the case. A basic reason for unwillingness to proceed with a decision may be a need to clarify one's objectives and the relationship of the predicted consequences of an action to these objectives. The traditional business decision involves a choice between high-profit–high-risk alternatives and low-profit–low-risk alternatives. For many decision makers, it is rather difficult to decide just how much possibility for profit they are willing to relinquish in return for additional certainty of obtaining a profit. Every new investor in stocks has experienced the difficulty of being explicit to his broker about the tradeoff between profit and risk consistent with his investment objectives. Similarly, the firm which considers installing a digital computer may find difficulty in balancing the potential monetary saving against the undesirable consequences of laying off a portion of its office staff. Again, the crucial question is how much effort to devote to value clarification before going on to other responses to the decision situation.

These responses, to whatever extent and in whatever sequence they are pursued, ultimately result in a modified conceptualization of the decision problem which the manager is willing to use as a basis for choice. The sorts of responses involved may easily be thought of as learning activities. Note also that they may be undertaken typically without committing oneself to a decision. One should not suppose that the manager reaches the point of being certain that he has considered all the possible courses of action, being certain about their consequences or about what his objectives are or how they will be served by the actions in question. Much as he would like to be certain, the pressure of ongoing affairs, the cost both in time and money of the responses involved, and the reasonable willingness to tolerate some uncertainty, lead the manager to something short of an indefinite postponement of the decision. Once again the crucial question is what degree of uncertainty he is willing to tolerate and what degree of uncertainty it would be "reasonable" for him to tolerate. When is it rational for him to stipulate that his current conceptualization of the decision is adequate and that he is willing to act "as if" his current conceptualization represented reality?

When the manager has reached the point of achieving a satisfactory basis for decision, presumably he decides, and ultimately his decision is implemented. The results of implementation are, in a more or less explicit manner, introduced into his own experience and into the firm's data bank, where they form a potential basis for subsequent decisions. When this assimilation of results is routinized, it is often called a *management control system*. Of course, it is basically just another sort of learning or adaptive system.

Science as a Learning Process

Science, like management, is a diverse, complex activity and any attempt to conceptualize it must admit to producing a simplified rendering of its nature. Yet it is useful to suggest that the work of the scientists is that of

1. Raising interesting hypotheses on the basis of both his own personal experience and intuition and the accumulated public knowledge of his discipline.

2. Designing experiments which test these hypotheses.

3. Assimilating the results both into his personal experience and the body of his discipline, thus preparing the way for new hypotheses and new experiments.

There may be some phenomena about which the scientist feels little uncertainty and thus little need for further hypothesizing and experimentation. Others, however, are matters of considerable uncertainty and thus become the subjects of extensive programs of experimentation and learning.

Viewed in this way, it may be reasonable to think of science and management as sharing certain broad common features as learning processes. If a manager's conceptualization of a decision problem is regarded as a hypothesis, then his activities aimed at testing the validity of the hypothesis may well be thought of as experiments. Management, like science, may be seen as a dynamic, experimental, self-correcting activity, involved essentially in the task of learning. One must be careful, however, to learn what is useful from such similarities without pressing them too far. There are interesting differences in the ways in which the two learning processes are carried on. These differences appear from this viewpoint, to be matters of degree and not matters of principle.

1. Explicit use of the hypothetico-deductive method. Since the time of Newton, physics has expressed its hypotheses and theories in mathematical language. This has the distinct advantage of permitting one to explore the deductive consequences of a hypothesis, the relations among hypotheses, and to work toward a unified theory in which everything of interest could be deduced from a small number of basic laws. Economics and, more recently, psychology and sociology have begun to emulate physics in its use of mathematical formulations or models.

If one's experimental data can be deduced from the model, if one can reach the same conclusions both deductively and experimentally, then it is said that the model *explains* the data. The data in turn lend credence to the model, although they do not unequivocally establish its truth. No matter how much data is obtained, some uncertainty remains about the future validity of the model. Nevertheless, there comes a point at which uncertainty about the model is limited and one feels confident in using it as a prediction of what will happen in future experiments. As will soon appear, agreement between model and evidence is not a trivial matter to decide and confronts the scientist with his most difficult decisions.

This learning process, which aims at both explaining and predicting, is the hypothetico-deductive method. Of course there has been nothing in management to compare with the well-developed mathematical theory which physics has produced. Yet it is the basic proposal of management science that management phenomena can be usefully captured in mathematical models and that the resulting deductive capability can be of considerable consequence for the learning process of managers. Sufficient progress has been made to create a justifiable optimism on the part of management scientists that this hypothesis will be progressively confirmed, and to moderate some of the skepticism of experienced managers.

2. Experiment and experience. Learning by experience on the job has been the traditional method of increasing one's appreciation of the intricacies of management phenomena. In science, however, the tradition of learning is by means of deliberate, carefully designed experiments. This distinction between casual experience and careful experiment is basic. Management science proposes to begin the transformation of the loose informality of management experience toward the designed experience or considered experiment of science.

Experimental design requires operational definitions of the concepts involved in one's hypotheses. To talk meaningfully of employee morale, customer satisfaction, military worth, or a fair day's work, one must be able to say explicitly how each of these concepts is to be identified in experience and to be measured. This, of course, does not always mean precise measurement in the tradition of physics. For some purposes it may be very useful to be able to distinguish operationally between high-morale and low-morale groups of employees, but there may be no particular need to scale morale through the assignment of numerical values.

Experimentation implies also a specific statement of one's beliefs before the experiment and an explicit examination of the impact of the evidence on these beliefs. Without statement and examination, science would be a mere accumulation of observations. With them, science can attempt to wring the maximum amount of information from any body of data. In this sense, experiment tries to use the data efficiently, whereas casual experience may use it wastefully or unreasonably. Beyond its marketable goods and services, the second most important output of a firm is likely to be information on how to improve its own operations. In moving from experience toward experiment, one hopes to move toward optimizing the production of this second output.

3. The uses of intuition. Management is well known to be an activity in which intuition plays a significant role. Indeed the really effective decision makers in many fields appear to operate in largely intuitive ways—and this includes, science. The more competent a mathematician or scientist, the more likely it is that his intuitive abilities will be highly developed and well used. An objective of considerable importance in training both scientists and managers is the development of intuitive skills.

Yet there is a major difference in the ultimate reliance placed upon intuitive decision making by scientists as opposed to managers. In management decision making, one is often required to place final reliance on intuitive processes and to evaluate managers on their intuitive skills alone. Lacking well-developed alternatives, pressed by the ongoing affairs of the firm, and taking considerable pride in "managerial judgment," managers are content to leave their decision processes on an intuitive level.

The scientist, however, makes full use of his intuition to reach conclusions, make discoveries, and raise hypotheses, but does not finally rely on intuition alone. Indeed, the meaning of "objectivity" in science is not that intuition is bad, but that it must be checked by logic and experiment. After reaching a tentative conclusion, the scientist undertakes to test it by logical deduction and experimental inference. Science as an activity may be roughly divided into the largely intuitive process of discovering and the formal process of justifying one's discoveries. For the scientist, intuition, however valuable is not to be trusted, but tested.

4. *The pressure of affairs.* It is the very nature of management that it involves decision making in the context of rapidly moving events. Opportunities must be grasped or they are lost; situations demand quick responses; and the size and complexity of his job strains the cognitive ability of the typical manager. The scientist, however, often finds himself working in a context which does not demand quick decisions and fast reactions, which permits throughtful and deliberate progress toward a conclusion, and which assures considerable freedom from distractions.

It is manifestly nonsense to propose anything to the manager which does not recognize clearly the pressures under which he must operate. It would be useless to suggest that the manager should behave as though he worked in the context of the stereotypic scientist, when in fact he does not. A further basic hypothesis of management science is that it can improve the learning-decision-making process within the constraints of the management environment, not simply by denying these constraints. Thus the problem is how to optimize learning, given the costs of getting information, the information-handling capacities, and the time deadlines which characterize the management situation. Perhaps this sensitivity to the "realities" of management decision making is one of the fundamentally distinctive features of management science. It is worth emphasizing again that these distinctions between management and science are matters of degree and not of principle. Managers and scientists differ, generally speaking, in the degree to which their hypotheses are mathematically expressed, the extent to which their experience is carefully designed, the amount of their final reliance on intuition, and the degree to which the pressure of affairs forces their decision making. Management science might be thought of as the program of reducing the degree to which management and science differ in an effort to enhance the effectiveness of management.

The Basic Proposal of Management Science

Our basic hypothesis is thus that improvement will occur if the methods of science are applied to the decisions which managers must make, that something is to be gained by making the learning-adaptive processes of management more nearly like those of science. It is not proposed that the manager become fully involved in the technical details of science, but rather that he adopt its strategy while delegating some of the tactical details to the trained management scientist.

Management science proposes to take seriously the task of giving explicit, reasonable answers to such questions as

1. When should a manager rely on his intuition in making a decision and when should he try to become very explicit and experimental about it? Clearly, not every decision will reasonably be subjected to a fully deliberated analysis.

2. When should the manager delegate a part of his learning process to a management scientist, to another manager, or to a digital computer? The basic aim is showing that he can delegate some tasks, thus giving himself more time to perform those for which he himself is uniquely qualified.

3. How prolonged should be the process of search for alternative courses of action? How much data should be obtained in predicting their consequences? How may these data be reasonably assimilated into one's experience? What predictions, inferences, or forecasts are reasonable in view of both data and experience?

In short, management science aims at optimizing the learning-adaptation process. It seeks to do this within the constraints and pressures of the ongoing affairs of the managerial situation. It seeks, further, to make full use of the most valuable asset in any decision situation, the rich experience and insight of managers themselves.

A very considerable body of evidence suggests that managers are intelligent and skillful decision makers, and that anyone who sets out to improve manager's learning-decision-making effectiveness is unwise to assume otherwise. There appears to be no particular support for the a priori assumption that management science can succeed in its program of contributing to management effectiveness. In fact, the reader is urged to regard the program of management science as a hypothesis which has some demonstrated effectiveness but which requires a good deal more validation, before the scope and magnitude of its contribution will become at all clear. In this sense, one may regard management science as an emerging science in rather early stages of development. The following chapter examines the management decision-learning process more carefully to see what grounds there are for expecting management science to enhance the process.

2

Logical
and Psychological
Decision Making

Individual and Group Decisions

It is often useful to identify a single manager as responsible for a given decision and begin the study of the decision-learning process with him. He may consult with others, weigh their opinions, and perhaps delegate parts of the process, but if authority and responsibility rest with him, one thinks of the decision as "his." This manager may, from time to time, experience conflict or "blocking" of his habitual decision-making processes. As seen in Chapter 1, this conflict may be attributed to uncertainty, to desire to search for additional alternatives, or to need to clarify his objectives.

One might expect that the greater the difference between the manager's decision-making achievements and his aspirations, the more likely he is to experience conflict. Similarly, the more complex the decision and the less relevant his past experience, the greater the chances that his habitual methods of choice will break down. In the case of the individual decision maker, management science has the task of contributing to the resolution of such conflict.

Alternatively, the decision may be made by a group or committee, and this may multiply difficulties. Sometimes, the membership of the group and the distribution of power among its members is reasonably clear and explicit. In other cases, it may be extremely difficult to find out who is involved and what influence each participant has. In group decisions, one expects conflicts to arise among those involved, reflecting their differing objectives, experience, and ways of viewing the situation. If the objectives of the organization are vague and lacking in operational definition, and if attainments are difficult to measure, then individuals are likely to focus on what they take to be the objectives of their own departments or subunits. The classic problem of conflict arises when what one person sees as consistent with the objectives of his department turns out to be detrimental to the achievement of the entire organization's goals. Such conflict frequently occurs when departments must share a limited common resource, such as capital funds or computer time. Where departments must coordinate their activities, as when the output of one department is the input to another, conflicts may also be expected to arise.

One of the most important uses of management science has been in the search for a reasoned resolution of conflict among the individuals in a decision-making group. Management science has tried to find analyses which will lead reasonable men toward a consensus that all can accept as "best" for the organization as a whole. This is a more desirable organizational response than the bargaining or "politics" which otherwise may become the method of resolving conflicts.

For simplicity, we speak of *the manager* or *the decision maker*. The reader, however, must be aware that this often represents something of an abstraction from the real nature of the decision processes he is studying. (At this point, one avoids the sociological complexity of decisions made in an actual organizational context.)

Simplification

Basic to understanding any decision-making activity is an appreciation of the way in which the decision maker simplifies his environment. He must do this in order to match his conception of it with the cognitive limitations of his mind. People do not perceive everything around them, but rather select from all the stimuli available some simplified set. Nor do decision makers conceptualize management problems in all the rich complexity of their nature. Instead those problems are thought about in simplified form, which makes them intellectually tractable. The capacity of the mind limits the number of alternatives, the list of constraints, the amount of past experience, and so on, with which that mind can consciously deal. The key to understanding choice behavior is understanding the pattern used in reducing the endless complexity of the actual situation to a manageable conception of the choice problem.

One may usefully raise some hypotheses about the ways in which this simplification takes place. For example,

1. Resort to "Rule of Thumb": A firm "ought to keep 30 days inventory on hand"; one "should expect an investment to pay out in three years"—these are examples of conventional simplifications which often serve in place of detailed analyses.

2. Appeal to a system of categories: Often policy categories are used to place decisions in broad classes. Each class is characterized by a particular response previously determined to be more or less appropriate for the members of the class. Generally speaking, the broader and more inclusive the policy categories, the less effective is likely to be the categorical response to any particular decision.

3. Suppress intangible values: Simplification may be sought by restricting consideration of the values of consequences to those dimensions which are most easily measurable or most "tangible." Thus one may consider profit, units of production, and so on, while suppressing the complexity of human attitudes and social, or moral values.

4. Adopt a near planning horizon: A decision often has consequences extending far into the future which a full analysis of the problem would examine. Typically, the further in the future an event, the greater one's uncertainty about it; the further in the future an income, the less one is willing to pay for it in the present. Much thinking about decisions is probably characterized by simplification through use of a relatively near planning horizon in which events are considered for a short period in the future but not beyond that point. Similarly one might simplify by limiting the consideration of past experience to only the rather recent past.

5. Suppress risk: As soon as an organization grows large enough to benefit from a division of labor in decision making, it becomes necessary to have some means of expressing the risk and uncertainty involved in decisions. This need arises when parts of the decision-making process are delegated to others or to computers. Yet surely one of the most widely observed facts of organizational life is failure to make risk and uncertainty explicit; rather, they are suppressed to an overwhelming degree. When information is passed from one organizational unit to another, very often all the variability in the data is omitted in favor of summarizing parameters. Expert and informed judgments of risk and uncertainty are lost when opinions are required and expressed as certainties. Managers deal with risk-taking situations in terms of their "best estimates" of the quantities involved, neglecting the uncertainties. Someone's rough order-of-magnitude guess becomes an accepted figure in the process of organizational choice. In fact, one might almost imagine that the more uncertainty associated with some estimate, the

less the tendency of the organization to recognize anything except the single-valued expression of the estimate.

The explicit expression of risk in large organizations would facilitate

    a. Communication for purposes of coordination.
    b. Delegation of parts of the decision-making process.
    c. Planning the information-gathering activities of the firm.
    d. Learning, teaching, and checking the subtle process of blending mature business judgment with explicit data which occurs when a decision is made.

Several plausible hypotheses help one to understand the suppression of risk. Managers who have no explicit way of dealing with risk in their choice processes may wish to suppress it. To acknowledge risk would require an explanation of how it is considered in making a decision. Lacking such a plan for explicitly considering risk, the manager might find himself on the verge of admitting that his decisions were somewhat irrational.

The suppression of risk allows the organization to communicate and reason in the language of certainty and this mode of expression may be attractive for several reasons:

1. Certainty represents the traditional academic view of many business decisions, and this may reflect a tendency to fit things into academic formulas and modes of thought.

2. Certainty may be associated with personality characteristics, such as boldness, aggressiveness, confidence, success, self-assurance, and feelings of power.

3. Certainty is surely related in part to the previously noted lack of language for thinking about or expressing uncertainty.

4. Certainty may be a part of an individual's need to preserve a self-image of the assured, confident, and successful man of affairs.

5. Certainty may in part explain the appeal to all manner of hunches, cues, habits, and rules of thumb with which a decision model may be simplified.

6. Most important, certainty may help to explain some of the nonrational relationships psychologists have pointed out between evidence, experience, and beliefs. Facts alone are seldom sufficient to change people's minds.

We are dealing here with a widely observed human tendency to convert assumptions into facts, doubts into certainties, and to revise images of decision situations so as to meet the need for certainty.

Perhaps one of the more interesting reasons that managers may seldom deal with risk explicitly is the insufficiency of language in which to express it. In order to make statements operational, one relies heavily on the language he has available. Clearly, managers recognize decisions made in the face of risk and speak about more or less risky future events. To translate these remarks into operational hypotheses, one must have in his vocabulary the concept of probability, which is the means by which science makes risk operational. In other words, the predictive content of statements involving ideas of risk can be specified only by giving directions for measuring risk. Interpretation of probability theory in terms of events in the conduct of business affairs is essentially the specification of a set of operations for measuring risk.

One would hypothesize that the terms *probability, risk,* and *the law of averages* are not fully operational in the ordinary usage of the person untrained in the theory and interpretation of probability. Thus, the manager who holds no operational conception of risk is at considerable disadvantage when he must make explicit his reasoning in risk-taking decisions.

The efforts of management science are directed toward meeting this general need to simplify by relieving the cognitive strain in several ways. It proposes explicit recording and analysis of past experience instead of a loosely organized and haphazard acquaintance with it. It proposes to offer a language with which uncertainty can be made explicit and shared among the participants in an organization. Management science suggests conceptual structures in the form of mathematical models which permit one to think systematically about complex decisions. In doing this, management science provides a basis for filtering the perceptual confusion in which experience comes to us and for making some sort of conceptual order out of a situation. It generally supposes that the more of a decision problem the manager can make explicit, the less he must keep in mind informally, thus the less he is required to simplify his concept of the actual problem.

Cognitive Distortion

It has just been suggested that one function of management science is to extend the range of the manager's intuition when it falters in the face of novelty or complexity. Closely related to this is the situation in which intuition leads to decisions by steps not understood nor made explicit and one wishes to check the reasonableness of those decisions. Are they based on wishful thinking, faulty logic, or neglect of some relevant past experience? These human failings which most decision makers would like to avoid may be regarded as instances of cognitive distortion. It is well known that in complex decisions people fail to discipline themselves according to the rules of logic and consistency with their past experience. The basic difficulty is perhaps that the processes of perceiving, remembering, and thinking are by no means free of the control of human needs and desires.

Among the most basic needs is clearly that for certainty. The manager shares the prevalent human desire to be certain of the consequences of his actions. If he cannot be sufficiently certain on the basis of the information available, he may, quite subconsciously, remake his own conceptualization of the decision, suppressing uncertainty and thus relieving his anxiety. His conceptualization may be distorted by factors like need to make a decision which will be defensible in the future, which confirms past positions and decisions he has taken, or need to see things in some conventional or socially acceptable way.

Learning

Of special interest are the sorts of cognitive distortion that one may expect to discover in the learning process. This is the process of assimilating new information into established conceptions. The basic problem is how much weight to give to past experience and how much to new data and information which may become available. Overconfidence and strong predispositions suggest that one may be giving too much weight to past experience. Decision makers may be distracted by irrelevant events or attach too much importance to critical incidents. Interesting evidence now suggests that when people have the opportunity to buy information which is relevant to a decision, they tend to pay more for information than consistent behavior would suggest, to buy more information than is consistent with their own opinions and objectives, and generally to fail to wring from the data all the uncertainty reduction that is logically possible. Here the special role of management science in optimizing the learning process supports expectations for improvements in decision-making effectiveness. Management science offers, in short, guides to clear thinking.

Guides to Consistent Decision

There are some things which no one can reasonably do for a decision maker. Management scientists cannot guarantee him a good outcome or the "right decision." They can only help him to work toward reasoned decisions which appear sensible in the light of the knowledge it is reasonable to have before acting. A good decision can be made with deliberation and care, but a good outcome depends upon chance. A man who must get from New York to Los Angeles, and for whom time is more important than money, may well decide to fly. If his plane crashes en route and he is injured, the outcome is not good, but this does not make the decision less reasonable. Indeed, one test is whether he remains satisfied with the decision, no matter what the outcome. The best one can hope for are decisions which will appear to be satisfactory to the decision maker, even from hindsight.

One cannot, of course, relieve a manager of need to sacrifice some of his objectives in order to achieve others. Seldom are courses of action found which simultaneously move a manager toward all his goals. One can, however, attempt to assist the decision maker in thinking more clearly about the relationships among his various objectives. One may be able to help him become more explicit about the tradeoffs he wishes to make between high-risk–high-profit opportunities and low-risk–low-profit ones.

Nor can management scientists relieve him of all uncertainty. They may be able to help the manager to express his uncertainty, to modify it reasonably in the face of new information, and to act with deliberation in spite of it. Management scientists cannot make the process of deciding easy for him. In fact, they may well make it more difficult. What they propose requires considerable effort and is clearly not something that will be used in every instance of management decision making. Their task is showing what benefits may be expected if one does invest the effort to be explicit and logical in deciding. Only by suggesting the possible payoffs, can management science give the decision maker a basis for deciding which of his problems are important and uncertain enough to warrant the required investment of effort.

The general strategy of management science is based on the presumption that one must first gain an understanding of both the decision maker's objective or values and of his judgments or opinions based upon his previous experience. One hopes to do this by asking him what choices he would make in certain kinds of rather simple situations. From his responses, one may be able to build an explicit theory of

1. His objectives, values, or preferences
2. His opinions or judgments about the chances of various kinds of events
3. His methods of combining values with opinions in order to arrive at choices

As is always the case, this theory does not claim to be a statement of what actually goes on in the conscious and unconscious mind of the decision maker. Others must be left to explore that. Management science will be content if it can develop a theory which, to a useful extent, explains and predicts his choice behavior. It will never claim more than the usefulness of thinking of the decision maker as acting "as if" he reasoned in certain ways.

If the manager wishes to act in future decisions according to some rather simple and acceptable principles of reasonable behavior, one can suggest consistent methods of dealing with novel and complex decisions. If he wishes to act in these cases in ways consistent with his judgments and opinions expressed in the simpler problems, one hopes to show how this can be accomplished by rather straightforward methods of calculation. Management scientists have nothing more to offer than a method of moving in a reasoned and consistent way from simple decisions which a manager can make satisfactorily without assistance, to complex decisions which are quite beyond his previous experience. Management scientists hope to include not only decisions about what course of action to select in the traditional range of management problems, but also decisions about how much search to undertake, how much information to obtain, how to assimilate the opinions of experts, and how to design management information systems generally.

Note that the manager need not become involved in the terminology or mathematical details of our theory. He need only respond to some questions about his preferences in the decision problems put to him. This may not be easy for him, nor will it fall immediately into the habitual patterns of his thinking. He must make the effort to give carefully considered answers. The test of his answers will come when he is helped to see some of their ultimate logical consequences. If the manager finds he cannot "live with" these consequences, then he must have the patience to go back again and see whether "he really meant what he said."

It must be very clear also that management scientists are not going to neglect his experience and insights, but rather consider them a primary input. They are not going to impose preferences upon the manager, but to help him to act more consistently in the light of his own or his organization's preferences. We seek a freeing of his intelligence, a full and effective expression of his capabilities, not a rigid mold into which his thought is to be compressed. If that objective is reached, the manager will be able to rid his decisions of some of the distortions and inconsistencies which plague us all. He will be able to delegate parts of the decision process with some assurance that the results will be close to those he himself would have achieved. Finally, he may find the satisfaction of knowing that his decisions are reasonable, no matter what the ultimate outcomes may be.

3

Management
Experience
and Learning

Scaling Judgments

The next problem to be confronted is making the decision maker's past experience explicit and useful as the first step in the sort of program just outlined. This chapter examines in its simplest form the central concept of a logical guide to learning, or the revision of opinion in the light of new information. The following chapter deals with the similar problem of scaling a decision maker's preferences. This will lead finally to assembling a theory of decision which combines judgments arising out of past experience, the revision of these judgments, and the manager's preferences, into a logically consistent pattern of choice.

In considering judgments, it is useful to keep in mind that people's past experience differs, and their processes for remembering and thinking about this experience also differ. Thus their judgments about the future will differ, and it has become customary to take note of this by describing these judgments as *subjective*. One should consider carefully before attempting any program aimed at eliminating "subjective" judgments in favor of some process called *objective*. Judgment based on experience is, after all, a fundamental asset which is highly valued in an executive. It is perhaps *the* significant ingredient in most interesting management decisions. Hence any program for supporting management decision making which does not recognize this fact is going to appear unrealistic and to be regarded by managers as "theoretical." Even though opinions may be properly described as subjective, one is not interested in haphazard, ill-considered opinion based on little or no experience. Rather one is dealing with the orderly opinions of intelligent and reasonable managers, often richly supported by experience.

The first task, then, is making explicit the decision maker's judgments about events, or "scaling" these judgments. Rather than select an arbitrary method of scaling, one adopts a particular method which allows checking, by means of rather direct calculations, whether his judgments are consistent with one another. Consistency here is defined according to some ordinary rules of logical behavior, but we shall postpone briefly a discussion of its exact nature.

It is not required that the decision maker become in any way involved in understanding the theory used to express his judgments. He need not understand such words as "probability" or "utility." It is required only that he be willing and able to make certain kinds of simple decisions. Since the manager is typically a man heavily involved in decision making, this requirement is not taken to be unreasonable. We have considerable freedom about how to confront him with the decisions involved. We may seek ways which are interesting and meaningful to him, which elicit carefully considered answers, and which lead to responses whose logical consequences he will be willing to accept. Again we emphasize that the decisions involved, however simple, may seem strange and difficult at first. The manager may indeed require some training and self-discipline before he can respond meaningfully to those decisions.

The Reference Experiment

The basic scaling device is an experiment which has several possible outcomes and elicits a special kind of decision-making behavior from the manager. One needs an experiment having, say, N possible outcomes numbered $1, \ldots, i, \ldots, j, \ldots, N$ such that, if the manager is offered the choice between

a_1: an important payoff if outcome i occurs; but nothing otherwise

a_2: the same important payoff if outcome j occurs; but nothing otherwise

he finds himself indifferent between the two actions, no matter what outcomes i and j are involved. *Indifference* means that if action a_1 is chosen for him by whatever method, he will be unwilling to exert any effort whatever to alter the selection in favor of action a_2. We might, for example, choose as the basic or reference experiment, a lottery in which there were N tickets, one of which was to be drawn and called the *winning ticket*. If, given a choice of any ticket, he is indifferent among them, choosing perhaps the first one at hand, then the experiment fulfills the requirements.

Assume that the decision maker's behavior toward the reference experiment satisfies one other rather acceptable condition. Given a choice between

a_1: an important prize if any one of x outcomes occurs, but nothing otherwise

a_2: the same important prize if any one of y outcomes occurs, but nothing otherwise

he will prefer a_1 to a_2 if and only if x is greater than y.

Notice very carefully several things about the reference experiment. The only requirement is that the manager exhibit certain decision-making behavior in connection with it. The manager himself is not required to think of the outcomes as being equally likely nor to regard them as having "equal probability," although he may think this way if he wishes. It is not required that the experimental outcomes have long-run relative frequencies which are in fact nearly equal.

On the other hand, as scientists we may choose whatever language and structure seem useful in formulating a theory to "explain" the manager's decision-making behavior. We aim, of course, at developing a theory which will predict how, if he acts consistently, he will choose in future decisions and thus formulate a theory which may be used as a guide for consistent choice.

It is natural to think of a manager's judgments about the outcomes of the reference experiment by saying that he regards them as "equally likely," and we shall do this. It is not necessary, however, for we might simply scale his judgments by associating a number or weight with each outcome. That is, we could reflect his indifference by associating with each experimental outcome the arbitrarily selected number k. It will be useful later on to choose k equal to $1/N$, although at the moment this may appear neither more nor less adequate than any other number.

For clarity, suppose that we have indeed found a lottery having N tickets toward which the decision maker exhibits the required sort of indifference. Using this reference lottery as the scaling instrument, we may now make explicit his judgments about events anticipated in the affairs of his business. Consider any such actual event, E_0. The manager is asked how he would choose between a contract promising an important payoff if E_0 occurs but nothing if it does not, and some number of tickets, x, in our reference lottery, where the winning ticket carries the same important payoff. We want to find the number of tickets, x, which he would regard as just as desirable as the contract involving E_0. One might try several values of x, adjusting it until one found him indifferent, or one might ask him directly for the value of x which would leave him indifferent. How one can most expeditiously obtain a meaningful value for x may be a matter of some psychological difficulty, but for the moment, one simply assumes that it can be done.

This particular decision-making behavior is summarized by associating with E_0 the number of "weight" x/N and representing this weight by $w(E_0)$. It may not be unreasonable to assume that, if he regards the event E_0 as impossible, he will be indifferent for $x = 0$; if he regards E_0 as certain, he will be indifferent only if he can obtain all the tickets making $x = N$. If he is uncertain about E_0, regarding it as neither impossible nor certain, he will be indifferent for some value of x between 0 and N. Thus in terms of weights, $w(E_0)$ will be a number in the interval 0 to 1 inclusive, 0 representing impossibility and 1 representing certainty.

Next consider two events, E_1 and E_2, which are mutually exclusive, and suppose the manager is offered a contract (called contract A) with an important payoff if either E_1 or E_2 occurs. As before, suppose that there exists some number of lottery tickets which he would be just willing to exchange for this contract, say, x_{12}. A second contract, B, offers the same payoff if E_1 occurs; a third, contract C, offers the payoff if E_2 occurs. Suppose he is indifferent between B and x_1 tickets and between C and x_2 tickets. One forms still another contract, D, which combines B and C. Since the conditions of A and D are identical, one assumes that he is indifferent between them. It is a principle of consistent behavior, to be made explicit later, that, since he is indifferent between B and x_1 tickets, one can form a contract D' which consists of x_1 tickets and contract C, and he will be indifferent between D and D'. Further, D' can be modified by substituting x_2 tickets for contract C, producing as a result contract D'', which consists simply of $x_1 + x_2$ tickets. By the same principle, one expects him to be indifferent between D'' and D', between D'' and D, and further, between D'' and A. This indifference we take to imply that

$$x_1 + x_2 = x_{12}$$

In terms of weights,

$$w(E_1) + w(E_2) = w(E_1 + E_2)$$

that is, if two mutually exclusive events are grouped to form a single event, the weight of this single event will be the sum of the weights assigned to the original events. Now the point of all this is to show that, if the assumptions being made hold, the properties of these weights are exactly the properties which constitute the basic axioms of the mathematical theory of probability. These are

a. A probability is a number in the inclusive range 0 to 1.

b. The probability of a set of collectively exhaustive events is 1.

c. The probability of either of two mutually exclusive events is the sum of their individual probabilities.

Thus one is justified in using the logic of probability theory in computing the weights that would be consistently assigned to events. For this reason, we customarily give our weights the name "probability."

Consistency

So important and so useful is this ability to draw upon the entire well-developed logic of probability theory in computing weights, that we shall adopt these axioms as conventions to be used in assigning weights. Further, if a decision maker's responses lack the sort of self-consistency required, one may point this out to him in the hope that he will want to reconsider his scaling decisions. We do not assume that people are naturally consistent in the sense of probability theory, but rather that the advantages of being so will motivate them to try to achieve consistency. We suppose that most decision makers share the widely held belief that to act effectively and in accordance with one's experience is to follow certain guides regarded as reasonable. To do otherwise is to expose oneself to the possibility of making decisions with which one would not be satisfied in the face of a careful exploration of the logical relations between beliefs, preferences, and actions. In other words, one assumes that managers prefer to make complex decisions in a manner which permits them to see what they are doing.

The man who believes that the probability of a coin coming up heads is one-half, but after seeing it come up tails ten times in a row, believes that the probability of heads on the next flip is different from one-half, holds inconsistent beliefs. Consequently, he can be lured into gambles which are more certain to leave him a loser the more often he accepts them. A man who believed that if a coin is flipped twice there are three equally likely outcomes (two heads, two tails, one head and one tail) might be trapped into a set of gambles which would make him sure to lose. Suppose he will accept any gamble which has a positive dollar expectation. He might be trapped into accepting four uncertain payoffs, each of which costs him $.80.

1. Receive $3 if two heads appear.
2. Receive $3 if two tails appear.
3. Receive $3 if the first flip is heads and the second, tails.
4. Receive $3 if the first flip is tails and the second, heads.

Now if he believes that each outcome has probability one-third, then each of the four opportunities will have a positive expected payoff for him, and he might accept all four. Clearly he pays $3.20 but will win only $3.00. In this simple example, the inconsistency is obvious and cries for correction; however, the possibilities in more complex decisions are ominous. Still, it is not difficult to find people who believe that there are three equally likely outcomes when a coin is flipped twice.

We shall, of course, be concerned with cases in which the inconsistencies are less obvious. For example, if a man wished to invest his money in stocks so as to maximize his expected dollar payoff, it is inconsistent to diversify his holding among several issues. He should hold a single stock if he really wants to maximize expected dollar payoffs. This is less obvious and potentially of greater importance.

The Naturalness of Weights

Suppose a man is told that the top card in a well-shuffled deck is either an ace or a club and that he will receive a prize if he can guess which. He guesses "club" and we regard his guess as "reasonable," "intuitively satisfying," "logical," or describe it in some such terms. We find it a natural, acceptable guess to make in such a situation. In this sense, our program of assigning weights simply tries to capture what reasonable people do anyway. Although most business situations do not have the simplicity of a pack of cards, similar thinking may be found. People buy a stock because they think it is "more likely" to go up ten points in six months than down ten points in the same period. Yet if pressed to say how much more likely, to quantify their beliefs, they typically find themselves in considerable difficulty. In management decisions, it is natural to think informally and qualitatively, and this kind of thinking serves well enough in many simple cases. In complex situations, it is no longer useful. Management science suggests that complexity can be dealt with by making the effort to move from natural, informal, qualitative, thinking processes toward formal, quantitative, but unhappily somewhat unnatural, conceptualizations of the decision. One questions, however, whether the decision maker will prefer to be intuitive about simple decisions or to be intuitive about complicated ones. We hypothesize that, with practice, he will come to prefer struggling with simple rather than with complicated decisions.

In sum, we suppose that we can find an experiment involving some imaginary or actual chance device toward which the decision maker behaves in a particular way. He makes decisions or behaves as if the outcomes of the experiment were equally likely. Further, we suppose that his judgments with respect to any event of actual interest in managing his affairs can be scaled by asking him how he would behave in some simple decision situations. The event may be winning a certain contract, realizing a 10 per cent increase in sales next year, meeting a production schedule, and so on. He must be able to indicate his preference between, say,

a_1: a substantial income if the firm wins a certain contract

a_2: x tickets in a lottery having N tickets, where the winning ticket yields the same substantial income as a prize

One must note several things about this method of scaling his judgments.

1. We assume that the information obtained through the decision maker's thinking about his response to such imaginary choice situations is valid,

in the sense that he will subsequently want to behave in actual decisions in a way consistent with this information. It is sometimes argued that the differences between what people say they will do and what they actually do are so great as to render useless any such study of imagined behavior. Consequently, one can infer a decision maker's judgments only by studying his behavior in a series of actual business decisions. This possibility should clearly be kept in mind, as should the very considerable difficulty of attempting to infer judgments from the complex and partially implicit process of actual business decision making. We must try to make it easy for the manager to think about and express his preferences so that the judgments we infer will not be the result of confusion or misunderstanding. We must also try to motivate the decision maker to think carefully about his responses and to report them accurately. There must be no reason for him to deceive us. He must understand that the whole program depends on scaling his judgments in such a way that he will be willing to "live with" their logical consequences.

2. We are not assuming that one can accomplish all of this in the first encounter with a manager. The stark simplicity of the decisions involved and their unfamiliarity mean that time, practice, and effort are required. Again, we must motivate compliance by suggesting the consequences which may follow.

3. Part of the needed practice may well be the imaginary testing of the decision maker's willingness to accept the logical consequences of his scaled judgments. If he is confronted with consequences which he finds unacceptable, then he may wish to revise his responses to the original scaling decision problems. In this sense, the process is an experimental one in which we continually test his willingness to accept the logical implications of his behavior.

4. We do not suppose that the manager would indeed be willing to give up his business and buy lottery tickets instead. We only raise the hypothesis that this will be a helpful device for thinking about the actual future events with which he must contend.

5. We have tried to suggest the "simplest" sort of questions which a decision maker must be able to answer in order to permit the assignment of weights or probabilities. He himself need not become involved in the assignment nor in associating weights with the logic of probability theory. He need only make some decisions. There are, of course, other ways of getting the same result. With practice, a decision maker may be able to assign probabilities directly, giving us statements of the form: "I believe that there is a 30 per cent chance of winning this contract," and so on. He may even be able directly to associate next month's

sales with a normally distributed random variable having some specified mean and standard deviation. As we proceed, we shall offer examples of various other ways of scaling his judgments. The point is to find the method which is easiest, most natural, and productive of consequences the decision maker wants to accept.

6. It may well be that, if we begin with a lottery or experiment having ten tickets or possible results, the decision maker will find that he prefers one alternative when x tickets are involved but the other alternative when $x + 1$ tickets are involved. His indifference point lies somewhere between x and $x + 1$. We can introduce a new experiment involving 100 outcomes, or 1,000, or however many seem needed to establish his indifference point. For the present, we assume that a unique indifference point can always be found. Later we shall examine the case in which the decision maker feels indifferent for a range of x values, a result which adds to the complexity of the program.

7. Finally, it should be clear that what we propose in no sense replaces management judgment. Instead it aims at utilizing judgment, policing it for inconsistencies, and extending it to situations more complicated than unaided intuition can approach.

Relation to Relative Frequencies

Many people strongly associate the idea of probability theory with the interpretation of this idea in terms of the relative frequencies of outcomes in repeated experiments or observations. Often they think of probabilities only as relative frequencies, and our use of the word "probability" then becomes confusing. To clarify this, Fig. 3-1 may be of some help. We may think of the mathematical theory of probability as we would think of any other branch of mathematics. It is an abstract, self-consistent body of deductions, proceeding from a small group of axioms. Of itself, it makes no reference to observable events, and for the mathematician, need not be interpreted in terms of events at all.

If, however, probability theory is to be "applied," in the sense of suggesting hypotheses about events, then it must be interpreted. We need a set of rules for associating the terms in the theory with what can be observed of the phenomena under study. *One* such interpretation is in terms of relative frequencies. A probability may be interpreted as the limit of the relative frequency of an outcome in a replicated experiment. It then turns out that we can use probability theory to deduce some relative frequencies from others. Typically, we can, by means of the theory, establish a relation between the relative frequency of heads when a coin is flipped repeatedly, and the relative

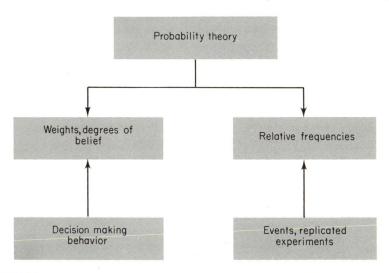

FIGURE 3-1

frequency of three heads in ten flips when the experiment of flipping a coin ten times is replicated. Clearly, however, we have proposed quite a different way of interpreting the mathematical theory of probability. Our interpretation does not associate it with relative frequencies, but rather with certain observed decision-making behavior. We are using it, not to calculate other relative frequencies, but rather to predict other decision-making behaviors. We are saying that, having interpreted the theory in some decisions, we can predict how the decision maker will act in others. If he acts in a way consistent with the theory of probability, our predictions will be correct.

Although there are two essentially different interpretations of the mathematical theory of probability, the weights or degrees of belief held by reasonable men are expected to be closely related to relative frequencies. If a *reasonable* man is defined as one whose weights or degrees of belief are consistent, in the sense of probability theory, then one can suggest the following result:

> Whatever his initial opinion may be, a reasonable man will modify this opinion in the face of relative frequency experience in such a way that his weights or degrees of belief approach relative frequencies.

People find it reasonable for a man, whose experience has been (or who accepts the reported experience of others) that the relative frequency of heads in repeated flips of a coin is very seldom greatly different from one-half in a long series of flips, to guess heads or tails indifferently when a coin is flipped once and a prize is offered for a correct guess. Thus we would expect

a. Reasonable men who have been exposed to similar experiences should hold similar opinions.

b. As long as sufficient data or experience can be obtained, one's initial opinion or assignment of weights may be quite unimportant, since the effect of this initial opinion will be negligible when modified by the additional experience.

c. When reasonable men disagree, it may mean that they do not have substantial common experience or shared data.

These remarks are of the utmost importance in management science and each of them will shortly be examined more carefully.

One must be clear that, although we cannot obtain a relative frequency value without actually making a series of relevant observations, weights or degrees of belief can be assigned without any such public or explicit experience being available. Suppose the decision maker in the coin-guessing problem just cited is informed by what he believes to be a reliable source that the coin to be used has either two heads or two tails. He might still find himself indifferent between guessing heads and guessing tails. We could thus establish weights without any explicit relative frequency experience in the usual sense. This indeed is the key to the usefulness of these ideas. We are not limited to situations involving replicated experiments, relative frequency data, and repeated decisions. We can deal with "one-shot" decisions and bring to bear *whatever* relevant experience the manager has in mind. Thus we can consider a far larger collection of management problems than the analyst who limits his interpretation of probability theory to relative frequencies. The reader should be clear that henceforth the term *probability* always implies weights which express a decision maker's opinions. When we wish to discuss relative frequencies, we will label them as such.

Consistent Learning

Having scaled the decision maker's judgments in a manner permitting use of the logic of probability theory, we may now see what guidance that logic offers for modifying judgments in the light of new experience. We need a consistent guide to the revision of opinion in the face of new data, or a theory of consistent learning. We begin with a basic theorem in probability theory which relates joint and conditional probabilities.

$$P(A \text{ and } B) = P(A \mid B) P(B) = P(B \mid A) P(A)$$

That is, the probability of the joint occurrence of both events A and B is equal to the conditional probability of A, given that B has occurred, multiplied by the probability of B, and so on. As an immediate logical consequence we may write

$$P(A \mid B) = \frac{P(B \mid A)\, P(A)}{P(B)}$$

which is called *Bayes' theorem*. This theorem is central to our theory of learning, and it may be well to pause for a careful interpretation of it.

The following example suggests the interpretation of Bayes' theorem in terms of relative frequencies: An automobile is produced in two body styles and two engine options. The accompanying table shows the number of each combination produced in a production run of N vehicles.

		Engine Option	
		B	D
Body Style	A	x	y
	C	z	w

Thus x cars were built having body style A and engine option B, and so on, where $x + y + z + w = N$. Interpreting Bayes' theorem in terms of relative frequencies, we obtain

$$P(A \mid B) = \frac{x}{x + z} = \frac{P(B \mid A)\, P(A)}{P(B)} = \frac{(x/x + y)(x + y/N)}{(x + z/N)}$$

which is clearly an identity.

In terms of weights, we might think of a choice between two gambles, both of which would be called off unless a certain event B occurs.

a_1: an important payoff if both events A and B occur: nothing otherwise

a_2: if B occurs, the decision maker receives x tickets in the reference lottery where the prize is the same important payoff; nothing if B fails to occur

If the decision maker were indifferent between these two acts, we should say

$$\frac{x}{N} = P(A \mid B)$$

If he also determines the unconditional probability of B as well as the joint probability of both A and B, then consistency would require that these quantities be related in the manner suggested by Bayes' theorem.

To show how this theorem provides a logical guide to the revision of opinion, consider a very simple experiment. It involves an ordinary coin and a special die, four sides of which are labeled "heads" and the remaining two, "tails." Out of your sight, the coin is flipped, the die is rolled, and one of the objects is covered with a cup. An important prize is offered if you guess correctly which object is uncovered. Let H_0 stand for the statement: "The coin is uncovered" and H_1 stands for "The die is uncovered." Using the methods suggested, one might assess the probability to be associated with each of these statements, interpreting it, if desired, as an expression of degree of belief in its truth. Many subjects in this experiment would be indifferent as to whether they guessed "coin" or "die," and this behavior could be represented by the assignment

$$P(H_0) = P(H_1) = \tfrac{1}{2}$$

We suppose that your opinion can also be expressed using this particular probability distribution.

Now the experimenter offers to look at the uncovered object (which is still hidden from your sight) and report whether its uppermost surface is heads or tails. The question is then, how much such a report would influence your opinion, or what you would learn from it. Clearly, the report of heads or tails on the uppermost surface will not remove all your uncertainty about which object is uncovered. It is not perfectly decisive information, since it does not remove all doubt. Yet such a report would be useful in that it would reduce uncertainty to some extent. The problem is, to what extent? If the experimenter reports that heads is showing, it is intuitive that one's opinion changes in favor of the die, but the degree or magnitude of this change is seldom intuitive.

To obtain a logical guide as to the new weight to associate with H_1, Bayes' theorem is used as follows. Let h stand for the report, "heads is showing," and t for the report, "tails is showing." If one assumes for a moment that it is in fact the coin which is uncovered, the conditional probability of h is, for most people, equal to one-half. That is,

$$P(h \mid H_0) = \tfrac{1}{2}$$

and similarly

$$P(h \mid H_1) = \tfrac{2}{3}$$

The unconditional probability of the report h may be computed from the relation

$$P(h) = P(h \mid H_0)\,P(H_0) + P(h \mid H_1)\,P(H_1)$$

Bayes' theorem suggests that your revised opinion, the probability of H_1 given that the experimenter has made the report h, should be

$$P(H_1 \mid h) = \frac{P(h \mid H_1)\,P(H_1)}{P(h)}$$

$$= \frac{(\tfrac{2}{3})(\tfrac{1}{2})}{(\tfrac{1}{2})(\tfrac{1}{2}) + (\tfrac{2}{3})(\tfrac{1}{2})} = \frac{4}{7}$$

Thus your probability for H_1 ought to rise from $\tfrac{1}{2}$ to $\tfrac{4}{7}$ if the experimenter gives the report "heads is showing," and if you wish to be consistent in the sense of probability theory. That the probability should rise is, as said earlier, intuitive. How much it should go up usually requires some assistance from probability theory in support of intuition.

In the same way, report t would reduce the probability of H_1 from $\frac{1}{2}$ to $\frac{2}{5}$. Notice that, before hearing the experimenter's report, one can calculate just what impact the various reports will have on your opinion. Should the experimenter decide to charge for the reporting service, he will want to be paid before he actually makes his report, and this sort of advance calculation will prove helpful in deciding whether to pay the price he asks.

To see the logic of Bayes' theorem from another viewpoint, one might list all ways in which this experiment could turn out. For example, let the symbols H_0, h stand for the outcome, "The coin is uncovered and its uppermost surface shows heads." If your prior probability for H_0 is one-half, then the probability for this outcome will be one-half times one-half, or onefourth. Listed herewith are all the outcomes and their prior probabilities:

$$H_0, h \quad \tfrac{1}{4} \qquad H_0, t \quad \tfrac{1}{4}$$
$$H_1, h \quad \tfrac{1}{12} \qquad H_1, t \quad \tfrac{1}{12}$$
$$H_1, h \quad \tfrac{1}{12} \qquad H_1, t \quad \tfrac{1}{12}$$
$$H_1, h \quad \tfrac{1}{12}$$
$$H_1, h \quad \tfrac{1}{12}$$

Notice that we have listed the two ways the coin may turn up and the six ways the die may turn up. The sum of all these probabilities is, of course, 1. Now if you are told that heads is showing, you know immediately that you are in the left-hand column. The probability that the coin's head is showing is simply the probability of the result H_0, h divided by the sum of the probabilities for the outcomes in the left-hand column. Thus,

$$P(H_0 \mid h) = \frac{\frac{1}{4}}{\frac{1}{4} + \frac{4}{12}} = \frac{3}{7}$$

This is, of course, exactly the same as applying Bayes' theorem.

A Management Example

To suggest the ease with which this sort of structure may be applied, consider a simple management decision situation in which the reliability of a missile system is of central concern. In most interesting management decisions, the uncertainty involved is determined partly by the experience of the decision maker and partly by the data and evidence which he can obtain. If he has considerable experience, he may elect not to gather any data and thus the uncertainty is characteristic of his experience. If he has little experience, he may be forced to put great weight on the data collected by his staff. In the typical case, however, some combination of explicit evidence and implicit experience goes into the decision. One of the most difficult aspects of the process is just how much weight to give to experience and how much to give to the data. Managers seldom wish to rely exclusively on either. Here again, the logic of probability theory may offer some assistance. If a decision maker can express his uncertainty about some relatively simple events and wishes to be logical in the sense of probability theory, then he can use that theory to guide him toward consistent conclusions in complex situations.

The manufacturer of a missile claims it is 98 per cent reliable. The missile has been evaluated by an independent agency which suggests that it is only about 90 per cent reliable. The decision maker, who is buying the missile, is about to conduct his own tests of the missile which will consist of actual firings. Suppose our decision maker, relying on his experience, is uncertain about the claims of the manufacturer and the testing agency. (If he were certain that one of them was right, he would need no further tests.) He can express this uncertainty based on experience in a statement: "The probability that the manufacturer's claim is right is .40; the probability that the independent agency's claim is correct is .60. (They might both be wrong, but we ignore this in order to achieve the utmost simplicity.) Now suppose the decision maker actually conducts test firings of two missiles. How should he combine these data with his experience? What weight should be given to each? Suppose the two missiles tested are both failures, what would be the decision maker's resulting opinion?

Bayes' theorem provides a logic for computing the probability that the testing agency is right, given that there have been two failures. The theorem suggests that this would be

$$P(R = .90, \text{ given 2 failures}) = \frac{P(2 \text{ failures, given } R = .90) \, P(R = .90)}{P(2 \text{ failures})}$$

The quantities on the right-hand side may be obtained as follows:

P(2 failures, given $R = .90$) = (.10)(.10) = .01

P($R = .90$) manager's original opinion based on his experience. The chance that the testing agency's claim is right is .60.

P(2 failures) is obtained as before; that is,

P(2 failures) = P(2 failures, given $R = .90$) P($R = .90$)
+ P(2 failures, given $R = .98$) P($R = .98$) = (.01)(.60) + (.0004)(.40)

Using these values, the probability that the independent agency's claim is correct, given that two tests resulted in failure, turns out to be .97. Thus the logic of Bayes' theorem suggests that the decision maker, originally believing, on the basis of his experience, that the agency had a probability of .60 of being correct, might now believe that this probability has risen to .97, based on both his experience and the data. Indeed, if he wished to modify his experience in a logical way, he might accept this as a guide to the reduction in his uncertainty. Table 3-1 shows the results of modifying opinion in the light of various sample results which might be observed.

TABLE 3-1

Sample result	Probability of sample $P(x \mid R = .90)$	Joint probability $P(x \mid R = .90) P (R = .90)$	Revised probability $P(R = .90 \mid x)$
Two failures	.01	(.01)(.60)	.97
One failure, one success	.18	(.18)(.60)	.87
Two successes	.81	(.81)(.60)	.56

Terminology

These are the conventional names given the quantities related by Bayes' theorem:

The probabilities which describe the decision maker's judgments about the states of the world, future events, or hypotheses, before obtaining additional information are called *prior* probabilities.

The revised values of these probabilities after receiving the additional information are called *posterior* probabilities. *Prior* and *posterior* are defined relative to a particular item of information or sample result. Thus, probabilities prior to one observation may also be posterior to a previous observation.

The probability of a given sample result, observation, or item of information, under the assumption that some particular hypothesis or state of the world prevails, is called a *likelihood*.

Thus in the coin-die example, $P(H_0)$ is a prior probability, $P(H_0 \mid h)$ is a posterior probability, and $P(h \mid H_0)$ is a likelihood.

Intuition and Logical Learning

The sort of logic which probability theory suggests as a guide to learning or the revision of opinion is in many ways confirmed by intuition. It is possible to explore some of these ways by considering a generalized situation in which there are two hypotheses, or possible futures, H_0 and H_1, letting x represent any information that the decision maker considers relevant to his opinion.

The posterior probability of, say, H_0 may be written

$$P(H_0 \mid x) = \frac{P(H_0)}{P(H_0) + LP(H_1)}$$

where L is the ratio of the likelihoods.

$$L = \frac{P(x \mid H_1)}{P(x \mid H_0)}$$

Now if the prior probability $P(H_0)$ is taken to be either 1 or 0, one says that he is certain beyond any doubt that H_0 is true or that it is false. To be certain is to be completely unwilling to learn and uninfluenced by any information whatever. The expression for posterior probability confirms this by indicating that if the prior probability is 1 or 0, then the posterior probability will be the same, no matter what information comes to the decision maker's attention. Hence it is useful to remember that, if there is any possibility of changing one's mind, prior probabilities of 0 and 1 should be avoided. In this sense there is an important difference between being almost certain and being absolutely certain.

The likelihood ratio gives some indication of how decisive or conclusive a particular sample result may be. If the ratio of the likelihoods is 1, then the posterior will simply equal the prior probability. Unless the information is more likely under the assumption that one hypothesis is true than it is assuming the other, it will not change one's opinion. The more the ratio of the likelihoods differs from 1, the greater the difference between the prior and the posterior probability.

Sequential Samples and Independence

Suppose the information which the decision maker considers relevant actually consists of two items or observations, x and y. One might imagine a case in which knowledge of x becomes available to him first, followed by y. If his beliefs about the likelihood of y are not influenced by his knowledge of x, then one would say that x and y are independent. Symbolically,

$$P(y \mid H_0, x) = P(y \mid H_0)$$

$$P(y \mid H_1, x) = P(y \mid H_1)$$

are the conditions for the independence of x and y. Of course, if the order in which the observations became known to him was reversed, we would want to interchange x and y in these statements.

We first remark that, as one would expect, it makes no difference whether the decision maker revises his opinions after learning x and again after learning y, or whether he revises them only once after learning both x and y. Either way, his final opinion will be the same. Bayes' theorem may be written

$$P(H_0 \mid x, y) = \frac{P(y \mid H_0, x)\, P(x \mid H_0)\, P(H_0)}{P(y \mid H_0, x)\, P(x \mid H_0)\, P(H_0) + P(y \mid H_1, x)\, P(x \mid H_1)\, P(H_1)}$$

Dividing numerator and denominator on the right-hand side by $P(x)$ and recalling the expression for the posterior probabilities, given x, permits this to be written

$$P(H_0 \mid x, y) = \frac{P(y \mid H_0, x)\, P(H_0 \mid x)}{P(y \mid H_0, x)\, P(H_0 \mid x) + P(y \mid H_1, x)\, P(H_1 \mid x)}$$

Thus it is clear that we get the same result if we compute the probability of H_0 posterior to x and y by either of two methods:

1. Compute $P(H_0 \mid x, y)$ in a single step.
2. Compute it in two steps, first finding $P(H_0 \mid x)$ and then using this result as a prior probability in applying Bayes' theorem for a second time.

Thus, as one's intuition would perhaps suggest, we arrive at the same final opinion whether we consider information in batches or sequentially.

Suppose, using the second method, we have computed the probabilities posterior to observing x. The impact of y on our opinions will depend on the likelihood ratio

$$L = \frac{P(y \mid H_1, x)}{P(y \mid H_0, x)}$$

As noted, the more the likelihood ratio differs from 1, the greater the change in the decision maker's opinions. Suppose that y and x are completely dependent and that after x is observed, one feels certain that y will follow. Then

$$P(y \mid H_0, x) = P(y \mid H_1, x) = 1$$

and the likelihood ratio equals 1. Thus in this case knowledge of y brings "no new information" and has no impact whatever on our opinions. Generally speaking, the effect of dependence of y on x is to make the likelihood ratio nearer to 1 than in the case of independence. This suggests the generalization that dependent samples have less influence on opinions, contain less information, or are less conclusive, than independent observations. This again agrees with intuition.

The Approach toward Relative Frequencies

Suppose you strongly believe that the long-run relative frequency of heads for a peculiarly deformed coin is $\frac{6}{10}$, but admit that there is some possibility that this relative frequency might be $\frac{1}{2}$. For simplicity, suppose you feel that no other values for the long-run relative frequency are possible. Your beliefs might be expressed as

$$P(H_0) = .9 \qquad P(H_1) = .1$$

where H_0 stands for the statement: "The long-run relative frequency is $\frac{6}{10}$" and H_1 for the statement that it is $\frac{1}{2}$.

Now you begin to flip the coin in question and keep a record of the observed relative frequencies. If in fact the long-run relative frequency is $\frac{1}{2}$, then as you make more and more observations, it becomes increasingly certain that the observed relative frequency will be close to $\frac{1}{2}$. That is, as the sample size grows larger, it becomes increasingly unlikely that the sample relative frequency of heads will differ from the true relative by more than any amount you wish to specify, however small. Thus it becomes increasingly certain that $P(x \mid H_0)$ will be close to 0 and $P(x \mid H_1)$ will be close to 1, where x is the observed relative frequency in an increasingly large number of flips. It follows from Bayes' theorem that $P(H_1 \mid x)$ is very likely to be close to 1 for large samples. If one learns from experience according to the logic of probability theory, one will eventually learn the truth. Whatever one's initial opinion (excepting, of course, complete certainty), with experience one will come to hold opinions in agreement with observed relative frequencies. Thus we find it reasonable to base our opinions on relative frequencies, and as suggested, we would expect reasonable men exposed to similar experience to hold similar opinions. As information accumulates, reasonable men tend to give less and less weight to their original opinions and more and more weight to the evidence becoming available. This is indeed the essence of what is meant by *science*. When there are enough data so that reasonable and informed men are in close agreement, we no longer refer to their opinions as *subjective* and may, if we wish, regard them as "objective."

What is perhaps less intuitive is the rapidity with which this convergence may take place. To pick an admittedly extreme example, consider two hypotheses about a coin:

H_0: the relative frequency of heads in the long run is p

H_1: the relative frequency of heads in the long run is q

Suppose $p/q = \frac{1}{2}$. Imagine two decision makers who have rather different opinions about these hypotheses. The beliefs of one may be expressed by the weight $P(H_0) = .5$; the other's beliefs may be expressed as $P(H_0) = .9$. Suppose both men begin to observe the flipping of the coin. If the coin were to come up heads seven times in a row, both would agree that the reasonable weight to associate with H_0 would be less than .07. Of course a less conclusive sample would not produce such a rapid convergence.

This very important effect will be examined in a number of instances as we proceed.

EXERCISES

3-1. Formulate your own prior distribution in several decision-making situations of interest to you. Choose some in which you have had considerable experience and some in which you have had little experience.

3-2. In one or more of the situations considered in Exercise 3-1, formulate your posterior distribution in the light of some particular data. Check your posterior distribution against that which would result from using the model discussed in this chapter.

3-3. Design and carry out an experiment to obtain explicit prior and posterior distributions in some decision situation, using as your subject a person not trained in probability theory.

3-4. Discuss the difficulties you would expect to encounter in attempting to obtain the prior distribution of a manager in some actual situation. What suggestions could you make for overcoming these difficulties?

3-5. Among the widely used conventional statistical techniques are hypothesis testing and confidence-interval estimation. What modifications of these techniques would you suggest in the light of the ideas discussed in this chapter?

3-6. Outline some methods of making decisions in the face of uncertainty which do not require the use of prior or posterior probabilities.

3-7. Relative frequencies are sometimes called *objective probabilities*. In what ways are they actually subjective?

3-8. A theory of learning is described in this chapter. What alternative theories of learning can you suggest?

3-9. A frequent objection to the idea of subjective probabilities is that people simply do not think in terms sufficiently precise to permit the assignment of such numbers to their opinions. What is your reaction to this comment?

3-10. One suggestion for obtaining a prior distribution is that the subject be asked to make some simple decisions *after* having received various sample results. From these decisions, posterior distributions are to be inferred, and from these, in turn, one may infer prior distributions. Show by means of an example how this would be done.

3-11. Many firms have considerable historical data on the *outcome* of past decisions, but very little data on the decisions themselves. Why, in your opinion, is this the case, and what would be the advantages of altering the situation?

4

Scaling
Preferences

Explaining Preference Systems

The manager's opinions about possible future events have been measured; we turn now to his preferences, and the way in which both opinions and preferences are to be combined into choices. It is assumed that the manager's preferences are relevant, in the sense that they may be taken to represent the firm's value system. We suppress questions as to whether or not the preferences of a particular manager fairly represent those of the stockholders, his associates, or his superiors. These are difficult and important questions, but for our purposes they may be neglected.

The method of scaling a manager's preferences is very similar to that which was used to make explicit his opinions. It makes the same sort of demands on his ability to think carefully about how he would behave in certain rather simply stated decision situations. The approach to this, then, is by means of an example in which the first attempt is to develop a theory to explain the manager's past behavior, then to offer this theory as a guide to consistent behavior in the future.

A manager is confronted with four courses of action which promise various profits and losses as indicated in Fig. 4-1, the probabilities included are to be understood as representing his opinions, and having been obtained by methods, such as those suggested in Chapter 3.

	$P(S_1) = .50$	$P(S_2) = .10$	$P(S_3) = .40$
a_1	$100,000	$-$50,000	$-$50,000
a_2	$-$50,000	$-$50,000	$100,000
a_3	$15,000	$15,000	0
a_4	0	0	0

FIGURE 4-1

The fourth action is thought of as "doing nothing"—although one always wants to avoid the general assumption that "doing nothing" will generally yield zero profit in a business context. Now, the manager is asked to rank the four actions in terms of his preferences. Assume that he can do this in a meaningful way. While he is doing this, we must attempt to explain what we think his preferences will be, and we begin with the rather common hypothesis: "He chooses among such actions so as to maximize the expected profit." Suppose that the results of this effort are

Action	His rank	Expected profit
a_1	2	$25,000
a_2	4	$10,000
a_3	1	$ 9,000
a_4	3	0

The hypothesis that he maximizes expected profit is clearly unsatisfactory. For he prefers action 3, with an expected profit of $9,000, to action 1, with an expectation of $25,000. He would rather "do nothing" than take action 2 although it has an expected profit of $10,000. Intuitively it can be supposed that he is somehow considering large losses to be more serious in the life of the firm than their dollar amount indicates. Perhaps also, large profits are not desirable to the firm in direct proportion to the dollar magnitudes. We require an operational method of making these considerations explicit. Hence we first indicate what the final result will be, then undertake to explain how it occurs.

An Equivalent Decision

We now examine a decision which, at first glance, appears quite unrelated to the one which our manager is considering.

a_1': $100,000 profit with probability = .50; $50,000 loss with probability = .50

a_2': $100,000 profit with probability = .40; $50,000 loss with probability = .60

a'_3: \$100,000 profit with probability = .55; \$50,000 loss with probability = .45

a'_4: \$100,000 profit with probability = .48; \$50,000 loss with probability = .52

In this decision it is quite natural to prefer the action with the greatest probability of producing the \$100,000 profit. Few people will argue with such a method of choice. In Chapter 3, we specifically assumed that a reasonable and consistent decision maker would choose in this way. Thus we could use the probability of the \$100,000 profit as an index or measure of preferences in this situation with considerable hope that it would explain the manager's preferences. Less obvious is the relation of this decision to the original situation. Clearly a'_1 is simply a restatement of a_1. If, however, a decision maker wishes to meet some rather acceptable criteria for consistency, it can be shown that he will be indifferent between a_2 and a'_2, a_3 and a'_3, and a_4 and a'_4. Thus the two decisions will be "equivalent" for him, and our method and our simple method of explaining preferences in the second decision may be used to understand the first as well. This is not at all obvious, and we must now see how it comes about.

The Reference Contract

As in Chapter 3, we select a basic decision problem as the scaling device for the manager's preferences. This consists of what we shall call the *reference contract* as one alternative and a riskless dollar profit as the other. The reference contract may be stated as follows:

a profit of \$100,000 with probability p; a loss of \$50,000 with probability $1 - p$

Logically it makes no difference what the two amounts of money are, although it is convenient to have one amount at least as large as any appearing in decision problems we will study, and the other at least as small as any amount appearing. Psychologically, however, we should avoid amounts which are too large or too small for the manager to consider meaningfully. We ask the manager how he would choose between

a_1: the reference contract in which the probability p takes some specified value

a_2: a sure profit (or loss) of x dollars

Assume that he can respond meaningfully to such questions and that we can find, for any value of x, a value of p which leaves him indifferent between the two alternatives. Selecting amounts that appear in the original decision, we thus discover, for each, what value of p would produce an indifferent reference contract. For example, he might be indifferent between the reference contract with $p = .60$ and a sure profit of $15,000. He might accept the reference contract with $p = .48$ as equally desirable as a certain profit of 0. Suppose that the results of this scaling effort are as follows:

Sure profit or loss	Value of p in indifferent reference contract
$-$50,000	0
0	.48
$15,000	.60
$100,000	1.00

Substitutability

We now introduce an axiom which defines in part the meaning of *consistency* in our theory of consistent decision. Since the manager has indicated indifference between zero dollars for certain and the reference contract with $p = .48$, we assume he will also be indifferent between a_4 and a new alternative formed by substituting for the zero dollars promised by a_4 the reference contract with $p = .48$. This new alternative we have already called a_4'.

Taking the original decision problem, we apply the principle of substituting indifferent reference contracts in each cell of the matrix. This will produce four new actions but they will be equivalent to, or indifferent with respect to, the four original actions. The symbol RC indicates the reference contract.

	$P(S_1) = .50$	$P(S_2) = .10$	$P(S_3) = .40$
a_1	RC with $p = 1.00$	RC with $p = 0$	RC with $p = 0$
a_2	RC with $p = 0$	RC with $p = 0$	RC with $p = 1.00$
a_3	RC with $p = .60$	RC with $p = .60$	RC with $p = .48$
a_4	RC with $p = .48$	RC with $p = .48$	RC with $p = .48$

FIGURE 4-2

Now in this transformed matrix, only two outcomes are possible, profits of $100,000 and losses of $50,000. If one chooses a_1 in the transformed matrix, for example, the probability of the $100,000 is

$$(.50)(1.00) + (.10)(0) + (.40)(0) = .50$$

Similar calculations yield

Action	Probability of $100,000
a_1	.50
a_2	.40
a_3	.55
a_4	.48

(In the case of a_3, we have rounded off the probability.) Looked at this way, the alternatives in the transformed matrix are simply those which we called $a'_1, \ldots, a'_4$. Thus we may argue that if the manager wishes to be consistent in the sense of the principle of substitution, he will behave in the decision involving these transformed actions in exactly the same way as he will behave in the original problem. Since the transformed decision simply offers the reference contract with various values of p, we can argue that

a. Any course of action can be reduced to an equivalent or indifferent reference contract

b. Since choice among reference contracts is based on maximimizing the value of p, this principle can be extended to any alternative.

Our theory of choice then becomes:

The consistent decision maker will choose among actions so as to maximize the probability of the larger outcome in equivalent reference contracts.

The quantity p thus becomes our indicator of preference or measure of value. Notice that this does succeed in explaining our manager's behavior in the example with which we began.

Utility

The quantity p in equivalent reference contracts which now serves as our scaled expression of the decision maker's preferences is conventionally given the name *utility*. We accept this convention, but remember that a utility is nothing more nor less than a probability in an equivalent reference contract. If we are scaling the decision maker's preferences for money, we may want to adopt a "smooth" or well-behaved function, $U(x)$, to represent the utility of x dollars. Having obtained utilities for some values of x, we may be willing to fit a smooth curve to them and obtain the decision maker's "utility function." Unless there are specific reasons for irregularities, or "bumps" in his utility function, the decision maker may be willing to accept a smooth curve as an expression of his preferences. If we are interested in his preferences toward any other set of outcomes which has some sort of structure, we may take advantage of this structure in establishing a utility function on the basis of some reasonable number of observations.

Expected Utility

The utility function, $U(x)$, gives utilities for sure sums of money, but our real interest is in obtaining utilities for actions which are in fact probability distributions. In other words, we need a workable way of reducing any complex action to its equivalent reference contract. Recall that when we computed the value of p in the reference contract equivalent to a_1, we wrote

$$p = (.50)(1.00) + (.10)(0) + (.40)(0)$$

Since we have changed the name of p from *probability* to *utility*, this equation may be rewritten as

$$U(a_1) = (.50)\, U(\$100,000) + (.10)\, U(-\$50,000) + (.40)\, U(-\$50,000)$$

Thus in calculating the utility of a_1, we simply calculated its expected utility. This is the especially useful feature of this particular method of scaling preferences. The utility of any complex action can be obtained by straightforward calculation of its expected utility. Our theory asserts that in any action, however complicated, the consistent decision maker will choose so as to maximize expected utility. (The reader may wish to confirm that the utilities of the other actions in our example may be obtained in this way.)

We now have a complete theory of consistent decision which indicates how opinions about future events are to be scaled; how preferences among outcomes are to be scaled; and how opinions and preferences are combined to determine choices.

Choice of a Reference Contract

When one chooses a reference contract, the smaller amount of money involved determines the zero point on the utility scale; the larger amount determines the unit of measure. Logically these choices are quite arbitrary. Utilities measured on one scale can be transformed into utilities on any other scale simply by adding a positive or negative constant or multiplying by a positive constant, or by both of these operations together. Thus, one would say that all utility scales are positive linear transformations of each other. Our scale does not permit us to say that if $U(x) = 2U(y)$, x is twice as desirable as y. We could alter this ratio by altering the reference contract or scale used to assign the utilities. Although logically we have considerable freedom to choose a reference contract, we stress again the importance of choosing one which permits psychologically meaningful responses. It would probably not be wise to use billions of dollars in a reference contract when the decision maker's problems involved hundreds or thousands.

Utility Function Shapes

The utility function of the manager in our example would, if plotted, increase at a decreasing rate. It might be said to exhibit a decreasing marginal utility for money; that is, the desirability of an additional dollar decreases as the total amount increases. This man, as we saw, valued the risky opportunities he was offered at less than their expected monetary value. Although a_1 had an expected profit of $25,000, he would not be willing to pay $25,000 for the opportunity to participate in it. He was conservative or risk averse. We would predict that such a man would buy various kinds of insurance against large risks and would pursue a policy of diversification in his business in order to reduce the risk or variability in its profits.

Alternatively, we might encounter a person whose utility function for money increased at an increasing rate. His marginal utility would be increasing; his behavior would contrast markedly with that of the previous manager. This man would be an avid seeker of risky opportunities. He might be willing to pay even more than $25,000 for the opportunity to participate in a_1, would not insure against large risks, and would avoid diversification, being perfectly willing to put "all his eggs in one basket."

Between these two would be the person whose utility function for money would be linear and whose behavior would be consistent with the maximization of expected profit. For this man, we could dispense with the utility notion in practice, and use monetary values.

Approximating Utility

It is easy to see that in a large firm there are many decisions whose largest possible profit and largest possible loss are small relative to the net worth or annual budget of the firm. Thus each of these small decisions involves only a small region of the firm's utility function. It is often possible to take the utility function to be linear in such a small region, to study the decision using expected profits and losses, and not lead the decision maker into any inconsistencies. This is the basic reason that many decisions having modest consequences may be delegated to lower management levels, whereas decisions involving larger amounts of money must be in the hands of top managers who presumably wish to control the degree of risk aversion in such cases.

Thus in any decision problem, we can make a rough test of whether we can use profit maximization as a guide to consistent behavior or whether we must develop a manager's utility function. If the manager is indifferent between a gamble involving the largest and smallest outcomes in the decision and a sure profit equal to the expected value of such a gamble, then we need not obtain utilities. If he values the gamble at more or less than its expected dollar profit, utilities will be required if we are to give a consistent guide to choice.

EXERCISES

4-1. Plot your own utility function in the range of amounts of money for which you have some decision-making experience.

4-2. Design and carry out the experiment of determining the utility function of some person not familiar with utility theory.

4-3. This problem and the three following concern the subject whose utility function is tabulated here.

x	$U(x)$
$-\$50,000$	0
$-40,000$	.08
$-25,000$	.24
0	.48
15,000	.60
50,000	.80
70,000	.88
100,000	1.00

Suppose this manager is given a choice between receiving a certain \$100,000 and a contract involving \$150,000 profit with probability p and \$50,000 loss with probability $1 - p$. Suppose he reports that he is indifferent. What utility would you assign to \$150,000? (*Ans.*: $U(\$150,000) = 1/p$.)

4-4. Plot the utility function tabulated in Exercise 4-3. Show that a risky contract promising x_1 dollars with probability p and x_2 with probability $1 - p$ may be represented by a point whose coordinates are

$$x_1 p + x_2(1 - p)$$
$$U(x_1)p + U(x_2)(1 - p)$$

and that this point lies on a straight line joining the points whose coordinates are

$$x_1, U(x_1)$$
$$x_2, U(x_2)$$

Show on the same graph the points which represent two risky contracts having equal expected profits but differing variances of profit.

4-5. The manager whose utility function is tabulated in Exercise 4-3 has a choice between

  a_1: a risky contract promising \$70,000 with probability .60 and $-\$40,000$ with probability .40

a_2: a diversified portfolio consisting of two contracts whose outcomes are independent, each of which promises \$35,000 with probability .60 and −\$20,000 with probability .40

Show that, although the expected profits are the same, this manager will prefer the diversified portfolio. Show that the diversified portfolio has a smaller variance of profit.

4-6. The foregoing manager is considering two possible opportunities. One promises a profit of \$100,000 with probability .45 and a loss of \$50,000 with probability .55. The second opportunity involves going into the first with a partner who will share equally in the profit or loss. Show that the manager would rather do nothing than undertake the first opportunity, but will be willing to take the second involving an equal partnership.

4-7. Repeat Exercise 4-4 but use a linear utility function and one which increases at an increasing rate.

5

Consistent

Management

Decision

The Value of Information

Henceforth, we assume that opinions have been made explicit by using methods like those of Chapter 3 and that the decision maker wishes to act in a manner consistent with the logic of probability theory. Further, we assume that preferences have been scaled as suggested in Chapter 4, and that the decision maker wants to choose so as to maximize his expected utility. To focus attention on other central issues, we will, in much of the following discussion, take the decision maker's utility function for money to be linear and seek the maximization of expected profit. We now examine the implications of this theory of consistent decision for the tasks of the manager.

The most important basic question to be faced is how much a manager should reasonably be willing to pay for information he considers relevant to his decisions. To illustrate our approach to this question in the simplest possible context, we return to the coin-die decision problem of Chapter 3. The basic elements of that problem were represented as follows:

$$H_0 = \text{the coin is uncovered}$$
$$H_1 = \text{the die is uncovered}$$
$$h = \text{heads is showing}$$
$$t = \text{tails is showing}$$

We now add the consideration that, if the decision maker guesses correctly which object is uncovered, he will receive a prize of \$1.00; he will receive nothing if he guesses incorrectly. If we assume that his prior probabilities (which we may now represent somewhat more suggestively) are

$$PR(H_0) = PR(H_1) = \tfrac{1}{2}$$

then without further information he would be indifferent as to which object he guessed, and his prior expected payoff would be 50 cents.

Imagine now that the experimenter offers the decision maker perfectly reliable information about which object is uncovered. The decision maker must, however, pay for this perfectly reliable reporting service before getting the information. How much would such information be worth? He may look ahead, ask what he would do in response to each of the two possible reports the service might furnish, and calculate his profit from the resulting responses. Weighting this profit with the prior probabilities of the possible reports would permit him to assess his expected profit if he paid for the perfectly reliable information before actually receiving it. Since this expected profit will be greater than the 50 cents he expects on the basis of prior information alone, the increase in profit would be the maximum amount he could reasonably pay for the information service.

If the report is "the coin is uncovered," his posterior probability for H_0 goes to 1. Although this is obvious, it is also in agreement with Bayes' theorem, since, if he believes the report to be perfectly reliable, the conditional probability of the report, given H_0, is 1. The best choice is then to guess "coin" and the resulting profit is \$1.00. If the report is to the effect that the die is uncovered, he will guess accordingly and again have a payoff of \$1.00. Based on his prior beliefs he would associate a probability of $\tfrac{1}{2}$ with the statement: "The perfectly reliable reporting service will indicate that the coin is uncovered" and also a probability of $\tfrac{1}{2}$ with the other report indicating the die is uncovered. Thus before receiving any report he feels that his expected profit if he subscribes to the reporting service is

$$EP \mid PI = (\tfrac{1}{2})(1.00) + (\tfrac{1}{2})(1.00) = 1.00$$

The symbol EP | PI suggests the expected profit, given perfect information. His gain in profit over that available to him on the basis of prior information will be called the *expected value* of perfect information (EVPI).

$$EVPI = EP \mid PI - \text{prior expected profit}$$
$$= 1.00 - .50 = .50$$

Thus the maximum he would find it reasonable to pay for this perfectly reliable reporting service is 50 cents. Most information in actual management problems is "imperfect," unreliable; it does not eliminate all uncertainty; hence, EVPI suggests the upper bound for the amount that can reasonably be spent on *any* information-gathering program. Since EVPI represents the profit increase from a complete elimination of uncertainty, it is sometimes called *the cost of uncertainty.*

Notice that we can compute EVPI in two other interesting ways. Since we would be indifferent, suppose the prior choice had been made by flipping a coin which resulted in the guess "coin." If the reporting service had indicated "coin," we would not have changed our behavior. Since our prior and posterior choices would have been the same, we argue that the information is of no value. If the report had been "die," we would have changed our guess, thus increasing our posterior payoff from zero, had we persisted with our prior guess, to $1.00 if we changed. Thus in this case the information brought a gain of $1.00. Weighting these gains by the probabilities of the reports again produces the EVPI.

Still another way of looking at the value of perfect information is to suppose again that our prior choice was "coin." If the guess was correct, we would have no cause for regret. If, however, that choice proved to be wrong, we get nothing instead of the $1.00 we would have received, had we only guessed "die." We may regard this $1.00 either as a measure of our "regret" or as an opportunity loss. Computing the expected regret or the expected opportunity loss for the best prior act also gives us the expected value of perfect information.

The Value of Imperfect Information

The same principles permit us to assess the value of imperfect or sampling information. Suppose the decision maker is offered a report on whether the uppermost surface of the uncovered object is showing heads or tails. If he wishes to subscribe to this reporting service, he must pay for it in advance, and we are concerned with how much he can reasonably offer for such imperfect information. As before, the decision maker can calculate his response to the various reports that might be received, the profit resulting from the best action in the light of each possible report, and the probabilities of the reports. We know from previous calculations that if the report is heads, the posterior distribution becomes

$$PO(H_0 \mid h) = \tfrac{3}{7} \qquad PO(H_1 \mid h) = \tfrac{4}{7}$$

the best guess is "die," and the resulting expected profit is $\tfrac{4}{7}$. If the report is tails, the posterior becomes

$$PO(H_0 \mid t) = \tfrac{3}{5} \qquad PO(H_1 \mid t) = \tfrac{2}{5}$$

the best guess is "coin," and the resulting expected profit is $\tfrac{3}{5}$. The probability of report h is $\tfrac{7}{12}$ and of t, $\tfrac{5}{12}$. The expected profit given sample information is

$$\text{EP} \mid \text{SI} = (\tfrac{7}{12})(\tfrac{4}{7}) + (\tfrac{5}{12})(\tfrac{3}{5}) = \tfrac{7}{12}$$

The expected value of sample information is

$$\text{EVSI} = \text{EP} \mid \text{SI} - \text{prior expected profit}$$

$$= \tfrac{7}{12} - \tfrac{1}{2} = \tfrac{1}{12}$$

As expected, the value of sample information is less than that of perfect information.

It is suggestive to examine an alternative method of obtaining EVSI. If we take our prior choice to be "coin," the report "tails" does not alter our choice; hence the information is valueless in terms of its impact on our behavior. If the report is "heads," however, we will switch our choice to "die." If H_0 is true, this change in our behavior will result in a decline of \$1.00 from what we would have made had we persisted in the guess "coin." If H_1 is true, the change will increase the payoff from 0 (if we had chosen "coin") up to \$1.00. Thus given the report t, we will have no change in payoff, but the report h brings a probability of $\tfrac{3}{7}$ of a \$1.00 decline in profit and a probability of $\tfrac{4}{7}$ of a \$1.00 increase in profit. Recall that these are the posterior probabilities, given the report h. Weighting the changes by the probabilities of the two reports yields

$$\text{EVSI} = (\tfrac{5}{12})(0) + (\tfrac{7}{12})[(\tfrac{3}{7})(-1) + (\tfrac{4}{7})(1)] = \tfrac{1}{12}$$

The Value of Information as a Function of Uncertainty

If $\text{PR}(H_0) = 0$ or 1, information of any sort will be valueless, since there is no possibility of changing the decision maker's mind or altering the chosen course of action. Suppose, however, that

$$\tfrac{1}{2} \le \text{PR}(H_0) \le 1$$

and the decision maker's prior choice is "coin." Then,

$$\text{EVPI} = \text{PR}(H_0)(1) + \text{PR}(H_1)(1) - \text{PR}(H_0)(1) - \text{PR}(H_1)(0) = 1 - \text{PR}(H_0)$$

Thus the maximum value of EVPI will occur for $\text{PR}(H_0) = \tfrac{1}{2}$, and one may think of this particular prior distribution as expressing the maximum amount of uncertainty.

Additional Sample Information

Next suppose that the decision maker is offered a more extensive, but still imperfect, reporting service. The uncovered object will be rolled or flipped n times, and each time a report will be given of what was showing on the uppermost surface. For a sample of size $n = 2$, there are four possible reports:

$$x_1 = h, h$$
$$x_2 = h, t$$
$$x_3 = t, h$$
$$x_4 = t, t$$

The conditional probability of a report, given that a particular hypothesis is true, may be calculated, using the binomial distribution. Henceforth we refer to such a conditional probability as a *likelihood* and symbolize it as $LK(x_i \mid H_j)$. Using the prior probabilities and the likelihoods, we may compute the unconditional probability of any sample result.

$$P(x_i) = LK(x_i \mid H_0) \, PR(H_0) + LK(x_i \mid H_1) \, PR(H_1)$$

Using Bayes' theorem, we may then compute the posterior probabilities, the best course of action, and the resulting expected profit. The results of these calculations are summarized in Table 5-1.

TABLE 5-1

Sample result x_i	Probability of sample $P(x_i)$	Posterior probability $PO(H_0 \mid x_i)$	Best act	Expected profit
$x_1 = h, h$	25/72	9/25	die	16/25
$x_2 = h, t$	17/72	9/17	coin	9/17
$x_3 = t, h$	17/72	9/17	coin	9/17
$x_4 = t, t$	13/72	9/13	coin	9/13

The expected value of sample information is

$$EVSI = \left(\tfrac{25}{72}\right)\left(\tfrac{16}{25}\right) + \left(\tfrac{17}{72}\right)\left(\tfrac{9}{17}\right)$$
$$+ \left(\tfrac{17}{72}\right)\left(\tfrac{9}{17}\right) + \left(\tfrac{9}{13}\right)\left(\tfrac{13}{72}\right) - \tfrac{1}{2} = \tfrac{7}{72}$$

Thus the expected value of sample information for $n = 2$ is greater than for $n = 1$, computed as $\tfrac{1}{12}$. Note that doubling the sample size does not double the EVSI.

Considering EVSI as a function of n, we would expect it to increase at a decreasing rate, approaching EVPI as a limit. If the cost of obtaining observations is simply proportional to n, say, kn, one might define the expected net gain from sample information as

$$ENGSI = EVSI - kn$$

There will be some value of n which maximizes ENGSI in our example. It might turn out to be $n = 0$, in which case we would conclude that sample information is entirely too expensive. The best thing to do is base the decision on the prior information alone. On the other hand the maximimizing value of n might turn out to be greater than zero (it will never be infinity unless

$k = 0$), in which case we would have the basic guide to planning a data-collection program or designing a management-information system.

The Likelihood Principle

We may note here a fact which will later warrant closer examination. The two reports, $x_2 = h, t$ and $x_3 = t, h$, both produced the same posterior distribution and the same posterior expected profit. Thus in reporting them to the decision maker, there is no need to distinguish between them. Indeed, we might consider *three* possible reports

report 1: the first observation was heads, the second, tails.

report 2: one head in two observations.

report 3: a series of observations was continued until the first tail appeared; this occurred on the second observation.

We have seen in the example that the first two reports will result in the same posterior, but what about report 3?

For report 3, the likelihoods are

$$\text{LK (report 3} \mid H_0) = (\tfrac{1}{2})(\tfrac{1}{2})$$

$$\text{LK (report 3} \mid H_1) = (\tfrac{2}{3})(\tfrac{1}{3})$$

From Bayes' theorem, we obtain

$$\text{PO}(H_0 \mid \text{report 3}) = \frac{(\tfrac{1}{2})(\tfrac{1}{2})(\tfrac{1}{2})}{(\tfrac{1}{2})(\tfrac{1}{2})(\tfrac{1}{2}) + (\tfrac{2}{3})(\tfrac{1}{3})(\tfrac{1}{2})}$$

Thus report 3 yields the same posterior distribution as reports 1 and 2. This is surprising because, so far as our decision maker is concerned, it makes no difference whether we decide to flip a coin twice and happen to observe one head, or whether we decide to flip a coin until the first tail appears and this happens on the second flip. So far as a management-information system is concerned, any of the three reports will do, and we may choose the one which makes most economical use of the system's resources. Clearly if a large number of observations were involved, there might be a substantial difference in the cost, say, of transmitting and recording reports 1 and 2.

We may generalize this idea by noting that two reports, r and r', will be *equivalent* if they result in the same posterior distribution. This implies

$$\text{PO}(H_j \mid r) = \frac{\text{LK}(r \mid H_j)\,\text{PR}(H_j)}{\text{P}(r)} = \text{PO}(H_j \mid r') = \frac{\text{LK}(r' \mid H_j)\,\text{PR}(H_j)}{\text{P}(r')}$$

which may be reduced to

$$\frac{\text{LK}(r \mid H_j)}{\text{LK}(r' \mid H_j)} = \frac{\text{P}(r)}{\text{P}(r')} = K$$

This must hold for all *j*. Thus we may say that two reports are *equivalent* if the ratio of their likelihoods is the same for all possible futures or for all hypotheses. This is called the *likelihood principle*.

One implication for management information systems is, as we have seen, that we may choose among equivalent reports those which are easiest and most economical to handle in our data-processing system. A second implication for the design of data-collection programs is also important. The example showed that, given the sample result *h, t,* it made no difference whether we had decided in advance to flip a coin twice or to flip until the first tail appeared. Thus it would have made no difference which of these two rules or policies had been used to terminate our data-gathering program. More generally, we can collect data until we run out of time, or money, or perhaps until we reach some particular level of certainty.

Responses to Uncertainty

Desire for certainty in decision problems is a fundamental human trait. We always wish we had more information to reduce our uncertainty, and the strength of this desire may well make it difficult to act reasonably in decisions involving the purchase of costly information. The coin-die decision problem, with several different payoff schedules, has been posed experimentally to groups of students before their introduction to our theory of consistent decision. Although such experiments are subject to a variety of interpretations, the results seem to confirm those obtained by other investigators using similar experimental problems.

Even in decisions as seemingly simple as the coin-die problem, consistent decisions about buying information are difficult to make without the aid of logic and explicit calculation. The most interesting result, however, appears to be the rather general tendency for the inconsistency to be in the same direction. The great majority of subjects appear willing to pay more for information than it is worth, where our theory is used as a standard. Alternatively, we may hypothesize that people rather generally fail to extract from the data all the information or uncertainty reduction which consistency would permit.

Should such results prove to be widely confirmed in management situations, our program for consistent decision making is clearly of considerable significance.

A Steel Strike Example

Consider the problem of a steel consumer who wonders how much extra steel to stock in anticipation of a possible strike in the steel industry. Again for simplicitly, assume that the steel consumer believes that the steel strike will last for 0, 30, 45, or 90 days. All his experience and his estimate of the current situation leave him uncertain about the duration of the strike. To obtain a specific problem, suppose he regards any of the four durations indicated to be equally likely. His decision is made explicit in Fig. 5-1. The cost figures in the matrix are only illustrative and are not supposed to be based on any particular underlying analysis. If, for example, no extra steel is stocked and a 30-day strike occurs, the additional costs resulting are assumed to be $200,000. If a 30-day supply of extra steel is stocked, and no strike occurs, additional costs of $50,000 are assumed. To keep the analysis simple, we restrict ourselves to a highly abstracted version of the actual decision problem. If the manager chooses so as to minimize expected cost, he will stock a 90-day supply of extra steel.

This consumer finds himself highly uncertain, in the sense that he sees no duration as more likely than another; thus he may feel a strong desire to obtain more information. Suppose he believes that his competitors have more experience than he and that it would be useful to find out what they are doing. They, however, are unwilling to make their beliefs public. By careful and costly investigation, the decision maker's staff can find out about some competitors' policies. If he tells his staff to proceed, he is explicitly or implicitly making some important assumptions:

 a. Knowledge of a competitor's policy is not useless. The probability of a competitor being right is more than .25.

 b. This knowledge is not to be followed blindly. The probability of a competitor being right is not 1.00.

 c. The cost of getting some data of this sort is less than its benefits.

 d. Both experience and data must go into the final decision.

THE STEEL STRIKE DECISION

Extra steel inventory (days' supply)		*Duration of strike (days)*			
		0	30	45	90
Extra	0	0	$200,000	$400,000	$600,000
steel	30	$ 50,000	0	$200,000	$400,000
inventory	45	$100,000	$ 50,000	0	$200,000
(days'	90	$150,000	$100,000	$ 50,000	0
supply)					

FIGURE 5-1

Suppose, for example, that the consumer wants to know how much effort or money it would be reasonable to expend to learn what a competitor is doing if it is believed that the competitor has a probability of .40 of being right. More specifically, we suppose that our decision maker believes that, if in fact there will be no strike, the probability of this competitor's preparing for no strike is .40; the probabilities that he will be preparing for a 30-, 45-, or 90-day strike are .20, respectively. In this situation, these likelihoods may well represent the decision maker's opinions.

If such a competitor was found to be preparing for no strike at all, the decision maker's posterior probability for a strike of 0 days duration would be obtained by direct application of Bayes' theorem.

$$PO(0 \mid 0) = \frac{(.40)(.25)}{(.40)(.25) + (.20)(.25) + (.20)(.25) + (.20)(.25)} = .40$$

This simply confirms that, if the decision maker believes the competitor has a probability of .40 of being right, and if the competitor indicates no strike, the decision maker's posterior probability for 0 days duration becomes .40. This is a result of his uniform prior distribution.

The probability of such an observation, given by the denominator in Bayes' theorem is .25. The remaining calculations are summarized in Table 5-2.

TABLE 5-2

Sample result	Probability of sample	Best action (days' supply)	Expected cost
0	.25	45 or 90	$90,000
30	.25	45 or 90	$80,000
45	.25	45 or 90	$70,000
90	.25	90	$60,000

Using the probabilities of the sample results and the expected costs for the best posterior actions, we may compute the expected cost given sample information. Notice that this turns out to be $75,000, which is also the expected cost for the best prior action (stock 90-days supply). Thus EVSI turns out to be zero in this case. In other words, no information about a competitor whose probability of being right is .40 would give our decision maker reason to change his prior decision; hence such information would be of no value to him in this context.

Now suppose that the decision maker has an opportunity to learn what a different competitor is doing, and this competitor is believed to have a probability of .60 of being right. As before, we assume that if the competitor is wrong, he is equally likely to be wrong in any one of three particular ways. The calculations for this case are summarized in Table 5-3.
In this case, each of the three sample results 0, 30, and 45 would lead the decision maker to alter his prior choice; thus the information would be of

TABLE 5-3

Sample result	Probability of sample	Best action (days' supply)	Expected cost
0	.25	45	$93,250
30	.25	45	$69,900
45	.25	45	$46,550
90	.25	90	$39,900

some value to him. Computing the EVSI in the usual way yields the result $12,600.

Finally, we consider the question of the value of information on two competitors, each of whom is believed to be right with probability .40. Assume the behavior of competitors to be independent, in the sense that the probability of their both being right is the product of their individual probabilities of being right. The posterior probability of no strike given, for example, that both competitors are preparing for no strike, would be

$$PO(0 \mid 0, 0)$$
$$= \frac{(.40)(.40)(.25)}{(.40)(.40)(.25) + (.20)(.20)(.25) + (.20)(.20)(.25) + (.20)(.20)(.25)}$$
$$= .5714$$

Although it is not necessary to become involved in the routine calculations, it is noteworthy that, with four possible futures and a sample of size 2, the amount of work begins to be burdensome. Clearly, if we had not abstracted our view of reality by drastically reducing the number of possible strike durations, and if we had considered larger sample sizes, the calculation of EVSI would quickly get out of hand. In the next chapter, therefore, we shall look for some ways around the sheer volume of calculations involved in even moderately realistic problems.

The results of these calculations are summarized in Table 5-4. From this table it is not difficult to compute the expected value of sample information, which proves to be approximately $6,000.

Thus these calculations suggest that knowledge of one competitor, whose probability of being right is .60, is more valuable than knowledge of two independently acting competitors, each of whom has a probability of being right of .40. As one might expect, if the two competitors do not act independently, their plans are of still less value to the decision maker.

It is worth emphasizing that the likelihoods in this example could have been expressions of the manager's opinion which others might very well not have shared. In dealing with coins, the likelihoods tend to be *public*, in the sense that reasonable men share the extensive common experience which supports the beliefs that the probability of heads is one-half and that flips are independent. There is so little disagreement about this, that we tend to describe it as *objective*. Belief that competitors are right a certain portion of the time and that they act independently, may rest on little explicit evidence and is probably not the consensus of any large group of reasonable persons.

TABLE 5-4

Sample result*	Probability of sample	Best act (days' supply)	Expected cost
0, 0	.07	45	$92,850
0, 30	.12	45	$83,340
0, 45	.12	45	$75,000
0, 90	.12	90	$75,000
30, 30	.07	45	$71,430
30, 45	.12	45	$66,670
30, 90	.12	90	$66,670
45, 45	.07	45	$50,000
45, 90	.12	90	$58,340
90, 90	.07	90	$42,860

* Nothing is implied about the order of the observations in this listing.

The Basic Points

With this highly simplified example, we attempt to suggest again the basic points concerning the role of management science in management decision making.

a. If the decision maker can express simple uncertainties, probability theory can help him move logically to complex ones.

b. The really basic problem in many management decisions is how to integrate rich management experience with the evidence produced by staff studies. Here we have some logic which may help intuition in this difficult step.

c. No attempt is made to replace or deprecate the valuable experince of managers. Instead, every effort is made to make maximum logical use of this most significant resource in the decision process.

d. The function of probability theory is to help the decision maker express his uncertainty and then to support his intuition in reasoning about his uncertainty in complex decision problems.

EXERCISES

5-1. Four men examine a mining property and consider the possibility of buying it. They take the view that a property is either profitable or unprofitable. Their respective degrees of belief that the property in question is profitable are .01,

.20, .80, and .99. They consider three methods of evaluating the profitability of the property. Method 1 is right 50 per cent of the time; method 2 is right 90 per cent of the time; method 3 is always right. Show how the beliefs of each man would change for each of the possible evaluation methods if consistent revision of opinion occurs.

5-2. A maintenance team makes a monthly helicopter tour of a group of remote, unmanned communications relay stations. There are N stations on the tour. A critical part of each station is called component *alpha*, which the team must sometimes replace. Whether an alpha needs replacing can be determined only by on-the-spot visual inspection. It is expensive and difficult to carry alphas on the tour, but if an alpha is required and none is available an expensive extra flight must be made. The team manager wonders how many alphas to take with him.

The cost of carrying each alpha on the tour (whether or not it is used) is $1,000. If an alpha is required but not available, the cost is $10,000. The manufacturer of component alpha claims that the probability of a unit failing in a month is .02. Independent tests indicate that this probability is .10. The team manager believes that either statement is equally likely to be true.

The team manager wishes to minimize expected costs for a tour of $N = 2$ stations.

a. Show that the best number of alphas to carry on the first tour is 1.

b. Suppose the first tour reveals that the alphas at both stations require replacement. Show that the best number of alphas to carry on the second tour is still 1.

c. Before the first tour, a telemetering system is proposed which will tell the manager, before he starts, exactly how many alphas need replacement. Show that such a system would be worth $930 per month.

5-3. A firm must purchase a large quantity of a commodity either today or tomorrow. Today's price is $14.50 per unit. The firm believes that tomorrow's price is equally likely to be either $10.00 or $20.00. Letting x_2 represent tomorrow's price, the prior probabilities are

$$f(x_2 = 10) = .50$$
$$f(x_2 = 20) = .50$$

A commodity market expert offers to give the firm his prediction on tomorrow's price. That is, he will say to the firm, "In my opinion tomorrow's price will be x_2" where x_2 will be either 10 or 20. The firm knows that the market expert is right 60 per cent of the time. For his prediction, he charges a commission which is equal to $0.15 per unit of commodity purchased.

Show that the firm would be willing to employ the market expert.

5-4. Demand for an item is a discrete random variable with a uniform distribution over the range $1 \leq d \leq 6$. The cost of having units left over at the end of a stocking period is $1,000 per unit; the unit cost of being unable to satisfy a demand is $2,000.

a. How many units should be stocked if one wishes to minimize expected costs? (*Ans.*: 4 or 5 units)
b. If a manager's utility function, $U(x)$, is known, write an expression for utility of an inventory level I.
c. How much would it be worth to know the exact demand in advance? (*Ans.*: $2,000)
d. If market research could reduce the range of the demand distribution from 6 to 3, how much would such research be worth? (*Ans.*: $1,000)

5-5. Show, possibly by means of an example, that the prior expected value of the mean of the posterior distribution is equal to the mean of the prior distribution.

5-6. Consider the "classical" hypothesis-testing procedure which tests whether the mean of a random variable is different from zero, based on a sample of observations. How would this problem be treated from the viewpoint of this chapter?

5-7. A firm buys an important component for its product from a supplier who sometimes has trouble with his production process. The components are shipped in lots of size 50, and it is believed that such a lot came from a process with mean per cent defective of either 3 or 8 per cent. At the outset these two possibilities are taken to be equally likely. For analysis, the cost of testing a component is taken to be $1,000; the cost of accepting a defective component is $15,000, and the cost of rejecting a good component is $1,000.

A plan is proposed which involves testing two components from a lot and accepting or rejecting the entire lot based on what is learned from these two tests. Show that this particular plan is not as good as simply accepting the lot without any tests.

5-8. Devise an example which illustrates the following effect: If the prior distribution strongly favors one of two possible future states, it is unlikely that small samples will greatly influence the decision. Thus the expected net gain from sample information may first become negative and subsequently positive as the sample size is increased.

5-9. Outlined later is an experiment based on the coin-die decision problem discussed in this chapter. The subjects are shown the coin, the die, and a cup used to cover one of them. In the first part, the experimenter simply covers one of the objects; in subsequent parts, he carries out the indicated procedures, such as flipping a coin, and so on. The subjects are asked to respond to various decisions as shown. It is instructive carefully to plan and carry out such an experiment, using a group of subjects who have not been trained in the logic of such decisions.

In planning the experiment, one might wish to consider how it could be used to shed light on such questions as the following. What explanations can be given of the decision-making behavior of various groups?

To what extent are the subjects consistent in the sense of Bayesian logic?

Is it reasonable to assume linear utility functions for the amounts of money involved?

Which of the decisions are most difficult? What characteristics of decision making are related to difficulty?

How is performance related to the time allowed for making the decisions?

Do the subjects generally tend to overvalue or undervalue information?

What characteristics of the subjects are related to their performance?

The coin-die decision experiment

This experiment is concerned with your reaction to three decisions, A, B, and C.

Decision A

	Coin showing	Die showing
Coin	$5.00	$2.00
Die	$1.00	$7.00

Decision B

	Coin showing	Die showing
Coin	$1.00	$5.00
Die	$3.00	$2.00

Decision C

	Coin showing	Die showing
Coin	$6.00	0
Die	$2.00	$2.00

Part 1

If you had no additional information, which action would you choose

in decision A?   _____

in decision B?   _____

in decision C?   _____

Part 2

If the item showing is determined by the flip of a fair coin, which action would you choose

in decision A?   _____

in decision B?   _____

in decision C?   _____

Under this condition, how much would you be willing to pay (at most) for absolutely reliable information as to which item is showing

in decision A?   _____

in decision B?   _____

in decision C?   _____

Part 3

Suppose the item to be covered is to be determined by a table of random numbers in such a way that the probability that the coin will be showing is .70 and thus the probability that the die will be showing is .30.

Under this condition, how much would you be willing to pay for absolutely reliable information as to which is showing?

in decision A?	_____
in decision B?	_____
in decision C?	_____

Part 4

Suppose, as in Part 2, the item showing has been determined by a flip of a fair coin.

I will look at the item showing and report to you what I see, heads or tails. Suppose I do this and report heads. Which action would you choose in

decision A?	_____
decision B?	_____
decision C?	_____

If I offered you this reporting service, how much would you be willing to pay me in advance of hearing my report

in decision A?	_____
in decision B?	_____
in decision C?	_____

Part 5

Suppose as in Part 3 the probability that the coin is showing is .70 and the probability that the die is showing is .30.

I offer to look at the item showing and report whether I see heads or tails. How much would you be willing to pay for this service in advance of hearing my report

in decision A?	_____
in decision B?	_____
in decision C?	_____

6

Continuous
Random
Variables

A Prediction Example

This chapter extends the theory of consistent decision to some of the situations in which the sources of uncertainty seem best modeled as continuous variables. Expressing uncertainty in the form of probabilities makes it necessary to extend analysis to include continuous random variables. In application, the normal and beta distributions are particularly useful; hence attention is concentrated on these. First we illustrate use of the normal distribution as an expression of a decision maker's uncertainty about forecasts on which he must base his choices.

Suppose that a manager feels confident of obtaining a certain important contract if he offers to do the work called for at a price, R. He is uncertain, however, whether the contract will yield any profit at this price. His firm has a method of estimating the cost of performing such contracts, but as is often the case, the manager is uncertain about these cost estimates and perhaps somewhat dissatisfied with them.

This cost-estimating activity might be regarded as a prototype of a variety of prediction or forecasting systems which are found in the typical firm. Estimates of production costs, sales volume, cash requirements, and so on, are routinely produced and offered as bases for significant decisions. The sources of these estimates may be single experts, management committees, or groups of specialists. The processes of estimating may involve experts relying largely on intuition, analysts using explicit data and mathematical models, or any imaginable combination of these.

The great tradition of such estimating activities has been the production of single-valued predictions: "The cost of performing this contract will be x"; "Our sales for the next six months will be y." These predictions make no attempt to express uncertainty. All uncertainty that may have been in the minds of those who made the predictions is suppressed as these single-valued statements are transmitted throughout the organization. Decision makers who have had experience with such predictions readily form impressions of their bias and precision or reliability. The opinion that sales forecasts produced by sales managers tend to be "optimistic" might be more formally expressed by asserting that, on the average, actual sales turn out to be somewhat less than the predictions made by sales managers. This average difference between an estimated quantity and the actual result measures the *bias* of an estimating process. If, on the average, the estimate and the actual quantity prove to be equal, the estimating process may be called *unbiased*.

There are many ways of making explicit the manager's uncertainty about the cost estimate in our contract example. He may wish to think of the actual cost of performing the contract as the sum of the estimated cost plus an error. We would then be interested in viewing the error as a random variable whose mean we took to be a measure of bias and whose variance measured the precision of the estimating process. If the mean of the error happened to be zero, we should say the process was one which produced unbiased estimates. If the mean of the error was, say, greater than zero, we could subtract this mean from any estimate and regard the corrected estimates as unbiased. No such simple adjustment can help if the process is imprecise.

This model suggests that errors are independent of the estimated costs of performing the contracts. Errors in estimates for large contracts are neither more nor less uncertain than estimates for contracts involving less money. It may seem more reasonable to the manager to take a different view and consider relative errors. He may feel that dollar errors will be larger on large contracts. We might suggest that actual cost be taken as the estimated cost multiplied by a random variable called the *error ratio*. In this case, an unbiased estimating process would be characterized by an error ratio having an expected value equal to 1. Which, if either, of these two models seems appropriate, is a matter for the manager's judgment based on past experience coupled with whatever explicit data he may accumulate on the performance of the estimating process in question. Whatever method he selects results, we shall assume, in regarding the cost of performing the contract as a random variable. If, as suggested, the manager is clear about the price at which the contract can be obtained, then profit becomes a random variable defined simply as the difference between price and cost.

If the manager had considerable experience with the cost estimates produced by his estimating processes, he might well be willing to act as if he were certain of their bias and reliability. Using the first model, in which actual cost is taken to be the sum of the estimate plus the error, he might be willing to act as if he were certain of the mean and variance of the error. We might well expect the error to be the result of a large number of small, independent effects and thus, on theoretical grounds, expect it to be normally distributed. We wish to consider, however, the more common case in which the manager does not have sufficient experience with the estimating process to act as if he were certain of the error distribution. How is he to get this experience, and how is he to act until it becomes available to him?

Suppose that the manager has had experience with estimating processes similar to that under consideration, and perhaps even has some explicit data on their performance. Yet he finds the process under consideration to be a source of uncertainty for one or more of the following reasons:

1. The process has been in operation only a short time.
2. A change—a new person, a new method of analysis, new data added—has occurred in the process.
3. The estimating process, made aware of its past performance, is expected to compensate for change, but in a manner which is not clear to the manager.
4. New conditions exist which the estimating process must consider, but it is not clear what effect these conditions will have on its performance.
5. The estimating process may be well-established, but the manager may simply have failed to take explicit note of its past errors.

The problem of designing a data-collection program that we will specifically examine assumes that the manager is willing to act as if he knows the variance of the error distribution but is uncertain about its mean. He may feel that something has happened to the process which alters its bias but not its reliability. He may feel that it is similar to other processes in his experience which have differed as to their biases, but had quite predictable precisions. Analytically, this assumption is of great importance, since without it the problem becomes technically very complex, although by no means impossible. In many situations in which some data can be obtained, the final results are quite insensitive to the assumption. Yet, if we can get on the order of 25 observations of the output of the estimating process, we can estimate the precision from them and have little fear of leading the manager astray.

Fitting Normal Priors

We now focus on the bias of the estimating process as measured by the mean of its error distribution. The manager, being uncertain about this, seeks to express his uncertainty in the form of probabilities or to regard the mean or the estimating error as a continuous random variable. Our task is to make it as easy as possible for him to establish such a prior distribution and to help him discover some of its consequences in the form of consistent behavior.

We consider first the case in which he does not have explicit data on the average errors of similar estimating processes. He must rely entirely on his general experience and judgment. We presume he has some such experience and is willing to think carefully about it, for otherwise he is not likely to be in a position of responsibility. He must consider how he would act in certain decision situations of the sort examined in Chapter 3. Letting m stand for the mean of the estimating errors, the problem is to establish a prior distribution for m. We may ask to consider a decision, such as

a_1: an important payoff if the true value of m is above m'; nothing otherwise

a_2: the same important prize if the true value of m is below m'; nothing otherwise

When we have established a value of m' which leaves the manager indifferent between these two opportunities, we have the median of a prior distribution. Similarly, we may invite him to consider decisions, such as

a_1: an important payoff with probability .25 (perhaps expressed in terms of a reference lottery); nothing with probability .75

a_2: the same important payoff if m is greater than m''; nothing otherwise

When we have established m'' so as to make the manager indifferent, we have the upper quartile of the prior distribution. How far we must continue this process depends heavily on the situation in which we are working. If it appears possible to get some information subsequently, then we need not expend too much effort developing the prior distribution, since our final results may be quite insensitive to its exact form. In other cases, as we shall shortly see, it is of greater importance to have a well-developed prior.

Suppose that the manager is willing to consider actions which are consistent with a "smooth" or "well-behaved" prior distribution, unless he has specific reasons for expecting "dips" or "humps" in it. Thus he will be willing to smooth out the distribution which is fitted to his imagined decision-making behavior. Further, suppose he has no objection to considering several prior distributions, all of which equally well represent the answers we have received to such questions. Since there are very strong analytical reasons for using a prior distribution which is normal in form, we suppose that the manager will often accept this form as long as it reflects his ideas about medians, quartiles, and so on. Of course, we must be careful to explore with him any special or unusual consequences of a particular prior distribution.

On the other hand, if historical data on the bias of a number of estimating processes are available, the manager might judge these data to be relevant and wish to base his prior upon them. We could then plot a histogram of observed values of m, and "fit" a prior to these data. One may raise all sorts of questions about the "best-fitting" distribution, but again in many situations the final results are somewhat insensitive to its exact form. We assume that the prior distribution will "smooth" the historical frequencies, unless there are specific reasons for doing otherwise. This brings to bear the manager's knowledge of the underlying phenomenon as well as the explicit data. Again, for our example, we also assume that a normal prior distribution is used to describe the available data.

Designing the Data-collection Program

We now face the really crucial management question. Should one decide on the basis of what is already known about the estimating process, or should one undertake some sort of data-collection program before making a final decision on the contract in question? A variety of learning programs might be considered, some of which doubtless are out of the question in any given management context.

1. If data on the past errors of the estimating process could be obtained but have not been, then we may consider how much delving into past records would be reasonable for the manager.
2. We might do some experiments in which the estimating process turns out cost estimates for contracts whose actual costs are known.
3. We might go ahead deciding on contracts as best we can in the light of prior knowledge, but set up a *management-information system* which will routinely generate the basic data needed to reduce the manager's uncertainty about the process bias.
4. We might wholly discard cost estimates from the process in question. Instead, the manager might seek out some other estimating process whose bias seemed less uncertain to him.

For simplicity, suppose that the first three of these programs can yield observations of cost estimates which the decision maker is willing to regard as having come from the process in question, and the actual cost of the work. Thus each observation permits calculation of a single error measurement. In the fourth case, the problem is really one of comparing the expected profit using the available estimating process with the profit to be expected if an alternative process is used. For the moment we shall consider the general problem posed by the first three cases.

The estimating process is viewed as a generator of the independent, normally distributed errors, whose variance is known. The decision maker is, however, uncertain about the mean. He expresses this uncertainty in the form of a normal prior distribution. One can obtain observations of the output of the process, and one can compute the likelihood of these observations under the assumption of any particular value for the mean error. Thus we would have all the ingredients for computing the posterior distribution of the process mean, using the logic of Bayes' theorem as a guide to learning or assimilating the data. From this we could move toward the expected value of sample information and, given some idea of the cost of gathering data, toward the design of an optimal data-collection program or management-information system. We now set out the basic analysis involved in this program, the general logic being identical with that seen in Chapter 5.

In following through this estimating example, a small simplification will be helpful. We assume that the manager wishes to maximize expected profit and that expected profit is the difference between the known price and the expected cost. If the cost is viewed as a normally distributed random variable, the profit will also be normally distributed, having the mean just noted and the same variance as cost. Henceforth in this example we simply take the profit on a contract to be the basic random variable, and the expected profit as the source of uncertainty. Thus a very large number of management situations might be viewed in these terms.

The Prior-posterior Relation

We shall model the basic phenomenon by taking it to be a random process which generates a sequence of independent, normally distributed random variables. Any one of these variables, x, has a distribution which will be symbolized by

$$f(x) = N(m, v)$$

where m is the mean and v the variance of a normal probability distribution. We shall often refer to this as the *process* distribution, and to m and v as the *process parameters*. The most useful situation to study is that in which the decision maker is willing to act as if v were known, but m uncertain. He expresses this uncertainty by regarding m as a random variable having a prior distribution which is normal, with mean m_{pr} and variance v_{pr}. Thus

$$PR(m) = N(m_{pr}, v_{pr})$$

The considerations which support this important set of assumptions will subsequently be examined in detail; for the present, we develop their deductive consequences.

Suppose a sample of observations of the output of the basic normal process is obtainable and is represented by $x_1, \ldots, x_i, \ldots, x_n$. The mean of the sample is simply

$$m_s = \frac{1}{n} \sum_{i=1}^{n} x_i$$

The sample mean is a normally distributed random variable in this case. For any particular value of the process mean, m, the likelihood of the sample mean is

$$\text{LK}(m_s \mid m) = N\left(m, \frac{v}{n}\right)$$

The effect of a particular sample of observations is to transform the prior distribution of the process mean into a posterior distribution according to the logic of Bayes' theorem.

$$\text{PO}(m \mid m_s) = \frac{\text{LK}(m_s \mid m)\,\text{PR}(m)}{\displaystyle\int_m \text{LK}(m_s \mid m)\,\text{PR}(m)\,dm}$$

It will be convenient to define

$$c = \frac{v}{v_{pr}}$$

which may be roughly interpreted as a measure of the decision maker's prior conviction or certainty about the process mean. If he is quite convinced or nearly certain of the value of m, c will be large, since the prior distribution will have a relatively small variance. On the other hand, little experience, small conviction, and great uncertainty will tend to produce large values of v_{pr} and thus small values of c. Returning to the expression for the posterior distribution and writing out the normal distributions in the numerator gives

$$\text{PO}(m \mid m_s) = \frac{e^{-a}}{\sqrt{2\pi v\, v_{pr}/n}\displaystyle\int_m \text{LK}(m_s \mid m)\,\text{PR}(m)\,dm}$$

where
$$a = \frac{n(m_s - m)^2}{2v} + \frac{(m - m_{pr})^2}{2v_{pr}}$$

$$= \frac{1}{2v}\left[n(m_s - m)^2 + c(m - m_{pr})^2\right]$$

We now expand this expression for a, add and subtract the quantity

$$\frac{(cm_{pr} + nm_s)^2}{2v(c + n)}$$

and rearrange terms. This yields

$$a = \frac{c+n}{2v}\left[m^2 - \frac{2cm_{pr}m + 2nm_sm}{c+n} + \left(\frac{cm_{pr} + nm_s}{c+n}\right)^2\right] + b$$

$$= \frac{c+n}{2v}\left(m - \frac{cm_{pr} + nm_s}{c+n}\right)^2 + b$$

Here

$$b = \frac{1}{2v}\left[nm_s^2 + cm_{pr}^2 - \frac{(cm_{pr} + nm_s)^2}{c+n}\right]$$

The posterior distribution of m may now be written in the form

$$\text{PO}(m \mid m_s) = Ae^{-\left(m - \frac{cm_{pr}+nm_s}{c+n}\right)^2\left(\frac{c+n}{2v}\right)}$$

Since the integral of this expression over the range from minus infinity to plus infinity must equal 1, it follows that

$$A = \frac{1}{\sqrt{2\pi v/(c+n)}}$$

Thus it may be seen that the posterior distribution of the process mean is also normal in form with

$$\text{mean} = m_{po} = \frac{cm_{pr} + nm_s}{c+n} \quad \text{and} \quad \text{variance} = v_{po} = \frac{v}{c+n}$$

Generally speaking, a normal prior is transformed into a normal posterior by normally distributed observations.

Interpreting the Posterior

The mean of the posterior distribution of the process mean turns out to be simply the weighted average of the prior mean and the sample mean. The weights are c, our rough measure of the decision maker's prior conviction or certainty, and n, the sample size. As the sample size increases, more weight is given to the sample mean and less to the decision maker's prior opinion. Similarly, the greater the variance of the prior, the smaller, the value of c; and the greater, the influence of subsequent observations. Thus one of the most interesting implications of the decision maker's assessment of his prior opinion is its leading directly to a guide to how much weight should be placed on prior opinion and how much on other data becoming available. One who says that he is willing to act as if his prior distribution had a large variance, is also saying he is willing to be heavily influenced by additional evidence. This provides a most useful operational definition of the concept of certainty or uncertainty. The more willing a person is to be influenced by new evidence, the more uncertain we take him to be.

The posterior variance of the process mean decreases as the number of observations increases. If n grows indefinitely large, the posterior variance will approach zero, and the decision maker will become completely convinced or certain as to the value of the process mean. Notice that the posterior variance grows smaller as the sample size increases, no matter what the value of the sample mean happens to be.

Although it is useful to interpret c as a measure of uncertainty or open-mindedness, be careful about using the term *vague* to describe the opinion which yields a small value of c. Notice that, whatever the variance of the prior, the decision maker has assessed his opinion by thinking how he would behave in some quite definite and clearly stated decision situations. There is nothing vague about these decision situations for the person who produces a broad prior as opposed to a tight one. Nor does a broad prior necessarily imply lack of experience. It is certainly true that the variance of the posterior does decrease with experience, but a broad prior may very well express the opinion of an experienced decision maker. A large prior variance may indicate inexperience with the particular random process in question, yet reflect the opinion of one who has a great deal of experience with similar random processes. Such a man may know from experience that the means of such processes may indeed occur over a wide range of values.

Sufficiency

Our analysis of the normal prior-posterior relationship, summarized the results of the sample in terms of the sample mean only. Was any information lost by not using the individual values of the n sample observations? If the same posterior distribution results from using the individual values, then the mean may be regarded as a sufficient statistic or a sufficient report. It would have the same influence on the decision maker's opinion, and in this sense, contain all the useful information in the sample.

A simple example will show that the sample mean is in fact a sufficient statistic under the conditions we have been studying. Suppose two observations have been obtained and two possible reports are being considered. Report 1 consists of the two observations, x_1 and x_2; report 2 consists only of the sample mean. Report 1 may be viewed as a sequence of two observations, yielding first

$$\text{PO}(m \mid x_1) = N\left[\frac{cm_{pr} + x_1}{c + 1}, \frac{v}{c + 1}\right]$$

This distribution may then be viewed as a prior and we may compute $\text{PO}(m \mid x_1, x_2)$. Noting that the new value of c becomes $c + 1$, it follows directly that

$$PO(m \mid x_1, x_2) = N\left[\frac{cm_{pr} + x_1 + x_2}{c + 2}, \frac{v}{c + 2}\right]$$

Since

$$x_1 + x_2 = 2m_s$$

this is the very same posterior that would result from report 2.

If the likelihoods of report 1 and report 2 are written out and their ratio formed, all the terms containing m cancel out. Thus we could claim that the ratio of the likelihoods would be a constant for all values of m. This, of course, is but another instance of the likelihood principle of Chapter 5 which suggested that if the likelihood ratio was a constant for two reports, then the reports were equivalent in the sense of leading to the same posterior distribution.

Preposterior Analysis

Certainly one of the most fundamental problems in management science is deciding in advance whether any data-collection program should be undertaken. How much data should one obtain in any decision situation, if indeed it is economic to collect any at all? What is the best kind of evidence to gather? Will a particular study be worth its cost? All these questions require that one consider the effect and value of information before it actually becomes available. In the terms we have developed, we must consider the various observations that might be made, the posterior opinions they would produce, and the actions we would then take. Yet we must consider all this before actually receiving the data. This sort of analysis is, for obvious reasons, called *preposterior analysis*.

For a particular sample mean, the posterior mean will be given by

$$m_{po} = \frac{cm_{pr} + nm_s}{c + n}$$

Before any data are obtained, however, m_s can be regarded only as a random variable. If we have chosen a sample size, then this uncertainty about the sample mean produces uncertainty about the posterior mean. Under these conditions, we shall speak of the posterior mean as a random variable with a distribution $PR(m_{po})$, the prior distribution of the posterior mean. Since m_{po} is a linear function of m_s, and since m_s is normally distributed, we can say that the prior distribution of the posterior mean will also be normal. It is also well known that if

$$m_{po} = a + bm_s$$

then

$$E(m_{po}) = a + bE(m_s)$$

$$V(m_{po}) = b^2 V(m_s)$$

where the function V signifies the variance. Using these results, we have

$$E(m_{po}) = \frac{cm_{pr} + nE(m_s)}{c + n}$$

However,

$$E(m_s) = \int_m E(m_s \mid m)\, PR(m)\, dm = \int_m m\, PR(m)\, dm = m_{pr}$$

Substituting this in the expression for $E(m_{po})$ produces

$$E(m_{po}) = m_{pr}$$

Thus we can say that the prior expected value of the posterior mean is the prior mean. Alternatively, the expected value of the mean of the posterior distribution, considered before sampling, is equal to the mean of the prior distribution.

The reader will do well to consider these statements carefully, attempting to keep clear in his mind the five distributions now involved in the analysis.

1. $f(x)$, process distribution
2. $PR(m)$, prior distribution of the process mean
3. $LK(m_s \mid m)$, likelihood of the sample mean, given a particular value of the process mean
4. $PO(m)$, posterior distribution of the process mean
5. $PR(m_{po})$, prior distribution of the mean of the posterior distribution of the process mean

Understanding from this point on rests heavily on being able to distinguish clearly among the distributions. This task is no easier because, under present conditions, all of them are normal in form, although with differing parameters in some but not all cases.

Returning to the prior distribution of the posterior mean, the prior variance of the posterior mean follows directly from the linear relationship between normal variables:

$$V(m_{po}) = \left[\frac{n}{c + n}\right]^2 V(m_s)$$

The variance of the sample mean, based on prior information, may be obtained starting with the definition of the variance.

$$\begin{aligned}
V(m_s) &= E[m_s - E(m_s)]^2 \\
&= E(m_s - m_{pr})^2 \\
&= E(m_s - m + m - m_{pr})^2 \\
&= E(m_s - m)^2 + E(m - m_{pr})^2 + 2E[(m_s - m)(m - m_{pr})]
\end{aligned}$$

The reader should assure himself that the value of the third term is zero and that the first two terms give

$$V(m_s) = \frac{v}{n} + \frac{v}{c}$$

$$= \frac{v}{n} + v_{pr}$$

The variance of the sample mean is the sum of the variance of the process mean plus the variance of the sample mean, given a particular value of the process mean. Alternatively, we may think of the sample mean as composed of two independent, additive components. It is the sum of the process mean plus the deviation of the sample mean around the process mean. Since this deviation is independent of the value of the process mean, the variance of the sum is simply the sum of the variances as just seen.

We may now use this fact to develop the previous expression for the prior variance of the posterior mean:

$$V(m_{po}) = \left[\frac{n}{c + n}\right]^2 V(m_s)$$

$$= \left[\frac{n}{c + n}\right]^2 \left[\frac{v}{n} + \frac{v}{c}\right]$$

$$= \frac{v}{c} - \frac{v}{c + n}$$

$$= v_{pr} - v_{po}$$

The prior variance of the posterior mean is equal to the prior variance of the mean less the posterior variance of the mean. As the sample size grows large, the variance of the posterior mean will approach zero. Thus the prior variance of the posterior mean will approach the prior variance of the mean as the amount of information grows toward perfect information.

Economic Analysis

To illustrate the computation of the expected value of sample information and the expected value of perfect information, we continue our very simple example. The profit from the contract in question is viewed as a normally distributed random variable with known variance but uncertain mean. The decision maker expresses his uncertainty about the mean profit by regarding it as a random variable with a normal prior distribution. His decision problem is whether to undertake the contract in question. He wishes to undertake it if the expected profit is greater than zero, but not otherwise. The expected profit associated with the best prior action is thus

$$\max (m_{pr}, 0)$$

First we suppose he is offered an opportunity to obtain perfect information about the mean profit. If the perfect information assures him that the expected profit is greater than zero he will undertake the venture, otherwise he will not. His payoff will then be m_{po} if m_{po} is greater than zero, otherwise his payoff will be zero. Before receiving the perfect information his expected payoff from the best act, given perfect information, is

$$\int_{m_{po}=0}^{\infty} m_{po} \, \mathrm{PR}(m_{po}) \, dm_{po}$$

where $$\mathrm{PR}(m_{po}) = N(m_{pr}, v_{pr})$$

The expected value of perfect information is the expected gain over the prior expected profit, resulting from the information.

$$\mathrm{EVPI} = \int_{m_{po}=0}^{\infty} m_{po} \, \mathrm{PR}(m_{po}) \, dm_{po} - \max(m_{pr}, 0)$$

The first term of this expression is an example of a *linear normal loss integral* which can be readily evaluated using the methods suggested in Appendix A.

The expression for the expected value of sample information is of the same form, although, of course, with sample data the variance of the preposterior distribution is different.

$$\mathrm{EVSI} = \int_{m_{po}=0}^{\infty} m_{po} \, \mathrm{PR}(m_{po}) \, dm_{po} - \max(m_{pr}, 0)$$

where $$\mathrm{PR}(m_{po}) = N(m_{pr}, v_{pr} - v_{po})$$

Here again the methods of Appendix A are helpful in evaluating the integral.

Next we introduce the expected cost of a data-collection program involving n observations, $C(n)$. We assume for the present that n is determined in advance and is not influenced by the observations themselves, nor does the cost of the program depend on what observations actually occur. The expected net gain from sample information is

$$\mathrm{ENGSI} = \mathrm{EVSI} - C(n)$$

To suggest the intuitive nature of this function, consider an example in which the prior mean, m_{pr}, is zero, and the cost of information is proportional to n, say, kn. In this case, the methods of Appendix A permit us to write

$$\mathrm{ENGSI} = (.3989) \, \mathrm{SD}(m_{po}) - kn$$

$$= (.3989) \left[\frac{v}{c} - \frac{v}{c+n} \right]^{1/2} - kn$$

$$= (.3989)(v_{pr} - v_{po})^{1/2} - kn$$

This example suggests some interesting confirmations of one's intuitive notions about data-collection programs.

1. The greater the variance of the prior distribution, the greater the expected net gain from sample information. The more uncertain one is, the more willing he will be to pay for information which will reduce that uncertainty.

2. If the cost of sampling is sufficiently large or the decision maker's prior uncertainty sufficiently small, ENGSI will be negative for all values of n greater than zero. If the decision maker is fairly certain as the result of his previous experience, or if the data are too costly, it is best not to obtain any additional data at all.

3. If ENGSI is positive for small n, it tends to increase at a decreasing rate, and there will be a sample size which maximizes ENGSI. The first information obtained has the greatest effect on one's uncertainty; each additional observation is less and less effective. If information is available at a constant unit cost, ultimately the effect of an additional observation will be to increase the decision maker's payoff by an amount less than the cost of obtaining it.

Known Process Variance

We have supposed that the decision maker is willing to act as if the process variance, v, were known. Hopefully this will be in accord with his beliefs, but if it is not, we place considerable reliance on the following formula which is offered here without proof. If data can be obtained, the quantity

$$s^2 = \left[\frac{1}{n-1} \right] \sum_{i=1}^{n} (x_i - m_s)^2$$

may be used as an estimate of v. If the sample size is of the order of 25, in most problems it would appear that little difference in the final results will occur if v is taken to be known and equal to s^2. If we must treat v as uncertain, then the analysis is somewhat more complex.

Sensitivity to the Prior Distribution

The amount of effort to be expended in developing a prior distribution depends on how sensitive consistent actions are to the form and parameters of the prior. The basic principle is intuitive. If considerable data will be available at modest cost, then exact specification of the prior is likely to be of little consequence, at least so far as determining the best posterior action is concerned. A broad or gentle prior, having a relatively large variance, places most of the weight on the data and thus tends to be of minor consequence itself. One may feel safe in using a normal prior in order to take advantage of its convenient analytic properties, as long as the prior variance is large relative to the process variance. We would expect the posterior to be little influenced by the exact form chosen for the prior.

Some insight into this effect may be obtained by imagining a decision maker who is considering two candidates for his prior distribution.

$$PR_1(m) = N(m_{pr}, v_{pr})$$

$$PR_2(m) = N(m'_{pr}, v_{pr})$$

The difference in the posterior means resulting from these two priors is

$$m_{po} - m'_{po} = \frac{cm_{pr} + nm_s}{c + n} - \frac{cm'_{pr} + nm_s}{c + n}$$

$$= \left[\frac{c}{c + n}\right](m_{pr} - m'_{pr})$$

Thus if c is small, the difference between the posterior means will decline rapidly as the sample size increases. One might develop similar statements regarding prior and posterior variances.

So far as the form of the posterior goes, we may offer the following rough suggestion: The posterior distribution will have a form which is relatively insensitive to the form of the prior if

1. The data obtained "favors" some particular range of m values, in the sense of having relatively large likelihoods in this range.

2. The prior chosen is "flat" in the favored region, meaning that the distribution function does not change much.

3. The prior chosen does not elsewhere greatly exceed its value in the favored region.

If these three conditions are met by some set of priors being considered, any one of them may be used with little danger of altering the best posterior action, since the form of the posteriors will be nearly the same for any of them.

It is most important to emphasize, however, that what we are saying concerns the posterior distribution and the best act, given that a sample has already been taken. More serious questions about the design of the data-collection program may *not* be so insensitive to the form of the prior. If data are costly, if there is a large set-up cost in order to start a flow of data, or if there is only one chance to obtain data, then a well-developed prior may be extremely important, since consistent data-gathering behavior may be markedly influenced by it. In such cases it will pay to expend considerable effort developing a prior distribution. Even if this should seem very difficult to the decision maker, he must strive to make his opinions explicit if he wishes to take advantage of our guides to consistency.

EXERCISES

6-1. Two methods of production for a certain product are available to a firm. The annual cost of production for the methods, called A and B, may be represented by the following functions:

$$\text{Method A: } 10,000 + 10x \qquad \text{(dollars)}$$
$$\text{Method B: } 20x$$

where x is the number of units produced in a year. The firm regards x as a normally distributed random variable with variance $= 2,500$ and uncertain mean. The mean of x is normal with expected value m_{pr} and variance $2,500/c$. It is possible although expensive to go back through records to find out how many units had been produced in previous years. The firm wishes to select the production method which will minimize the expected annual cost.

Find the expected value of perfect information for all combinations of the following values for m_{pr} and c:

$$c = .1, .5, 1.0, 2.0$$
$$m_{pr} = 900, 950, 1,000, 1,100$$

Find the expected value of sample information for the foregoing combinations, using sample sizes of 1 and 4.

Arrange the results in tabular form and discuss the various generalizations which are illustrated by the data.

To see how this goes, we outline the computation of EVPI for the case

$$c = .1 \qquad m_{pr} = 900$$

Since the two methods have equal expected annual costs for $m = 1,000$, the best prior action is to select method B, yielding a prior expected annual cost of

$$20\,m_{pr} = (20)(900)$$

If the posterior mean turns out to be greater than 1,000, we choose method A, otherwise method B. Thus,

$$\text{EVPI} = (20)(900) - \int_{m_{po} = -\infty}^{1000} 20\,m_{po}\,\text{PR}(m_{po})\,dm_{po}$$
$$- \int_{m_{po} = 1000}^{\infty} (10,000 + 10\,m_{po})\,\text{PR}(m_{po})\,dm_{po}$$

Recalling that

$$(20)(900) = 20\,m_{pr} = \int_{m_{po} = -\infty}^{\infty} 20\,m_{po}\,\text{PR}(m_{po})\,dm_{po}$$

we may simplify the expression for EVPI to obtain

$$\text{EVPI} = 10 \int_{m_{po} = 1000}^{\infty} (m_{po} - 1000)\,\text{PR}(m_{po})\,dm_{po}$$

For perfect information and the parameters selected, we have

$$\text{PR}(m_{po}) = N\left(m_{pr} = 900, v_{pr} = \frac{2500}{.1}\right)$$

Using the methods of Appendix A, we may write

$$\text{EVPI} = (10)(\sqrt{v_{pr}})\,L_N\left(\frac{1000 - m_{pr}}{\sqrt{v_{pr}}}\right) = (10)(158)\,L_N(.63)$$

$$\text{EVPI} = (10)(158)(.1606) = \$254$$

6-2. In establishing a prior distribution it is often assumed that the "tails" of the distribution are of little importance if the decision maker's utility function is linear or nearly so. Discuss the plausibility of this assumption.

6-3. We have indicated that the process standard deviation or variance can reasonably be assumed to be known if we have a sample of size 25 or more on which to base an estimate of it. Discuss ways in which one might test this assertion. What would the analysis of a simple decision problem look like without the assumption of known process variance?

6-4. Discuss the relation between the concept of sufficiency outlined in this chapter and the idea of a sufficient statistic as presented in conventional statistics texts.

6-5. We have indicated that five distributions may appear in decision problems as we are viewing them. Which of these distributions appear in ordinary statistical hypothesis tests?

6-6. We wish to choose between two methods of production in the face of uncertainty as to what volume of production will be required. The cost of method 1 is given by the function, $a + bx$, and that of method 2 by $v + wx$, where x is the production volume. Assume that $a < v$ and $b > w$. The production volume, x, is regarded as a normally distributed random variable with known variance but uncertain mean. The prior distribution of the mean of x is itself regarded as normal. Show explicitly how one would compute ENGSI, including use of the methods of Appendix A to obtain actual quantitative results.

What other management problems can you think of which might have this same sort of linear cost structure?

6-7. Refer to the illustrative example discussed in the chapter involving the decision whether to undertake a contract. Suppose the prior mean is zero and the cost of information is proportional to the sample size. Find an expression which could be solved for the sample size which would maximize ENGSI.

6-8. It is important for a firm's planning to estimate the average monthly sales of a given product. Monthly sales of the product in question are viewed as a normally distributed random variable with known variance and uncertain mean. The prior distribution of mean monthly sales is also normally distributed. A single-valued estimate must be given, and there is a loss to the firm which is proportional to the square of the difference between the estimate and the true mean monthly sales. The firm wishes to minimize expected loss.

Show that, based on prior information, the best estimate is the mean of the prior distribution. Show also that the expected loss using this best estimate is proportional to the variance of the prior distribution.

What would be the best estimate and expected loss based on a posterior distribution?

Show how you would find the optimal sample size if the cost of sample information is proportional to the sample size.

II

Applications

7

Capital
Investment
Planning

Evaluation Policies

We examine now the problems faced by the firm which, from time to time, undertakes to formulate plans for investment in plant and equipment. Typically, investment plans of this sort may be made for the coming year based on the capital funds which the firm expects to have available and the proposals for investment opportunities which it is currently considering. The term *search* describes the process by which possible capital investment opportunities are discovered or identified. We suppose that the search process produces opportunities which are described in terms of some preliminary or basic information. For example, we think of the search for possible machines to carry out a particular step in the production process as resulting in a list of several machines described by manufacturer, approximate price range, and rough statements of technological capabilities. From this point on, the process of obtaining additional detailed information and verifying that already in hand is undertaken, in preparation for the actual decision step. This data-gathering step we shall call *evaluation* of the possibilities. It is basically a process aimed at reducing the uncertainty in the decision to be made.

As an example of the questions involved, consider the manager who is faced with the classical problem of choosing among mutually exclusive investment proposals.

1. Should he accept one of the proposals immediately on the basis of his experience and the evidence now in hand?

2. If not, how much should be spent on getting further information on each of the proposals? Some proposals will be well supported and characterized by low uncertainty. Money will not be spent on these. Others appear more uncertain, yet if they are obviously good or obviously bad proposals, little money need be spent to establish this further

3. Answering question 2 implies knowing something about how data-gathering effort would be employed if it were expended on a given proposal. Should one get more data on near-term cash flows or those further in the future? (The latter are traditionally the most uncertain.) Should one try to make better predictions of service life or the rate of technological obsolescence?

4. One can ask
   a. What is the optimal amount of money for the manager to spend and how should it be allocated?
   b. If the manager has only a limited amount of money (or time) to devote to evaluation, how should that be allocated?

Evaluation Policies in Practice

In discussing highly refined policies for evaluating projects, it is perhaps wise to keep in mind certain difficulties which may be associated with implementing those policies. For example,

1. Evaluation may tend to be a "lumpy" process in that it is more economical to undertake a single evaluation effort for a given project than to conduct an evaluation based on a sequential policy. Important "set-up" costs may dictate that the amount of evaluation should be decided in advance and accomplished in one effort. This may preclude policies in which the amount of evaluation depends on what is known about the project in question or what is known about other projects subsequently studied.

2. There may be costs which dictate that evaluation of a project must be carried out essentially at the time the project is discovered.

3. The cost of information is difficult to estimate, since in many instances it is highly nonlinear, and sometimes has value for more than one project being considered by the firm. Indeed the availability of certain kinds of information might lead the firm to search for projects which could benefit from its use.

The models with which we deal here are rich models and as such require rather rich input data. One can well ask whether such data are, or could be available at a cost reasonable enough to make the analysis useful. This is a difficult question to answer, and perhaps the present discussion should be considered a preliminary step in answering a slightly different question: "If the necessary input data were routinely available, of what consequence would that be?" That is, the analysis might be viewed as a step in considering what justification might be given for making the necessary input data available. Clearly, it would be surprising to find them currently available on a routine basis in many firms in explicit form. Yet, to the extent which the analysis does reflect what is going on, one may infer that the necessary data or something like them, are available in implicit form.

Some basic distinctions are helpful in considering the various problems of evaluation which follow. The term *ample funds* describes the situation where the firm has more capital available than investment projects which it is willing to consider. This is roughly the situation in those companies which have large pools of capital invested in government bonds or some such "near cash" asset. In some cases, such funds are clearly set aside for some future project, such as a major acquisition; in others, at least a portion of these funds is available for current investments of the sort being studied. The opposite situation is referred to as the *ample-projects* situation. Here the firm is ordinarily confronted with more projects that it has funds to undertake. We are thus considering the firm which sets an upper limit on the funds to be invested and finds that it must budget these funds by choosing some, but not all the projects available. It may, for example, limit its investment in any one year to an amount equal to the sum of depreciation charged plus earnings retained for that year.

Evaluation policies may be classified as static or dynamic, according to the following conceptions. If the decision on how much evaluation effort to devote to a project, depends only on the characteristics of the project itself, then evaluation is called *static*. Thus a fixed-sample-size experiment, or a sequential experiment might be conducted in evaluating the project, and as long as the design of these experiments did not require knowledge of other projects, the policy would be considered a static one.

If on the other hand, the amount of evaluation effort expended on a project depends on the previous discovery and evaluation of other projects, then the evaluation policy is called *dynamic*. For example, if a number of very good projects have already been discovered and evaluated, and if these projects would more than utilize the available funds, the firm may reduce the amount of evaluative effort expended on projects subsequently discovered.

Ample Funds

To illustrate approaches to these problems, consider a project which has been discovered and is to be evaluated. Suppose that ample funds are available and the decision to invest or not depends simply on whether the final estimate of the project's present worth after evaluation is positive or negative. If perfect information were available, the present worth of the project, P, would be computed according to the relation

$$P = \sum_{t=0}^{N} a^t R_t$$

where R_t = net cash flow at time t
a = present worth factor
N = duration of the project

We suppose that under even the most favorable conditions of knowledge attainable, the decision maker would regard the R_t as random variables. For simplicity, we consider the case in which the R_t are viewed as independent normally distributed random variables, with means $m(t)$ and variances $v(t)$. The expected value of the present worth of the project is then

$$m = \sum_{t=0}^{N} a^t m(t)$$

In order to deal with a specific problem, we suppose that the values of the $v(t)$ are known, but that the decision maker is uncertain about the means, $m(t)$.

This may be interpreted as saying that, before actually undertaking the project, even if all conceivable information were obtained, the cash flow at the end of period t would be regarded as a random variable with mean, $m(t)$, and variance, $v(t)$. One simply cannot find out in advance exactly what the value of R_t will be. Further, although for illustration we assume that the variances are known, the decision maker knows the means only imperfectly or uncertainly. He is therefore interested in considering possible programs of data collection which will reduce his uncertainty (give him better knowledge) as to the means, $m(t)$.

His uncertainty about the $m(t)$ is expressed by regarding them as random variables which are independently normally distributed with means, $m_{pr}(t)$ and variances, $v_{pr}(t)$. Based on these prior distributions and the assumptions of independence among them, we can write the prior distribution of the expected, or mean, present worth of the project. It will be a normally distributed random variable with mean given by

$$m_{pr} = \sum_{t=0}^{N} a^t m_{pr}(t)$$

and variance given by

$$v_{pr} = \sum_{t=0}^{N} a^{2t} v_{pr}(t)$$

To reduce uncertainty about the mean cash flows, various sorts of observation programs might be undertaken. For example,

1. Data might be obtained on the cash flows from similar projects which the decision maker regards as coming from the same population as the project under study.

2. Since the cash flow in any period is the sum of a number of components of income and expense, data might be obtained on these individual components from situations regarded as being from the same population as the project under study.

3. Instead of observing cash flows or their components directly, one might obtain indirect evidence which is known to be correlated with the cash flows. For example, if the revenue from a certain project is thought to be correlated with the level of disposable personal income, one might secure data on the latter quantity. This in turn might be used to project disposable personal income to the time periods anticipated in the project, and the correlation used to produce a projection of cash flows.

Whatever the data obtained, the Bayesian evaluation process requires that we be able to state its likelihood. That is, it is necessary to be able to give, for any data y, the probability of y conditional on a particular value of $m(t)$, say, $LK(y \mid m(t))$. In other words, one needs to know the likelihood of the sample on the assumption that a particular hypothesis about $m(t)$ is true.

If, for example, one observes the cash flow in a particular period, t, for another project believed to be of the same statistical population as the project under study, then this observation, say, R_t, may be regarded as a normally distributed random variable with mean, $m(t)$, and variance, $v(t)$.

If a component of a cash flow is observed, then the required likelihood is that conditional on various hypotheses about the component. For example, if we take a particular cost, C_t, as the subject for study, we may consider the mean cash flow to be

$$m(t) = I_t - C_t$$

Given prior probability distributions for I_t and C_t and perhaps the assumption that these two random variables are independent, we can write the prior probability distribution of $m(t)$. When an observation c_t is obtained, we will require the likelihood of c_t conditional on C_t.

Choosing Between Two Projects

We now turn to analysis of the choice between two investment projects, only one of which is to be undertaken. We regard each project as a normal process with known variance but uncertain mean. We take the decision maker's principle of choice to be maximization of expected present worth, although other measures may easily be substituted for this.

Let

m_i = expected present worth for project i $(i = 1, 2)$
v_i = variance of present worth for project i
m_{pri} = prior mean of m_i
v_{pri} = prior variance of m_i
n_i = number of observations made on project i
m_{poi} = posterior mean of m_i
c_i = ratio of v_i to v_{pri}

We suppose the projects are numbered such that

$$m_{pr1} > m_{pr2}$$

and we define

$$d = m_2 - m_1$$

Clearly d is a random variable with a normal prior and normal posterior distribution. We are interested in the prior expected value of the posterior mean of d, which is

$$E(d_{po}) = m_{pr2} - m_{pr1}$$

The prior variance of the posterior mean of d is

$$V(d_{po}) = V(m_{po2}) + V(m_{po1})$$

$$= \frac{n_1}{c_1(c_1 + n_1)} v_1 + \frac{n_2}{c_2(c_2 + n_2)} v_2$$

$$= v_{pr1} - v_{po1} + v_{pr2} - v_{po2}$$

These are the parameters of the normal prior distribution of the posterior mean of d.

Based on prior knowledge, project 1 will be chosen. After data are accumulated, the decision maker's perference will change in favor of project 2 only if d_{po} is greater than zero. Thus

$$\text{EVSI} = \int_{d_{po}=0}^{\infty} d_{po} \, \text{PR}(d_{po}) \, dd_{po}$$

(This may be computed using the methods of Appendix A.)

Allocating Investigative Effort

The next problem is allocating the firm's data-gathering efforts in the most effective manner. We want to gain some insights into how best to allocate a fixed budget for information gathering under various conditions of capital-investment planning. We would also like to know what would be the best data-collection expenditure and how it should be allocated. We begin with the simplest problem, allocating investigative effort among the various cash flows which are combined to form an evaluation of a single project.

The basic issues may be illustrated with a project that involves only two cash flows, R_0 and R_1. The problem is deciding how much data-gathering effort to expend in reducing uncertainty about each of these cash flows. Suppose we can choose any combination of n_0 observations of R_0 and n_1 observations of R_1. For simplicity also, we take the unit cost of any of these observations to be k. If the expected present worth of the project is positive, it will be undertaken, otherwise it will be discarded. The expected net gain from sample information may be written

$$\text{ENGSI} = \int_{m_{po}=0}^{\infty} m_{po}\, \text{PR}(m_{po})\, dm_{po} - \max (m_{pr},\, 0) - k(n_0 + n_1)$$

In order to suggest the intuitive aspects of the problem, we examine the case which permits analytic expression, that is, the case for $m_{pr} = 0$. Using the ideas in Appendix A, we may obtain

$$\text{ENGSI} = (.3989)\, \text{SD}(m_{po}) - k(n_0 + n_1)$$

The prior variance of the posterior mean is a function of n_0 and n_1.

$$V(m_{po}) = \frac{n_0}{c(0)(c(0) + n_0)}\, v(0) + \frac{a^2 n_1}{c(1)(c(1) + n_1)}\, v(1)$$

where $v(t)$ = variance of R_t

$c(t)$ = ratio of $v(t)$ to the prior variance of the mean of R_t

Suppressing knowledge that the number of observations is a discrete variable, we may take the partial derivatives of ENGSI with respect to n_0 and n_1, and set them equal to zero. If we take the variances of the R_t to be equal, $v(0) = v(1)$, then the resulting equations permit us to show that the relation between n_0 and n_1 should be

$$n_0 = \frac{c(1) + n_1}{a} - c(0)$$

From this relation we may draw the following generalizations: The more prior information we have about a particular R_t (as measured by $c(t)$), the smaller the additional amount of information we wish to obtain. Contrariwise, if we have relatively little prior information about a particular R_t we are more inclined to obtain further information about it. As the interest rate increases, the value of a decreases. Thus the greater the interest rate, the greater the tendency to seek information about R_0, and the less the tendency to seek information about R_1. Since one would often expect that the prior information about R_0 would be more complete than the prior information about R_1, these two effects tend to offset each other.

One could, however, solve both the problem of allocating a fixed investigative budget among the R_t, and the problem of finding an optimal budget combined with an optimal allocation.

In the case of ample funds then, the optimal amount and allocation of data-collection effort can be calculated based on the prior distribution of the project's present worth. If the opportunity population in which the firm was searching could be characterized by distributions for the prior parameters, one could compute in advance the expected value of the optimal data-collection (risk-reduction) expenditure for a project. This amount might simply be added to the cost of search, and the two steps in project evaluation treated as one.

Ample Projects and the Value of Sample Information

Considering the value of sample information requires consideration of the decision problem in which the project appears. Clearly, if we were dealing with a project which was sure to be funded or sure not to be funded, then the decision would already be made; there could be little point in gathering additional information about the project. The value of sample information is zero. In the ample-funds case, one might use the decision rule that the project will be funded only if the mean present worth is positive. In this case, we can compute the expected value of sample information in the usual way. If we are going to fund the better of two projects, again, a method is available for computing the expected value of sample information.

The difficulty arises when we consider evaluation of a project, whose funding does not depend simply on the value of the posterior mean. Thus whether a project is funded may depend on the posterior means of other projects which have not yet been evaluated (or even discovered), or projects which are to be evaluated and submitted by another unit of the organization. We require then some method, necessarily approximate, for dealing with this situation.

Suppose, for example, one had on hand more project proposals than funds available to undertake them. The general strategy for evaluation would be to dispose of projects which are clearly bad on the basis of prior information without further evaluation. Similarly, projects which are clearly very good on the basis of prior information might be put down for funding without further evaluation. If projects were ranked on the basis of prior information, the nearer a project to the cut-off point between projects that would be funded if no further evaluation were made and projects which would not be funded, the greater the expected value of sample information. Projects near the cut-off level would tend to receive most of the evaluation effort.

One approach might be to suppress differences among projects as to the amount of investment required, and treat the problem as one of selecting the best N of M projects. This would require a generalization of the analysis of the best of two projects discussed previously. Instead, we will consider a number of approximate methods which appear to have some suggestive value in connection with the ample-projects case.

1. Choose a critical value for the project mean (other than zero). If posterior mean is greater than the critical value, assume that the firm will invest, otherwise assume it will not invest. The critical value may be chosen by relating past experience on the distribution of the means of evaluated projects to the current budget amount available. This tends to show that when there are ample projects only *good* projects will actually be funded.

2. Choose a critical value for the variance of the posterior mean. Evaluation effort is expended on each project up to the point where the variance of the posterior mean reaches this critical value.

3. Evaluate projects further only if the probability of reversing the decision, given perfect information, is greater than some value, P_c. Projects which are evaluated further are subjected to

   a. Optimal sample size experiments
   b. Methods 1 or 2 above

   Thus clearly good projects are considered without further evaluation and clearly bad projects are discarded without further evaluation.

4. Assume the probability that a project will be funded is p, independent of any information about the project. The factor p is applied to calculation of the expected value of sample information in the case of ample funds, to determine a good evaluation program.

5. The probability that a project will be funded is taken to be a function of its expected present worth per dollar of investment. This probability is applied to calculation of the expected value of sample information in the case of ample funds.

An Example

As an example of the first of these approximate policies, suppose the firm ranks projects according to the ratio of present worth to investment required. A critical or cut-off value of this ratio is chosen. We then assume that if a given project is found upon evaluation to have a present worth per dollar of investment greater than this critical value, it will be funded, otherwise it will be discarded. This assumption may reflect what happens if the firm operates on a basis of continuous budgeting. That is, as projects are discovered and evaluated, those whose ratios exceed the critical value are immediately funded; others are immediately discarded. This process continues until the available funds for investment are exhausted.

If, however, the firm uses batch budgeting the foregoing assumption will be only approximately correct. Thus, if the firm accumulates evaluated projects until the end of the budget period, and then invests in the best of those available, up to the point permitted by the available budget, some projects with ratios exceeding the critical value may not be funded. On the other hand, some projects with ratios below the critical value may be funded if sufficient funds remain available.

To make such a policy explicit, let

G = critical value of the ratio of present worth to investment
I = investment in a particular project
$Q = IG$ = corresponding critical value of present worth
m_{pr} = prior mean of P

Suppose $m_{pr} < Q$; thus the prior choice is discard. The expected value of sample information is given by

$$\text{EVSI} = \int_{m_{po}=Q}^{\infty} m_{po}\, \text{PR}(m_{po})\, dm_{po}$$

If $m_{pr} > Q$, the prior choice is invest. In this case,

$$\text{EVSI} = \int_{m_{po}=Q}^{\infty} m_{po}\, \text{PR}(m_{po})\, dm_{po} - m_{pr}$$

Thus as Q increases, EVSI tends to decrease and the amount of effort devoted to evaluation decreases as well.

If divisions of the firm perform search and evaluation, then the critical value of G (and thus Q for any project) may either be fixed by headquarters or established by the divisions themselves. Clearly, the results of these two methods need not be the same.

This model would be most logical if the critical value, G, were indeed chosen so that the probability of funding a project was very nearly 1 if its ratio exceeded G and very nearly 0 if its ratio did not exceed G. In the continuous budgeting case, this will in fact be true up to the point where the budget is exhausted. It would, however, be desirable to choose G so that it represented the highest ratio likely to permit full utilization of the budget. In the case of batch budgeting, it would similarly be reasonable to choose G so that those projects whose ratios were above it would very nearly match the budget available for investment.

Ranked Projects

A different sort of policy is exemplified by that of evaluating a proposal only if the chances of reversing the prior decision about it exceed some specified value. In this case, we assume that a group of projects is on hand and that management has drafted an initial budget based on prior information. To illustrate with a simple case, suppose all projects require roughly the same investment. The prior budget will contain a worst (lowest-ranked) project with present worth having a prior mean of P_1. Among projects not included in the budget will be a best (highest-ranked) project with present worth having a prior mean P_2. If a project is included in the prior budget, the chances of excluding it (approximately) after evaluation are the chances that the posterior mean of the project will fall below P_2. Actually, of course, if the project were thus excluded, it might later be reincluded on the basis of further evaluation of the other projects. Hence the foregoing probability is approximate. Similarly, if a project is not included in the budget on the basis of prior information, the probability of reversing this decision is approximately the probability that its posterior mean will fall above P_1. Thus the firm might choose an evaluation policy but apply it to only those projects for which the probabilities of decision reversals exceed some specified value.

This raises the question of the order in which projects should be evaluated since the amount of evaluation effort expended may depend on that order. We shall not explore this question but simply suggest that the process might well be begun with those projects whose prior means are nearest P_1 and P_2. These are the projects for which EVSI will tend to be the greatest. For example, the two projects most likely to interchange positions (one included and one excluded from the prior budget) might be considered, using the analysis for choosing the better of two projects. This process might be repeated until there are no more pairs of projects for which further investigation can be justified.

Evaluation Dynamics

We have previously defined a *dynamic evaluation policy* as one in which the amount of evaluation effort expended on a proposal depended in part on the characteristics of projects previously discovered and evaluated. We have already encountered one type of dynamic problem: Given a batch of projects to be evaluated in what order should they be studied? One might propose various approximate solutions, such as allocating evaluation effort sequentially, always seeking to maximize the marginal ENGSI. Here ENGSI might be calculated on the basis of some assumption about the probability of funding a project of the sort we have used earlier.

We may consider two other versions of dynamic evaluation problems.

1. Instead of batch evaluation as suggested earlier, one may adopt a policy of sequential evaluation of projects as they are discovered. This would be necessary in the case of continuous budgeting, for example. If we permit a return to projects previously evaluated for further evaluation

in the light of those which subsequently emerge, then the problem of developing a good policy may be rather complex.

2. One might modify the policy of sequential evaluation of projects by not permitting a return to projects previously evaluated. That is, the amount of evaluation effort devoted to a given project may depend on projects previously discovered and evaluated, but not on projects subsequently discovered.

The second problem may be approximated by making the additional assumption that once a project is in the budget, it will not be later displaced. This assumption is made for computing EVSI, and is approximate since in batch budgeting later displacement could occur. We suppose that when a project is discovered its size is known with certainty. (*Size* refers to the investment required.) For any given size, one could compute the value of the present worth which must be exceeded if the project in question is to displace the lowest-ranked project of projects in the budget. Then one might assume that if the posterior mean exceeds this value, the project will be funded; otherwise it will not be funded. This would provide a basis for computing EVSI and thus establishing the amount of evaluation effort to be expended.

Search and Evaluation

It will often be useful to consider search and evaluation as a single process which serves to produce projects for budgeting consideration. In doing this note two general points: First, before the discovery of a project, those attributes which will determine the amount of evaluation effort devoted to it in the case of a static evaluation policy are unknown. These attributes may, however, be viewed as random variables characteristic of the opportunity environment in which search is carried on. This would permit one to consider the average amount of evaluation effort expended on project from the opportunity environment in question. This average amount of evaluation effort might then be added to the cost of search in the environment in order to produce a combined average cost for the search-evaluation process. This cost could then be used in planning a combined search-evaluation policy.

Second, in some cases the evaluation process reduces the number of proposals reaching the budgeting stage. For example, in the case of continuous budgeting with ample funds, projects which failed to meet some specified criterion after evaluation might simply be discarded. Thus a portion of the projects discovered would not be funded. One would, of course, need to consider this loss in planning a policy for search and evaluation.

As indicated in some examples of evaluation policies, search and evaluation may often interact; thus one might face the task of designing search and evaluation policies compatible with each other and with other aspects of the system. Suppose, for example, one uses an evaluation policy which reduces the amount of evaluation effort as the probability of funding a proposal decreases. The larger the number of projects available, the smaller the probability of funding, if this probability is based on the number of proposals competing for a fixed budget. Thus, the larger the number of proposals, the smaller the amount of evaluation effort expended per proposal. The marginal cost of search and evaluation tends to fall as the number of proposals increases; this encourages the production of large numbers of proposals and may lead to the situation in which a relatively small number of high-quality projects are chosen from a large number of proposals without much evaluation effort. We shall subsequently consider more carefully several instances of the problem of matching search and evaluation policies with other aspects of the system.

The system design problem is really that of matching policies for

> search
> evaluation
> budgeting

with the allocation of these tasks and budgets throughout the system.

A Digression on Sufficiency

Consider two modes of observation;

1. Observe the present worth of a project considered to be from the same population as the project under study.
2. Observe the cash flows from situations considered to be the same statistically as those for the project under study. That is, observe the values, $R_0, \ldots, R_N$. We continue the assumption that these are independent random variables.

Are these two modes of observation equivalent, in the sense of conveying the same amount of information? Put another way, can one summarize the values $R_0, \ldots, R_N$ by computing

$$P = \sum_{t=0}^{N} a^t R$$

without loss of information?

To illustrate that the answer to these questions is negative, consider a situation in which $N = 1$ and $a = 1$. The prior mean of P is

$$m_{pr} = m(0) + m(1)$$

Now let

$$c(t) = \frac{v(t)}{v_{pr}(t)}$$

$$c = \frac{v(0) + v(1)}{v_{pr}(0) + v_{pr}(1)}$$

The basic question is then: "Is a report of P equivalent to a report of R_0 and R_1?"

If P is reported, then

$$m_{po} = \frac{cm_{pr} + P}{c + 1}$$

$$v_{po} = \frac{v(0) + v(1)}{c + 1}$$

If R_0 and R_1 are reported, then

$$m_{po} = \frac{c(0)m(0) + R_0}{c(0) + 1} + \frac{c(1)m(1) + R_1}{c(1) + 1}$$

$$v_{po} = \frac{v(0)}{c(0) + 1} + \frac{v(1)}{c(1) + 1}$$

If these two reports are equivalent, then m_{po} and v_{po} should be independent of the report given. If $c = c(0) = c(1)$, this will be so. This reduces the problem to that just given where the sample mean was shown to be sufficient, with the exception that $v(0)$ need not be equal to $v(1)$. This says roughly that if we have equally good "relative" information (as measured by $c(0)$ and $c(1)$) about R_0 and R_1, then the two reports are equivalent.

If, however, the relation

$$c = c(0) = c(1)$$

does not hold, then it may be shown that the two reports are not generally equivalent; thus P cannot be regarded as a sufficient report. Intuitively, the report of R_0 and R_1 contains "more information." If this is interpreted to mean that the posterior variance will be smaller with this report than with report P, it may be shown in a rather straightforward manner that this intuition is indeed correct.

EXERCISES

7-1. Consider the problem of choosing the best of three investment possibilitites. How might the expected net gain from sample information be found in this case? Can the analysis in the chapter be usefully extended to three possibilities?

7-2. What rationale might be offered for adopting a planning horizon in the analysis of investment proposals?

7-3. What are the implications of the concept of sufficiency for the design of a management-information system to assist in carrying out the capital-budgeting function?

7-4. What justifications can be suggested for the rather common industrial practice of suppressing risk in the analysis of investment decisions?

7-5. What would be the impact of a nonlinear utility function on the analysis of this chapter?

7-6. Three possibilities were suggested for approximating the value of sample information in the case of ample projects. The first of these was based on a selection of a critical value of the project mean. Discuss how this critical value might be chosen in the case of continuous budgeting. In the case of batch budgeting.

7-7. The second of these possibilities (referred to in Exercise 7-6) for dealing with the ample-projects case involved choosing a critical value of the variance of the posterior mean. How might this reasonably be chosen?

7-8. Which of these ways of dealing with the ample-projects case seems most suggestive of what is actually being done in an industrial situation of which you have some knowledge?

8

Inventory
and Related
Decisions

The Basic Inventory Structure

This chapter deals with a group of decisions which are found in somewhat diverse management contexts but which share a similar analytical structure. The most prominent member of this group, from the viewpoint of both managers and analysts, is perhaps the basic policy problem of determining an inventory level in the face of uncertain demand. We shall explore the structure of this problem and then suggest its relationship to various other decision situations.

Consider the problem of inventory level determination for an item which can be stocked at the beginning of a time period only. If the inventory level proves insufficient for the demand which develops during the period, additional stock cannot be routinely obtained until the beginning of the subsequent stocking period. We assume that whatever stock level we wish to have at the start of a period can be obtained without any concern for lead time, delivery time, or delivery quantities. The demand for the item in question during a period is viewed as a random variable. In particular, we suppose that one can have knowledge of demand, in the sense of the total number of requests for the item, as opposed to knowledge of "sales" only, in the sense of the total number of satisfied requests. This is sometimes called the *mail order* situation, since in that case one typically has data on demand by customers which are independent of the inventory level maintained.

To make the problem especially simple, we adopt a set of assumptions which permits the problem to be studied as a one-period problem and avoids need to consider the impact of what we do in a given period on what will happen in subsequent periods. We may assume that stock left over at the end of a period is useless because it spoils or becomes obsolete. Thus left-over material cannot be used to satisfy later demands. We may also assume that unsatisfied demands are not back-ordered to a future period. This might reflect that demands not met out of inventory are lost, or are satisfied in non-routine ways at additional cost. These or other similar assumptions are taken to lead to a problem in which there is cost of having excess inventory at the end of a period which is proportional to the amount of that excess, and a cost of failing to meet demands which is proportional to the amount of the shortage occurring during the period.

Analysis of the Single-period Problem

To represent this problem, let

x = demand during a period
$f(x)$ = probability distribution of x
I = an inventory level (I_0 = the optimal level)
C_1 = unit cost of excess stock at the end of a period
C_2 = unit cost of a shortage of stock
$E(I)$ = expected cost per period using an inventory level of I

We develop the model on the assumption that x is a continuous variable, or can reasonably be modeled as such. The discrete case follows directly analogous steps. The expected cost is given by

$$E(I) = C_1 \int_{x=0}^{I} (I - x)f(x)\, dx + C_2 \int_{x=I}^{\infty} (x - I)f(x)\, dx$$

To find the optimal inventory level, we take the derivative of this function with respect to I and set the result equal to zero. The details of this process may be explored through Exercise 8-1. The result suggests that the optimum value of I satisfies the following expression.

$$\frac{dE(I_0)}{dI_0} = C_1 \int_{x=0}^{I} f(x)\, dx - C_2 \int_{x=I}^{\infty} f(x)\, dx = 0$$

This may be written more simply as

$$\int_{x=0}^{I} f(x)\, dx = F(I_0) = \frac{C_2}{C_1 + C_2}$$

In words, we want the value of I at which the cumulative of the demand distribution is equal to the ratio of the shortage cost to the sum of the shortage and overage costs. It is evident that the greater the shortage cost relative to the overage cost, the greater will be the optimum inventory level. To compute the expected cost when the optimal inventory level is used, we may write

$$E(I_0) = C_1 \int_{x=0}^{I_o} If(x)\,dx - C_1 \int_{x=0}^{I_o} x f(x)\,dx + C_2 \int_{x=I_o}^{\infty} x f(x)\,dx$$

$$- C_2 \int_{x=I_o}^{\infty} If(x)\,dx$$

We know from the optimality condition for I_o that

$$C_1 F(I_o) - C_2 [1 - F(I_o)] = 0$$

Using this result, the expected cost may be reduced to

$$E(I_o) = C_2 \int_{x=I_o}^{\infty} x f(x)\,dx - C_1 \int_{x=0}^{I_o} x f(x)\,dx$$

The integrals in this expression are known as *partial expectations* since they represent the expected value of the random variable taken over only a part of its range.

If we add to the problem the assumption that x is a normally distributed random variable, we may then make use of linear normal loss integrals from Appendix A to compute $E(I_o)$.

Define

$$z_o = \frac{I_o - E(x)}{SD(x)}$$

where

$$SD(x) = \text{standard deviation of } x$$

In terms of unit normal loss integrals we have

$$E(I_o) = [C_1 L_N(-z_o) + C_2 L_N(z_o)]\, SD(x)$$

In doing this we have ignored that x will typically not take on negative values. Instead of truncating the normal distribution at zero, we have assumed its tail below zero is so small as to be safely neglected.

A useful alternate form for this expected cost may be obtained using the expression from Appendix A which suggested

$$L_N(z_o) = f_N(z_o) - z_o[1 - F_N(z_o)]$$

Recalling in addition that

$$F_N(z_o) = \frac{C_2}{C_1 + C_2}$$

we may substitute these two expressions in the previously developed form of $E(I_o)$ to obtain

$$E(I_o) = \left[C_1 f_N(z_o) + z_o \frac{C_1 C_2}{C_1 + C_2} + C_2 f_N(z_o) - z_o C_2 \right.$$

$$\left. + z_o \frac{C_2^2}{C_1 + C_2} \right] SD(x)$$

This may be reduced directly to

$$E(I_o) = (C_1 + C_2) f_N(z_o) \, SD(x)$$

The expected cost of operating with the optimal inventory level is thus seen to be directly proportional to the standard deviation of the demand distribution.

Uncertainty and the Value of Information

We now enrich the problem by supposing that the demand distribution has a known variance but an uncertain mean. Assume that $f(x)$ is normal with mean m and variance v. Uncertainty about m is expressed by regarding it as a normally distributed random variable with prior parameters, m_{pr} and v_{pr}. The prior distribution of demand is then normal with mean m_{pr} and variance given by

$$v + v_{pr} = v + \frac{v}{c}$$

The optimal inventory level, based on prior information, will be of the form

$$I_o = m_{pr} + z_o \left(v + \frac{v}{c} \right)^{1/2}$$

Uncertainty may arise because we are dealing with a new product for which there is limited information or experience on which to base predictions of demand. Alternatively, uncertainty may arise in dealing with an established product for which major changes in the marketing situation limit the relevance of past data and experience.

If we could obtain perfect information about the *demand* in a given period, we would take the optimal inventory level equal to the known demand and incur no shortage or overage cost at all. The value of such information would be the expected cost of an optimal policy based on prior information. That is,

$$E_{pr}(I_o) = (C_1 + C_2) f_N(z_o) \left[v + \frac{v}{c} \right]^{1/2}$$

If, alternatively, we obtain perfect information about the *mean demand*, then the value of this information is the difference between the expected cost based on prior information and the expected cost of an optimal policy when uncertainty about m has been eliminated.

$$\text{EVPI} = E_{pr}(I_o) - (C_1 + C_2) f_N(z_o) v^{1/2}$$

$$= (C_1 + C_2) f_N(z_o) \left\{ \left[v + \frac{v}{c} \right]^{1/2} - v^{1/2} \right\}$$

The Economics of Imperfect Information

If we are dealing with what is indeed a single-period problem, then it would be consistent to assume that any information about demand in the period in question would be of no value on any other occasion. More commonly, however, the problem is really a multiperiod one. Any information obtained about demand may be relevant to more than one period; hence to calculate its value, we must have some notion of how many periods of operation will benefit from it. Simply operating through a period gives an observation of demand which may be used to revise one's opinion about demand in future periods. Whether it is worthwhile to record demand and make such revisions, depends in part on how many future periods one anticipates. Questions about the value of information in multiperiod problems will be treated in a later chapter. For the present we suppose that any information obtained is relevant only for the single period in question; its value is to be based on its use in this period alone. It may be possible, for example, to obtain from past records some data relevant to the period we are planning for. The question is, "How much effort ought to be expended in obtaining and assimilating these historical data?" It may be possible to do some market studies which would be relevant, and we would be interested in the value of such studies. Nevertheless, we suppose the data consist simply of a sample of demands, a sample containing observations of x.

Given such information, say, in the form of a sample mean, we can transform the prior distribution of m into a posterior distribution. This in turn, permits us to obtain the posterior distribution of demand and compute the optimal inventory level. For a sample of size n, the posterior expected cost of an optimal inventory level is

$$(C_1 + C_2) f_N(z_o) \left[v + \frac{v}{c + n} \right]^{1/2}$$

This does not depend on the particular sample mean observed nor on a posterior mean of m, but only on the sample size. In other words, the posterior expected cost using an optimal policy will be the same for all samples of size n. Note of course, that the optimal inventory level based on posterior information *does* depend on m_{po} and thus upon m_s. The expected cost depends on the variance of the demand distribution only; thus the posterior expected cost just computed is also the prior expected value of the posterior expected cost. The expected value of sample information may then be found in the usual way, by subtracting the prior expected value of the posterior expected cost from the prior expected cost.

$$\text{EVSI} = (C_1 + C_2) f_N(z_o) \left[\left(v + \frac{v}{c} \right)^{1/2} - \left(\frac{v}{c} + \frac{v}{c + n} \right)^{1/2} \right]$$

In short, the expected value of sample information is proportional to the amount by which it reduces the standard deviation of demand.

The Optimal Sample Size

If the expected value of sample information is considered to be a function of n and one assumes that the cost of sampling is proportional to n, then the expected net gain from sampling is

$$\text{ENGSI} = \text{EVSI} - kn$$

Taking the first derivative of ENGSI with respect to n and setting the result equal to zero yields

$$\frac{d\,\text{ENGSI}}{dn} = 0 = \frac{C_1 + C_2}{2} f_N(z_o) \left[\frac{v}{(c + n + 1)(c + n)^3} \right]^{1/2} - k$$

This may be put in the form

$$(c + n + 1)(c + n)^3 = \frac{v[(C_1 + C_2) f_N(z_o)]^2}{4k^2}$$

Although this is not a particularly handy form for computing the optimal sample size, it does confirm some intuitive expectations about the problem:

1. As the cost of a sample observation, k, goes up, the optimal sample size comes down.

2. As c, our measure of the decision maker's prior conviction or knowledge goes up, the optimal sample size comes down.

3. As the costs involved, C_1 and C_2 go up, the optimal sample size goes up.

4. As the prior variance of m increases, the optimal sample size increases.

The reader may find it useful to consider the expression for the derivative of ENGSI and see what similar statements can be made about the sensitivity of ENGSI to sample size. Note also the possibility that the cost of sampling may be so great as to make the optimal sample size zero.

Learning and Adaptation in Multiperiod Problems

Although the economics of information processing in multiperiod problems has been postponed to a later chapter, it is useful to examine briefly the learning or adaptation process as involved. As each inventory period comes to a close, demand for that period becomes known, we suppose. Further, we assume that this information is relevant in making predictions of demand in future periods. In the simplest case, demands in future periods are regarded as a sequence of identically distributed normal random variables. That is, at any given moment the decision maker's prior distribution for demand is the same for every future period. In a slightly more plausible case, the variance of the decision maker's prior distribution increases as one considers periods further and further into the future. In many situations it will be economic to use demand data as they become available to revise these prior distributions. If one does not make such revisions, one is acting as if

1. Current data are irrelevant to future demand.
2. The cost of recording current data and revising one's priors is more than the savings to be obtained.
3. There is no uncertainty about future average demand; hence no revision is required.

In the case in which the priors for future periods are the same, each period's demand, x, as it becomes known leads to a new prior mean

$$\frac{cm_{pr} + x}{c + 1}$$

and a new prior variance

$$\frac{v}{c + 1}$$

As time goes on, the variance of the prior mean becomes smaller and smaller, and the weight given to each new observation of demand will also decline. This is fine as long as the situation is characterized by a stationary mean demand. If, however, the mean demand should change, reflecting changes in market conditions, then the smaller the prior variance, the less responsive this policy will be to any such change.

Now if management expects changes in the true mean demand, it may avoid this lack of responsiveness in several ways. It may, for example, simply revise the prior variance from time to time as conditions in the market suggest increased uncertainty as to the mean demand. Unquestionably this should be done in any case. Certain routinized procedures are also of interest.

One possible policy is to throw out demand data more than c periods old. The prior mean, m_{pr}, will then be simply the average of the demands for the last c periods. A new observation will result in

$$m_{po} = \frac{cm_{pr} + x}{c + 1}$$

Thus the mean of the prior distribution for the next period, m_{po}, relative to the last period, is simply a $c + 1$ period moving average. Thus if we modify the Bayesian learning process by assuming that old data are no longer relevant, we obtain the familiar and widely used moving average method of adapting predictions to events.

Another possible policy is to keep the variance of the prior constant, thus keeping c constant, but not actually throw away the old data as in the foregoing discussion. In this case we have

$$m_{po} = \frac{cm_{pr} + x}{c + 1} = \frac{c}{c + 1} m_{pr} + \frac{1}{c + 1} x$$

and the weight given the new data will always be the same. This may be recognized as the familiar exponential smoothing method of revising a prediction.

The point is simply that by modifying the Bayesian learning process in some simple, common-sense ways in order to make it more responsive to possible changes in the true mean demand, we arrive directly at two prediction methods which are already widely known in management practice.

From the Bayesian viewpoint, a more direct way of maintaining sensitivity to possible future changes in the mean demand, is to reflect this possibility by adopting prior distributions for future periods having variances which increase with time. Suppose, for example, we take the prior variance for the current period to be v/c and the prior variance for mean demand n periods in the future to be $v/c - n$. By the time that future period arrives, we will have n additional observations of demand and its prior variance will have been reduced to v/c. Thus as the system progresses through time the prior variance for the current period is always the same.

Modifications of the Single-period Model

We return now to the single-period model to suggest some modifications and enrichments which might be of interest in adapting it to various situations. We consider first various cost structures which might occur.

1. There may be a cost proportional to the stock level held at the beginning of the period, in addition to the shortage cost previously used. Thus

$$E(I) = C_1 I + C_2 \int_{x=I}^{\infty} (x - I) f(x) \, dx$$

2. There may be costs which depend only on the occurrence of overages or shortages, but not on the amount of these overages or shortages. Thus,

$$E(I) = C_1 \int_{x=0}^{I} f(x) \, dx + C_2 \int_{x=I}^{\infty} f(x) \, dx$$

3. Costs might depend on the square of the amount of overage or shortage, or some such function of these quantities.

4. We may be interested in maximizing expected profit when the cost of procuring each item of inventory is C_o and the revenue per unit is R. Thus,

$$\text{expected profit} = \int_{x=0}^{I} [Rx - C_1(I - x)] f(x) \, dx$$
$$+ RI \int_{x=I}^{\infty} f(x) \, dx - C_o I$$

We might also enrich the inventory analysis by considering other sources of risk, beyond that of demand itself. It may be necessary to place our "order" for inventory somewhat in advance of the start of the period. The time between placing the order and its delivery may be uncertain. The order may be delivered in parts, yielding uncertain amounts at uncertain points in time. Indeed, one may be able to control only the average rate at which material becomes available. The quantity delivered may be a matter of uncertainty, either because some of the items delivered turn out to be defective or because the supply mechanism simply does not respond precisely to the amount requested.

From a larger point of view, a firm may have some choice beyond simply inventorying as a way of meeting demand. When demand exceeds some "normal" production level, the firm may hire additional workers, use overtime, influence demand through various sales and marketing strategies, and so on. The problem is thus of a more general policy for matching output with demand.

Some Related Management Problems

The basic nature of the single-period inventory problem requires management to choose a single action in the face of uncertainty as to the future. The penalties for inappropriate actions depend on the deviations between the act and the event. This implies that act and events can be quantified and described on the same scale. We describe several management problems which are related in their structure to the inventory problem and which may yield to similar analyses. Many of these problems have to do with designing a system with appropriate capacity or fixing some resource at a suitable level.

1. A basic problem in plant design is that of how many machines to have in the plant or in a department in the face of an uncertain work load. Too many machines results in idleness; too few necessitates overtime, subcontracting, or some typically costly method of supplementing capac-

ity. How large a computer, how much generating capacity for an electrical system, how many fork-lift trucks, how many employees of a certain skill, and so on, are questions of a very similar nature. In many of these situations, as in some which follow, we would want to relax the assumption that demands not met in one period are lost. Indeed we would want to explore the additional complications arising when such demands are "back ordered" or held to be satisfied in some future period.

2. In designing a transportation system to operate according to a fixed timetable, there is the question of how much capacity or service to schedule out of a given terminal in the face of uncertain demand for transportation at that terminal. Too much or too little outbound capacity has obvious drawbacks in many systems.

3. The general problem of point estimation in statistics may be related to the inventory structure. If we must choose a single estimate of an uncertain parameter, then the "best" estimate is not necessarily an unbiased one. If we would establish a cost associated with various degrees of overestimation and underestimation, then we could choose an estimate which would minimize expected cost.

4. Many scheduling problems may appear in a similar context. Suppose we wish to complete job A at the same time that job B is completed, and that we have some choice as to the starting time of A. We may be uncertain about how long it will take to complete A and uncertain also about when B will be accomplished. If we can say something of the cost of having A completed before B and something of the cost of the opposite result, then we can decide on the best time to begin job A.

To see how this problem might be formulated, let

$$x = \text{time to complete job A}$$
$$f(x) = \text{probability distribution of } x$$
$$y = \text{time at which job B is completed}$$
$$g(y) = \text{probability distribution of } y$$
$$S = \text{time at which A is started}$$

Then

$$E(S) = \int_y \int_{x=0}^{S-y} C_1[S - (y - x)] f(x) g(y) \, dx \, dy$$
$$+ \int_y \int_{x-S-y}^{\infty} C_2[(y - x) - S] f(x) g(y) \, dx \, dy$$

By methods similar to those used in solving the inventory problem, we may obtain the expression

$$\int_y \int_{x=0}^{S-y} f(x) g(y) \, dx \, dy = \frac{C_2}{C_1 + C_2}$$

The value of S which satisfies this expression will be the starting time for job A which will minimize the expected cost.

5. Consider a production process, the output of which is characterized by some critical dimension x. The dimension x may, for example, be length, diameter, weight, specific gravity, conductivity, and so on. Although we cannot control the actual value of x, we can regulate the process in such a way as to control the mean of x. The problem then is how to fix the mean of x if there is a cost associated with having x fall above some upper specification limit, LU, and a cost of having it fall below some lower specification limit, LL. We may view this as a problem of choosing m so as to minimize

$$E(m) = \int_{x=0}^{LL} C_1 f(x, m)\, dx + \int_{x=LU}^{\infty} C_2 f(x, m)\, dx$$

Seen in this way, the problem is, in a sense, the opposite of the inventory problem. In that problem, the parameters of the distribution were fixed and we were required to choose the upper limit of the first integral and the lower limit of the second. Here, the limits on the integrals are fixed and we are required to choose a parameter of the distribution. By a slight alteration in viewpoint, however, we can make the problems similar. We might consider the expectation to be a function of LL, taking m to be fixed and LU = LL + k, where k is the required "spread" in the specification limits. This would place the problem in the inventory framework and we could obtain the best value of LL for any specified m. We need only determine for what value of m, our originally given specification limits are best.

Multilevel Inventory Systems

In the discussion so far we have concentrated on information gathering and learning as the basic method of influencing the uncertainty in a decision. There is a group of interesting problems in systems design in which the well-known phenomenon of "pooling the risk" plays a central role. Here the systems design itself may have interesting effects on the risk experienced by the decision makers who must manage the system. The basic principle may be applied whenever any resource must be provided in anticipation of an uncertain demand. By establishing a common pool of the resource to serve an aggregation of such demands, savings may be realized, since a smaller pool may afford the same level of protection as would be provided if each demand was protected by its own reserve. A distributor, for example, who must establish a reserve inventory in anticipation of uncertain demands at various retail outlets, finds that, if the number of retail stores is increased, the reserve inventory need not be increased proportionally in order to provide the same level of protection. Thus his centralized inventory can provide equal "insurance" for a larger number of stores at a smaller cost per store served or per unit sold. The same effect permits large firms to realize savings in face of uncertain demands for cash, inventories, plant capacity, manpower, specialized management service, and so on. This effect explains in part the tendency to aggregate uncertain demands by centralizing certain activities through the formation of equipment pools, secretarial pools, centralized computer facilities, and the like. The basic principles involved may be illustrated by means of a two-level inventory system in a divisionalized firm. We suppose that the firm consists of several operating divisions and a headquarters division. Demands for a certain commodity arise at the operating divisions, and since these demands are uncertain, there is a problem of where and in what quantities inventories should be carried. How much inventory should be held by each of the operating divisions and how much by the headquarters division?

Assume that the situation is a direct extension of that examined earlier in this chapter. Let

x_j = demand for the commodity at division j during a stocking period

$f(x_j)$ = prior probability distribution of x_j, having a mean m_j and standard deviation $SD(x_j)$

$D = \sum_j x_j$ = total demand experienced by the firm during a stocking period

I_{oj} = optimal inventory level for division j

I_{oh} = optimal inventory level for headquarters division

Suppose that, as before, there are storage costs and shortage costs and that these costs are the same throughout the firm. Any inventory system design is to be evaluated in terms of its expected cost.

Consider first a fully decentralized design in which no stock is held by the headquarters division and each operating division holds an inventory for its exclusive use. High shipping costs are assumed to prevent the movement of material from one division to satisfy demands arising at another. Each division chooses an inventory level which will satisfy the relation

$$F(I_{oj}) = \frac{C_2}{C_1 + C_2}$$

The quantity inventory resulting may be, as we have seen, expressed in the form

$$I_{oj} = m_j + z_o \, SD(x_j)$$

The expected cost associated with the optimal inventory level is proportional to the standard deviation of demand, a result we express here simply as

$$E(I_{oj}) = k \, SD(x_j)$$

For the entire firm this decentralized system will result in a total inventory of

$$\sum_j I_{oj} = \sum_j m_j + z_o \sum_j \mathrm{SD}(x_j)$$

and a total expected cost per period of

$$E(I_{oj}) = k \sum_j \mathrm{SD}(x_j)$$

Compare this with a completely centralized design in which all inventory is held at headquarters and none by the operating divisions. We neglect for the present any additional costs or delays which result from serving the demands from the headquarters stock as opposed to the divisional stocks. The demand experienced at headquarters may then be viewed as a random variable, D, with mean

$$m_h = \sum_j m_j$$

The crucial point is the relation between the standard deviation of demand at the divisions and the standard deviation of demand at headquarters. If the demands at the divisions are *independent*, then the variance of the total demand is equal to the sum of the variances of the divisional demands. Thus,

$$\mathrm{SD}^2(D) = \sum_j \mathrm{SD}^2(x_j)$$

The inventory held by the headquarters division will be

$$I_{oh} = m_h + z_o \, \mathrm{SD}(D)$$

and the expected cost per period for the firm will be

$$E(I_{oh}) = k \, \mathrm{SD}(D)$$

Under our assumption of independence,

$$\mathrm{SD}(D) < \sum_j \mathrm{SD}(x_j)$$

and thus the cost for the centralized design will be less than that for the decentralized one. This saving results from "pooling" the uncertain demands and serving them with a single central stock.

It is interesting to note that if

$$\frac{C_2}{C_1 + C_2} > .5$$

the amount of inventory held under the centralized design will be less. If, however, this cost ratio is less than .50, the centralized design will call for more inventory but still achieve lower average costs per period.

The amount of savings due to the centralization of stocks may be calculated most easily in the case where each division is assumed to have the same standard deviation of demand.

$$\mathrm{SD}(x_j) = \mathrm{SD} \qquad \text{for} \quad j = 1, \ldots, N$$

Under this assumption, the difference in cost for the two designs will be

$$E(I_{oj}) - E(I_{oh}) = kN\,\text{SD} - kN^{1/2}\,\text{SD} = kN^{1/2}\,\text{SD}\,(N^{1/2} - 1)$$

Since k is positive, this difference will always be positive as long as more than one division is involved. As the number of divisions, N, increases, the amount of the savings possible through centralization of stocks increases.

If the divisional demands are not independent as assumed but are in fact positively correlated, then the savings will not be as great. In the simple case of the firm with two operating divisions, the variance of demand at the headquarters division may be written

$$\text{SD}^2(D) = \text{SD}^2(x_1) + \text{SD}^2(x_2) + 2r_{12}\,\text{SD}(x_1)\,\text{SD}(x_2)$$

where r_{12} is the coefficient of correlation between the demands at the two divisions. If the correlation coefficient is positive, the larger it becomes, the greater the cost of the required inventory at headquarters and thus the less the savings to be achieved through centralization. If the demands are negatively correlated, however, high demands at one division tend to be compensated by low demands at the other, and the savings due to centralization become even greater than in the case of independence. The maximum possible savings occur with perfect negative correlation, that is, $r_{12} = -1$.

The important assumption has been made that the centralized design produces no additional costs resulting from serving the divisional demands out of the headquarters stock. In addition, it has been assumed under the decentralized design that there are to be no transfers of inventory among the operating divisions. One can modify these assumptions now in order to suggest some of the conditions under which the decentralized placement of stocks would be preferred.

If an added penalty cost is incurred when demands are met from headquarters inventory, then it is possible that this penalty could negate any advantages due to complementarity. Suppose that for every unit of demand met from the headquarters supply there is a cost for shipping and delay of C_3. Then the cost of a centralized design will be

$$E(I_{oh}) + C_3 \sum_j m_j$$

Assuming some complementarity, as C_3 increases, the least costly design will shift from a centralized one to a decentralized one. If the cost of C_3 is considered and one assumes that cross shipments are permitted between operating decisions at no cost, then the preferred design is a decentralized one. Free cross shipment permits a decentralized design to take advantage of exactly the same degree of "pooling" that could be utilized in a centralized system.

Assuming an equal charge for cross shipments between any two divisions or between headquarters and any division, it can be shown that the preferred system will be decentralized. As the cost of cross shipments is increased, the preferred system will have inventories and expected costs approaching those of the previously discussed decentralized system with no cross shipments permitted. The lower the cost of cross shipment, the smaller the total amount of inventory held by the firm. As long as some cross shipment does occur, one may predict that, if the divisions have equal standard deviations of demand, as the number of divisions increases, the inventory per division will decrease.

In considering these systems, it is wise to remember the sort of communication or the coordination problems which they imply. In a fully centralized system, for example, the headquarters division must have information on demand at all the divisions in order to formulate policy for the firm. Presumably this information must be revised from time to time. The divisions on the other hand, cannot know whether a particular demand will be satisfied until headquarters has informed them of the situation. In a fully decentralized system with no cross shipments, complete self-containment has been achieved, and the divisions may proceed with their own formulations of inventory policy without reference to the activities of other divisions or of the headquarters group. In a fully decentralized system with cross shipments, no division can fix its own inventory policy without knowing what is being done at all the other divisions. Any division is in the position of having part of its inventory potentially supplied by the other divisions; therefore, it acts in part as an inventory holder for the other divisions. Inventories cannot be fixed optimally in this case without complete centralization of information and policy making. Only through full and complete coordination can minimum inventory costs be achieved.

EXERCISES

8-1. A manager views monthly demand for a given commodity that must be stocked as a normally distributed random variable with uncertain mean and standard deviation 20. His "best estimate" of the mean monthly demand is 100 and he thinks that there is a 50 per cent chance that this mean is greater than 90 but less than 110. He is willing to use a normal distribution to represent his uncertainty.

If $C_1 = \$10$ and $C_2 = \$20$, find the optimal inventory level, the cost associated with this level, the expected value of perfect information, and the expected value of sample information for a sample size of 5.

After five months' experience, it is found that the average demand during the period was 120 units per month. Given this experience find the optimal inventory level.

8-2. Suppose in the single-period inventory model, the cost in a period is given by a constant times the square of the deviation between inventory and demand. Find an expression for the optimal sample size in this case.

8-3. By introducing procurement costs and sales revenues convert the single-period inventory model to a profit-maximizing model. Find an expression for the optimal sample size.

8-4. This chapter proposes several methods for making the demand distribution less sensitive to past data and more sensitive to current data. Discuss the sort of work required to implement each of these proposals in a specific situation. How could the effectiveness of such "forgetting" methods be tested?

8-5. Consider the problem of establishing the capacity of a new plant in the face of uncertainty as to the demand for its output. Suppose there are fixed costs which are proportional to plant capacity and shortage costs which depend on the amount by which demand exceeds capacity. Show how this problem might be formulated and obtain an expression for the optimal sample size.

8-6. Suppose in the single-period inventory model that some of the units stocked turn out to be defective and thus cannot be used to satisfy demand. The number of defectives is uncertain. Suggest how this additional source of uncertainty might be added to the analysis. What factors would influence the value of information about the number of defectives?

8-7. What other management decision problems might be regarded as having structures similar to those discussed in this chapter?

8-8. A dispatcher sends ready-mix concrete trucks from his plant to a construction job and may choose the departure time for each truck. The travel time to the job is a random variable. The time at which the contents of each truck are required on the job is also seen by the dispatcher as a random variable. There is a cost associated with having the truck arrive on the job too early, as well as a cost associated with late arrival. Suggest how the problem of selecting a departure time might be formulated. How would you go about estimating the value of a communication system which would give the dispatcher better information as to the time trucks would be needed at the job?

8-9. When we use an unbiased estimator, what sort of assumptions are implied about the costs of estimating errors?

8-10. Refer to the discussion of the problem of adjusting the mean of a production process so that its output meets certain specifications. Suppose that the cost of exceeding either specification limit is the same. Obtain an expression for the optimal sample size in this case.

8-11. In the discussion of possible "forgetting" systems, one was proposed in which the value of c was to be kept constant, independent of the amount of experience obtained. What is the effect of choosing large or small values of c? Begin with a specific c and m_{pr} and suppose after three periods you have the observations x_1, x_2, and x_3. Write an expression for m_{po} in terms of these quantities.

8-12. Discuss extending the analysis of multilevel inventory systems from two to three organization levels.

8-13. What would be the effect of a nonlinear utility function on the two-level inventory system analysis given in the chapter?

8-14. What other sorts of complementarities available to a large firm have mechanisms similar to that of the inventory systems discussed in Chapter 8?

9

Bidding
Decisions

The Prevalence of Bidding

Nearly all the goods and services sold to the various
levels of government by private firms involve submitting
sealed bids. Much of the business transacted among
firms also involves more or less formal bidding. For
the buyer, the essence of the process is preserving uncertainty among the bidders and thus eliciting the bid most
nearly related to the cost of performing the contract.
This chapter deals with the question of what a firm
should bid for a given contract in the face of this and
other sources of uncertainty. The firm must balance
two basic considerations: uncertainty about the actual
cost of performing the contract and uncertainty about
whether a given bid will be the winning one. Low bids
have a relatively high probability of winning, but may
involve little or no chance of a profit if they do win.
Higher bids increase the certainty of profit if they win,
but have less probability of winning. Thus, as the firm
increases its bid, the chance of profit goes up, but the
probability of winning goes down. The question arises:
Can a "best" bid be found which combines these considerations and maximizes expected profit or utility.
This chapter discusses how this problem may be struc-
tured in the decision-learning framework previously developed. The mathematical functions involved do not
lend themselves to simple, explicit analyses; in actual
application, numerical results involving a digital computer would usually be required.

The case of closed or sealed bidding, rather than auction bidding is to be considered. It is assumed that, in a given competition, the bids promise equivalent quality and certainty of performance of the contract in question, and that the award will be made to the lowest bidder. In many situations, winning a competition may involve considerations more complex than simply submitting the lowest bid. Suppose that, in a particular competition, a firm faces three sources of uncertainty. Given a specification, however complete, of the goods or services to be furnished under a specific contract, some uncertainty typically remains as to the actual cost of performing the contract. The firm may have records of the actual cost of performance of similar contracts in the past and have experienced persons who can add judgments about the costs of a particular contract under consideration. Yet some uncertainty as to the final cost remains. Suppose, further that the firm is also uncertain about who will bid against it in a given competition, and most importantly, what its competitors will actually bid. In some large or highly specialized contracts there may be little or no uncertainty about the bidders, but uncertainty about what the competing bids will be is typically preserved. In many instances, the opening of the sealed bids submitted to governmental agencies, is public. Thus, a firm could compile data on who had bid in various competitions in the past and what their bids were. Such data may well become the basis for expressing uncertainty on these points in future competitions. In addition, of course, there will typically be managerial judgments about who is going to submit what sort of a bid in any particular anticipated competition.

The Lowest-Competing-Bidder Model

First, in order to make the basic issues explicit, a model with a particularly simple structure is presented. A firm wishes to bid in a certain competition so as to maximize its expected profit. The cost of actually preparing and submitting the bid is taken to be small enough to be neglected. Thus if the firm fails to win, its profit is zero. Uncertainty about the cost of performing the contract is expressed by regarding this cost as a random variable. Perhaps cost estimates and actual costs for similar contracts won in the past have been compared, as suggested in the analysis outlined in Chapter 6. Further, judgments about the cost of performing the particular contract at hand may have been combined with these historical data.

Uncertainty as to who will bid and how much, is expressed by focusing on the notion of the lowest competing bid. Here again there may be historical data on the lowest bid on contracts of the size and type in question. There may also be managerial judgments to be combined with these data in order to yield an expression of uncertainty as to the lowest competing bid upon which management is willing to base its bidding behavior. Assume the probability distribution of the lowest competing bid which expresses this uncertainty to be independent of the bid the firm decides to submit. If it were thought that competitors had some way of finding out in advance what was to be bid, this would be a poor assumption. With these assumptions, the decision-learning problem may be expressed using the following symbolism: Let

x = lowest competing bid on the contract in question

$f(x)$ = probability distribution of x, having mean = m and variance = v

$PR(m)$ = prior distribution of m

c = mean of the prior distribution of the cost of performing the contract upon which the firm is bidding

If a bid in the amount B is submitted, the prior expected profit may be written

$$E(B) = (B - c) \int_{x=B}^{\infty} PR(x) \, dx$$

Thus, if $B = c$, the expected profit will be zero; if the bid is sufficiently high, the probability of winning will be zero. Hopefully, somewhere between one can find a bid which maximizes the expected profit. If, to take a computationally simple example, the prior distribution of m combined with the distribution of x (v is assumed to be known) should yield a prior distribution of x which was uniform over the range $a \leq x \leq b$, the expected profit would be

$$E(B) = (B - c) \int_{x=B}^{\infty} \frac{1}{b - a} \, dx = (B - c) \frac{b - B}{b - a}$$

Taking the derivative with respect to B, setting it equal to zero and solving, yields an optimal bid

$$B_o = \frac{b + c}{2}$$

If the prior distribution of the lowest competing bid were normal, it would be necessary to program a digital computer to evaluate the expected profit for various bids and to select the optimum bid on the basis of these computations. Hence no solutions are given to many of the problems formulated here.

The Value of Perfect Information

Suppose one could obtain perfect assurance about the lowest competing bid. Knowing that the lowest competing bid would be x, one would submit a bid just less than x, say, $x - e$, as long as $x - e$ was greater than one's expected cost of performance, c. If $x - e < c$, then the best thing to do would be not to bid at all. For the winning bid would produce the expected profit, $x - e - c$. Since e may be made very small and is included only to assure that the bid is indeed perceptibly lower than the lowest competing bid, it may be neglected in computing the expected profit. The expected value of perfect information may be expressed as the difference between the prior expected value of the maximum profit, given perfect information, and the maximum prior expected profit.

$$\text{EVPI} = \int_{x=c}^{\infty} (x - c)\, \text{PR}(x)\, dx - (B_o - c) \int_{x=B_o}^{\infty} \text{PR}(x)\, dx$$

It may be computationally useful in some instances to rearrange this expression so that the terms take the familiar form of linear-loss integrals:

$$\text{EVPI} = \int_{x=B_o}^{\infty} (x - B_o)\, \text{PR}(x)\, dx - \int_{x=c}^{B_o} (x - c)\, \text{PR}(x)\, dx$$

If instead of being given perfect information as to the lowest competing bid, one anticipated obtaining perfect information about the expected value, m, of the distribution of the lowest competing bid, the value of this information would be

$$\text{EVPI} = \int_{m} E(B_o(m))\, \text{PR}(m)\, dm - (B_o - c) \int_{x=B_o}^{\infty} \text{PR}(x)\, dx$$

where $B_o(m)$ stands for the optimum bid for a given value of m.

Sample Information

If one can observe the results of past bidding competitions or perhaps postpone action until several future competitions have been studied, the value of such imperfect information may be computed in the usual way. Suppose the sample of lowest bids observed has a mean, m_s. This information transforms the prior distribution of m into a posterior using the logic of Bayes' theorem. The optimal bid based on the posterior distribution may then be obtained, and the maximum of the posterior expected profit determined. If $B_o(m_s)$ is the optimal bid based on the posterior distribution resulting from observing a particular sample with a mean m_s, then EVSI is given by

$$\text{EVSI} = \int_{m_s} E(B_o(m_s))\, \text{PR}(m_s)\, dm_s - E(B_o)$$

Here $E(B_o)$ is the maximum of the prior expected profit. Again, the computational difficulties of finding optimum bids and the associated expected profits suggest the use of machine computation at this point.

Alternate Models

Next, consider briefly the problem of choosing among alternate models or expressions of the same decision-learning problem. One might approach the bidding problem by obtaining data and opinion on the bidding behavior of specific possible competitors; that is, one could have considered a particular firm, competitor 1, and sought an expression of uncertainty about what he would bid on the contract in question, assuming that he would in fact make a bid. This might then have been coupled with an expression of uncertainty as to whether competitor 1 would bid in the competition being studied. These expressions of uncertainty imply a somewhat different model of the problem than suggested by the lowest-competing-bidder model which did not consider specific competitors. To examine differences that arise in the use of these two models, a simple example may be given.

Suppose there are only two potential opponents in a particular competition. Suppose, too, historical data and managerial opinion enable one to obtain the following expressions of uncertainty:

$$f_1(x_1) = \text{prior probability distribution of competitor 1's bid}$$
on the contract, assuming that he does bid (a similar prior distribution is defined for competitor 2)

$$g(1), g(2), g(1, 2) = \text{probability of being opposed by 1 alone; 2 alone;}$$
both 1 and 2

The expected profit from a bid of B is then

$$E(B) = (B - c) \left\{ g(1) \int_{x_1 = B}^{\infty} f_1(x_1)\, dx_1 + g(2) \int_{x_2 = B}^{\infty} f_2(x_2)\, dx_2 \right.$$

$$\left. + g(1, 2) \int_{x_1 = B}^{\infty} f_1(x_1)\, dx_1 \int_{x_2 = B}^{\infty} f_2(x_2)\, dx_2 \right\}$$

It is interesting to note in this model how the probability of winning decreases as the number of competitors increases.

This model appears more complex than the lowest-competing-bidder model and might be less desirable on that basis alone. Note, however, that, starting from the same basic expressions of uncertainty and proceeding in a manner consistent with the logic of probability theory, the two models lead to the very same behavior so far as the optimal bid is concerned. To see this, begin with the distribution just assumed and compute the probability distribution of the lowest competing bid. If competitor 1 is the only opponent, the distribution of the lowest competing bid is the distribution of x_1. Similarly, if competitor 2 is the only opponent. If both competitors submit bids, the probability that the lowest competing bid will exceed our bid is simply the product of the probabilities that each competitor's bid exceeds ours. These probabilities, weighted by the probabilities of the conditions included in their statements and added, give the probability distribution of the lowest competing bid. It will immediately be noted that this is precisely what is written for the probability of winning in the foregoing model. If one proceeds consistently, the two models will be equivalent. If it seemed unlikely that one would learn anything specific about who would be involved in a given competition, nor anything about the bidding behavior of a specific competitor in a specific competition under consideration, there would be little point in preserving the uncertainties associated with each opponent. It would be equally useful to process the data and judgments as indicated by the lowest-competing-bidder model.

If, on the other hand, one anticipated opportunities to obtain information about who was going to bid in a specific competition and how much, then one would require some conceptual structure into which to fit this information. Under these conditions, the second model might well be preferred. In other words, the richer model might be needed in order to compute the value of such specific information. For example, working with past data on bids submitted and aggregating these data into a distribution for the lowest competing bid, one can do little with the specific information that only competitor 1 will bid. To make use of this information, one needs some model of the bidding behavior of competitor 2, which is not directly available in the lowest-competing-bidder framework.

Computation of the value of certain knowledge as to who opponents will be can be shown by a simple example: Suppose

$$g(1), g(2) \neq 0, \qquad g(1, 2) = 0$$

$$f_1(x_1) = \text{uniform over the range } a \leq x_1 \leq b$$
$$f_2(x_2) = \text{uniform over the range } f \leq x_2 \leq e$$

If one were reliably informed that 1 would be the only competitor, the optimal bid would be

$$B_o(1) = \frac{b + c}{2}$$

and if one were informed that 2 alone would be competing, the optimal bid would be

$$B_o(2) = \frac{e + c}{2}$$

The maximum expected profits are given by

$$E(B_o(1)) = (B_o(1) - c)\frac{b - B_o(1)}{b - a} = \frac{(b - c)^2}{2(b - a)}$$

Similarly, if competitor 2 alone is the opponent. Computing the best bid on the basis of the prior information expressed by $g(1)$ and $g(2)$ gives

$$B_o(1, 2) = \frac{g(1)(b + c)/[2(b - a)]}{g(1)/(b - a)} + \frac{g(2)(e + c)/[2(e - f)]}{g(2)/(e - f)}$$

The best prior bid is thus a weighted average of the best posterior bids. It follows in the usual way that the expected value of perfect information about who will be one's competitors is given by

$$EVPI = g(1) E(B_o(1)) + g(2) E(B_o(2)) - E(B_o(1, 2))$$

where the last term stands for the maximum prior expected profit.

Allocation of Information-gathering Efforts

In order to illustrate once again the problem of allocating information-gathering effort among the various sources of uncertainty which appear in a decision problem, return to the lowest-competing-bidder model. There one has uncertainty about the cost of performing the contract as well as uncertainty about the lowest competing bid. Perhaps one could obtain further information about the cost of performance and so partly reduce the uncertainty from that source. In addition it might be possible to obtain more information about the lowest competing bid. The value of information about one source of uncertainty might be expected to depend on knowledge about the other. Clearly, very precise knowledge of what the lowest competing bid will be is of little value if one is very uncertain about the cost of performing the contract. As a simple example, suppose that uncertainty about the cost of performing a contract is expressed by regarding it as a uniformly distributed random variable over the range from v to w. The prior expected cost of performance is thus

$$\bar{c} = \frac{v + w}{2}$$

The maximum prior expected profit is then

$$E(B_o) = \frac{(b - \bar{c})^2}{2(b - a)}$$

Assuming $w < b$, the expected value of perfect information as to the cost of performance is

$$EVPI = \int_{c=v}^{w} \frac{(b - c)^2}{2(b - a)(w - v)} \, dc - \frac{(b - \bar{c})^2}{2(b - a)}$$

This may be reduced to the expression

$$EVPI = \frac{1}{2(b - a)} \text{Var}(c)$$

The expected value of perfect information is proportional to the prior variance of the cost of performance. Note, however, that the expected value depends also on the range of the prior distribution of the lowest competing bid. If this range be taken to be a rough indication of the prior state of knowledge about the lowest competing bid, one can say also that the value

of perfect information about the cost of performance is inversely proportional to uncertainty about the lowest competing bid.

In order to design a carefully conceived data-collection program in this
situation, one is interested in the expected net gain from sample information
for both types of data. Thus one needs an expression for

$$\text{ENGSI }(n_1,\, n_2)$$

where n_1 is the amount of data on the cost of performance and n_2 is the
amount of data relative to the lowest competing bid. One then takes the
partial derivatives of this function with respect to each of the two variables,
sets them equal to zero, and solves the resulting pair of equations. The
result would indicate the optimal amount of data of each kind to obtain.
In practice this task may well require the use of machine computation. Of
course, this difficulty in computing the value of various kinds and amounts
of information should not be allowed to obscure the many cases in which the
data-collection system does not require such detailed study. It is often rather
clear on common-sense grounds that it is worthwhile to gather certain types
of data. The really interesting part of the analysis then becomes the assimilation of this data into managerial thinking. The most useful product
of the management-information system may then be the sort of revisions of
opinion that can be suggested by a rather straightforward application of the
normal theory of Chapter 6.

Some Data-processing Problems

The complexities of producing a prior distribution for the bid of a particular competitor or a prior distribution for cost of performance on a particular
contract have been ignored until this point. One approach to establishing
these prior distributions may now be outlined. Suppose, for example, one is
concerned with estimating the unit cost of production for a particular iron
casting. Data and experience might support the belief that the unit cost
depends on, say, the number of castings to be made, the weight of each,
and the complexity of the casting as measured by the number of gates and
risers. As a first hypothesis, one might suppose that these three "predictor
variables" are related to unit cost by a linear function of the form

$$y = b_o + b_1 x_1 + b_2 x_2 + b_3 x_3 + e$$

where y = unit cost of a particular type of casting
   x_1 = number of castings to be produced
   x_2 = weight of each casting
   x_3 = number of gates and risers
   e = a normally distributed random variable with mean = 0 and
       known variance

Roughly speaking, the more terms in the function and the larger the absolute values of the coefficients, the smaller the variance of e. One might consider the variance of e to be "unexplained" variance in y, or variation in y not attributable to its relation with the predictor variables. The general objective might be to obtain models which make this variance small.

The procedure would be to assign prior distributions to the coefficients $b_o, \ldots, b_3$ based on available data and managerial judgments. Then as additional data become available, the prior distributions of these coefficients are transformed into posterior distributions in the usual way. It would, of course, be convenient to assign normal prior distributions to the coefficients so as to use the well-developed theory for that distribution. Given the distributions of the coefficients and the error term, e, one has the distribution of y, the unit cost. Although the computational details are somewhat complex, the general method of assimilating additional knowledge is roughly this: As data on y and the corresponding values of the predictor variables x_1, x_2, and x_3 are obtained, a set of coefficients is computed. This set will be those coefficients which provide the "best fit" for the sample data and may be obtained by solving the "normal equations" familiar to students of linear regression analysis. The coefficients computed from the sample are then used to revise the prior distributions. In practice this process would generally be routinized and performed with the aid of a computer.

The same type of model might well be used in obtaining a distribution for the bid of a certain competitor on a particular contract. In one study involving a company bidding on major interstate highway construction work, it was found that bidders' behavior could be usefully thought of as depending upon such variables as

amount of work already undertaken by competitor

distance of job from competitor's home office

distance of job from competitor's nearest active project

estimate of the amount of pavement work involved

estimate of the amount of bridge work involved

estimate of the amount of drainage work involved

One may suggest that such analysis can be of considerable assistance to a manager in assigning and revising the necessary prior distributions.

Sequential Dynamics

Consider a sequence of bidding competitions in which the firm has some interest. Each competition that the firm experiences or lives through provides data on who is likely to bid

the bidding behavior of those who actually participate

Each competition won provides additional data on the firm's cost-estimating accuracy and reliability. Clearly these data tend to become available only as the contract performance moves along and may not be ready for use when the very next bid must be submitted. Now if the cost of submitting a bid is negligible or is somehow reimbursed to the firm, then there is no reason why it should not bid on every competition. Note that

1. We assume that there is no operational limitation on design engineering, cost estimating, and such other resources as are involved in the preparation of the bid.

2. The cost of performing a given contract may depend on how much business the firm already has in hand. In some cases, one knows how much business is in hand at the time a certain contract would be performed if won. In other cases, one may be uncertain about how much business will be on hand at a given future time, since this depends on how many jobs are bid on and won in the interim.

If the cost of submitting a bid is not zero, then there will be some competitions on which it will not be profitable to bid. Even if the firm does not bid, it may have the opportunity to obtain information on the bidding behavior of others simply by attending the public opening of the bids or reading about it in the paper.

We can define several problems:

1. Several competitions occur almost simultaneously. We must decide which m of n to bid on. This is of precisely the same form as the capital-investment problem discussed in Chapter 7.

2. Several competitions occur sequentially in time and we must decide which one of them to bid on.

3. One wishes to bid on m of n occurring sequentially in time. The latter two problems in the dynamics of a sequence of bidding decisions are dealt with in Chapter 11.

EXERCISES

9-1. Graph the prior expected profit as a function of the amount of the bid for some easily handled case. What sort of explanation can be given for the behavior of the function?

9-2. Specify the steps which must be carried out (perhaps by a computer) to find an approximate value for EVSI in the case of a normal prior distribution for the lowest competing bid.

9-3. What complications arise if we believe that our competitors are using the very same type of analysis that we are using in order to determine their bidding policies?

9-4. Consider a firm which regularly bids in some area of interest to you. Outline the main features of a management information-learning-decision system which you might propose to the firm.

10

Learning
in Binary
Data Systems

Binomial Experiments

The next issues involve learning-decision problems in which the basic principles are identical with those already developed, but the form of the data to be processed is somewhat different. If one is inspecting units of product being produced or purchased, the items may be classified as good or bad, effective or defective, acceptable or not acceptable. The inspection of a unit results in one of two possible reports, and the data from a series of such inspections may be reported in the form of the number of defectives, r, found in the inspection of n units. If the probability of being defective is the same for all items, then it is well known that the probability distribution of r is binomial. Similarly, in the study of consumer buying habits, a given consumer may be classified as a user or nonuser of a certain product. Missions may be successful or unsuccessful, a worker may be busy or idle, a machine may be operating or out of commission. All these are examples of situations in which the basic data are binary and with suitable assumptions, the basic random process may be modeled using the binomial distribution. These sorts of problems may be illustrated by means of an example from the field of quality control.

A Rectifying Inspection Example

Suppose that lots consisting of L units of product are received from a supplier and that some uncertainty exists over the quality of the material. If one were reliably informed that some proportion, p, of the items was defective, one could decide without difficulty between

a_1: accept the lot, permitting it to move into the production process

a_2: examine every item in the lot, replacing or repairing all defective items, so that the lot finally enters the process consisting entirely of good units

Assume a simple cost structure which depends essentially on the proportion of defectives. There is a cost of C_1 dollars per unit for material which is defective when it enters the production process. There is a cost C_0 for every unit which is inspected when the lot is subjected to 100 per cent screening, and a cost C_2 for the repair or replacement of each defective. Thus if p is known, one chooses the minimum of

$$E(a_1) = C_1 p L$$

$$E(a_2) = C_0 L + C_2 p L$$

If $C_0 > 0$ and $C_1 > C_2$, setting the preceding expectations equal leads to the conclusion that one will be indifferent for

$$\hat{p} = \frac{C_0}{C_1 - C_2}$$

The decision problem is interesting only if there is some uncertainty about the proportion of defectives in the lot and if there is the possibility of examining a sample of items from the lot before making the decision.

The Beta Prior Distribution

Suppose that typically there is uncertainty as to the proportion of defective items in the lot. If the lot is large relative to the size of any sample one may consider taking, then the binomial (rather than the hypergeometric) distribution can be used to compute the probability of r defectives in a sample of size n. Thus one requires a distribution for use in expressing the decision maker's prior uncertainty which

permits expression of a wide variety of prior attitudes

combines easily with the binomial sampling distribution according to the logic of Bayes' theorem.

The beta family of distributions, it turns out, will meet these requirements very well. The prior distribution of the proportion of defectives may be taken to be a random variable with a beta distribution having the form

$$PR(p) = \frac{(n_{pr} - 1)!}{(r_{pr} - 1)! (n_{pr} - r_{pr} - 1)!} p^{r_{pr}-1} (1 - p)^{n_{pr}-r_{pr}-1}$$

The prior mean of p may be obtained in the usual way:

$$m_{pr} = \int_p p \, PR(p) \, dp$$

This may be written

$$m_{pr} = \frac{r_{pr}}{n_{pr}} \int_p \frac{(n_{pr})!}{(r_{pr})! (n_{pr} - r_{pr} - 1)!} p^{r_{pr}} (1 - p)^{n_{pr}-r_{pr}-1} \, dp$$

Since the expression under the integral is a proper beta distribution itself, its integral has the value 1 and one has

$$m_{pr} = \frac{r_{pr}}{n_{pr}}$$

The prior variance of p turns out to be

$$v_{pr} = \frac{r_{pr}(n_{pr} - r_{pr})}{n_{pr}^2(n_{pr} + 1)}$$

Now suppose a sample of n items results in the observation of r defectives. The posterior distribution of p may be obtained using Bayes' theorem.

$$PO(p) = \frac{LK(r \mid p, n) \, PR(p)}{\int_p LK(r \mid p, n) \, PR(p) \, dp}$$

Here the likelihood is given by the binomial distribution.

$$LK(r \mid p, n) = \frac{n!}{r! \, (n - r)!} p^r (1 - p)^{n-r}$$

Substituting previous expressions for the beta prior and the binomial likelihood into the posterior distribution of p yields

$$PO(p) = \frac{p^{r_{pr}+r-1} (1 - p)^{n_{pr}+n-(r_{pr}+r)-1}}{\int_p p^{r_{pr}+r-1} (1 - p)^{n_{pr}+n-(r_{pr}+r)-1} \, dp}$$

Comparing the denominator with the definition of a beta distribution function suggests that the value of the integral must be

$$\frac{(r_{pr} + r - 1)! \, (n_{pr} + n - (r_{pr} + r) - 1)!}{(n_{pr} + n - 1)!}$$

It may then be seen that the posterior distribution of p is itself a beta distribution with parameters

$$r_{po} = r_{pr} + r$$

$$n_{po} = n_{pr} + n$$

The posterior mean of p is then

$$m_{po} = \frac{r_{po}}{n_{po}}$$

Thus by choosing a beta distribution to express the decision maker's prior uncertainty, one may take advantage of the very convenient result that the posterior distribution will also be a beta with parameters which may be obtained in this particularly simple way. (We will return shortly to the problem of expressing the attitudes of a particular decision maker in terms of a beta prior distribution.)

The Preposterior Analysis

If it has been decided to take a sample of n items but one has not yet actually done so, the number of defectives which will be found may be regarded as a random variable. For a given value of p, the distribution of the number of defectives, r, is, under our assumptions, a binomial distribution. Since p itself is taken to be a random variable with a beta prior distribution, the unconditional distribution of r is

$$f(r) = \int_p \mathrm{LK}(r \mid p, n)\, \mathrm{PR}(p)\, dp$$

Substituting the beta and binomial expressions and combining terms gives

$$f(r) = \frac{n!\,(n_{pr} - 1)!}{r!\,(n - r)!\,(r_{pr} - 1)!\,(n_{pr} - r_{pr} - 1)!}$$

$$\int_p p^{r_{pr}+r-1}\,(1 - p)^{n_{pr}+n-(r_{pr}+r)-1}\, dp$$

Comparing the expression under the integral with the form of a beta distribution permits one to obtain the value of the integral. The result is that the unconditional distribution of r turns out to be

$$f(r) = \frac{n!\,(n_{pr} - 1)!\,(r_{pr} + r - 1)!\,(n_{pr} + n - (r_{pr} + r) - 1)!}{r!\,(n - r)!\,(r_{pr} - 1)!\,(n_{pr} - r_{pr} - 1)!\,(n_{pr} + n - 1)!}$$

which is called the beta-binomial distribution. The mean and variance of r may then be obtained

$$E(r) = n\frac{r_{pr}}{n_{pr}}$$

$$V(r) = n(n_{pr} + n)\frac{r_{pr}(n_{pr} - r_{pr})}{n_{pr}^2\,(n_{pr} + 1)}$$

The prior expected value of the posterior mean of p is then

$$E(m_{po}) = \frac{r_{pr} + E(r)}{n_{pr} + n} = \frac{r_{pr}}{n_{pr}}$$

This confirms the result previously obtained suggesting that the prior expected value of the posterior mean is the prior mean.

The prior variance of the posterior mean of p is

$$V(m_{po}) = \frac{1}{(n_{pr} + n)^2} \, V(r) = \frac{n}{n_{pr} + n} \, \frac{r_{pr}(n_{pr} - r_{pr})}{n_{pr}^2(n_{pr} + 1)}$$

$$= \frac{n}{n_{pr} + n} \, v_{pr}$$

Here again we see the result that as the sample size, n, grows large, the prior variance of the posterior mean approaches the variance of the prior distribution.

The Value of Perfect Information

Returning to the rectifying inspection decision, one may first compute the expected value of perfect information. Suppose on the basis of prior information it is the case that

$$m_{pr} = \hat{p} = \frac{C_0}{C_1 - C_2}$$

thus the best prior action is a_1, accept the lot. If we were to discover that the true value of p was in fact greater than $\hat{p}$, this would change our opinion as to the best act, suggesting that we should screen and rectify. The expected value of such perfect information is

$$\text{EVPI} = \int_{p=\hat{p}}^{1.0} (C_1 pL - C_0 L - C_2 pL) \, \text{PR}(p) \, dp$$

$$= (C_1 - C_2)L \int_{p=\hat{p}}^{1.0} (p - \hat{p}) \, \text{PR}(p) \, dp$$

The latter expression is a linear loss integral involving a beta distribution.*

The Value of Sample Information

If one decides to take a sample of n items, the best posterior action will depend on the posterior mean of p, m_{po}. Assume once again that the prior mean of p is less than, or equal to, $\hat{p}$, thus if no further information can be obtained, the choice would be accept. If the posterior mean turns out to be greater than $\hat{p}$, one's posterior preference will be to screen and rectify the

* This chapter does not deal with the computational details of either beta or beta-binomial loss integrals. These may be found in D. V. Lindley, *Introduction to Probability and Statistics from a Bayesian Viewpoint*; Part 2, *Inference* (Cambridge: Cambridge University Press, 1965), pp. 143–52; and Robert Schlaifer, and Howard Raiffa, *Applied Statistical Decision Theory* (Boston: Harvard University Graduate School of Business Administration, 1961), pp. 220, 241, 263, 267.

lot. One knows that the prior distribution of the posterior mean is the beta-binomial, thus the expected value of sample information is

$$\text{EVSI} = \int_{m_{po}=\hat{p}}^{1.0} (C_1 m_{po} L - C_0 L - C_2 m_{po} L)\, \text{PR}(m_{po})\, dm_{po}$$

$$= (C_1 - C_2)L \int_{m_{po}=\hat{p}}^{1.0} (m_{po} - \hat{p})\, \text{PR}(m_{po})\, dm_{po}$$

Here again is a linear loss integral, this time involving the beta-binomial distribution

Fitting Beta Priors

Some members of the beta family of distributions appear in Fig. 10-1. Clearly it is a "rich" family, in the sense that a considerable variety of prior

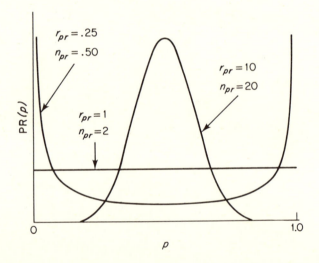

FIGURE 10-1

attitudes may be expressed by adjusting the parameters. Taking $r_{pr} = 1$ and $n_{pr} = 2$, one obtains a uniform prior distribution for p. As n_{pr} increases, the variance of the prior tends to decrease, representing less and less uncertainty about p. The decision maker may well be able to select, from such sketches of various members of the family, a prior which will adequately express his opinions about p. If data on historical values of p are available, adjustment of the parameters may lead immediately to a reasonably good model for these data. If estimates are available on the mean and variance of p, one can solve directly for the parameters of the beta distribution which have the same mean and variance.

One may also obtain from Fig. 10-1 some feeling for the rapidity with which the form of the distribution changes with changes in n_{pr} and r_{pr}. This suggests what was seen previously, that the posterior distribution resulting from a considerable amount of information does not depend very much on the exact shape of the prior distribution.

Quadratic Cost Functions

In the rectifying inspection example, it was difficult to obtain an immediate feeling for the relationships among the prior distribution, the sample size, and the value of sample information because of the computational effort required for the loss integrals. If, however, one examines decision problems in which the cost structure is quadratic rather than linear, considerable simplification results.

Consider the class of problems in which the cost of taking an action is given by

$$C(a - p)^2$$

where

a = action taken ($0 \leq a \leq 1$)
p = parameter of a binomial distribution
C = constant or proportionality

For example, the proportion of defectives or reliability of a lot of product might be estimated to be a. If this estimate differs from the true value p, the cost in terms of the price paid for the material and the use made of it may be approximately proportional to the square of the difference between a and p. A proportion, a, of men on a particular project team may be estimated to leave during the project. In anticipation of this one may take various actions, such as hiring additional men in advance. If the estimate is in error, one may have too few or too many men, with costs approximately proportional to the square of the estimating error. In production planning, a proportion a of the items produced in a run may be expected to be defective. To meet a fixed requirement for the number of good units produced, the size of the planned production run is increased to allow for the defectives. Turning to the field of marketing, a proportion a of the recipients of direct mail advertising may be estimated to become buyers. Producing in anticipation of the direct mail campaign on the basis of the estimate may result in too much or too little product on hand. These are but a few of the many instances of decision problems in which the cost structure might be reasonably approximated by a quadratic function of the sort just suggested.

Suppose that uncertainty exists about the value of the binomial parameter, p, but that this uncertainty may be expressed in the form of a prior distribution. The prior expected cost of action (or estimate) a is given by

$$E(a) = \int_p C(a - p)^2 \, \text{PR}(p) \, dp$$

This may be operated on as follows

$$E(a) = C\left[a^2 - 2aE(p) + E(p^2)\right]$$
$$= C\left[a^2 - 2am_{pr} + E(p^2)\right]$$

To find the best prior action, take the first derivative of the prior expected cost, set it equal to zero, and solve.

$$\frac{dE(a)}{da} = C(2a - 2m_{pr}) = 0$$

$$a_0 = m_{pr}$$

Thus the best prior action, a_o, is to estimate p to be the mean of the prior distribution. In statistics, a_o would be called an *unbiased estimate* of p; thus one meaning of an unbiased estimate is one that will minimize expected cost in the face of a quadratic cost function.

Computing the expected cost using the optimal value of a gives

$$E(a_o) = C \int_p (m_{pr} - p)^2 \, \text{PR}(p) \, dp$$

$$= Cv_{pr}$$

Thus the expected cost, using the best value of a, is proportional to the variance of the prior distribution of p. It follows immediately that, if additional information were obtained, the prior would be transformed into a posterior, the best posterior action would be to take $a = m_{po}$, and the posterior expected cost, using the best action would be Cv_{po}.

The value of additional information is thus

$$\text{EVSI} = C\left[v_{pr} - E(v_{po})\right]$$

$$\text{EVPI} = Cv_{pr}$$

These results satisfy the intuitive expectation that the expected value of sample information should increase as the posterior variance decreases and thus as the sample size increases. The value of sample information decreases as the variance of the prior distribution decreases. The more certain one is, the less additional information is valued. Since with perfect information, the variance of the posterior becomes zero, EVPI is the limiting value of EVSI as the sample size increases. Notice that none of these results depend upon any particular assumption about the form of the prior distribution. They hold equally well for a normal or for a beta prior.

The Optimal Sample Size

With a quadratic cost structure, an expression for the optimal sample size can be obtained directly. Consider the expected net gain from sample information to be a function of the sample size. The cost of sampling is taken simply to be proportional to the sample size.

$$\text{ENGSI}(n) = C\left[v_{pr} - E(v_{po})\right] - kn$$

To evaluate $E(v_{po})$ the following result is employed.

The prior variance of the posterior mean is equal to the variance of the prior mean minus the expected value of the posterior variance.

Rather than prove this generally, it is simply shown that the statement holds for the case of the normal distribution discussed in Chapter 6. Recall that for the normal, the prior variance of the posterior mean was given by

$$V(m_{po}) = \frac{v}{c} - \frac{v}{c + n}$$

Now v/c is, by definition, the variance of the prior distribution. The variance of the posterior distribution is

$$\frac{v}{c + n}$$

and since this does not depend on the observed value of the sample mean, it is also the expected value of the posterior variance. Thus the result holds for the normal. Although this is no proof that it holds generally, we shall assume that it does.

Applying this result in the case of a beta prior distribution involves recalling a previous result. The prior variance of the posterior mean was found to be

$$V(m_{po}) = \frac{n}{n_{pr} + n}\, v_{pr}$$

Thus the result may be stated

$$V(m_{po}) = v_{pr} - E(v_{po})$$

or

$$E(v_{po}) = v_{pr} - V(m_{po})$$

$$= v_{pr} - \frac{n}{n_{pr} + n}\, v_{pr} = \frac{n_{pr}}{n_{pr} + n}\, v_{pr}$$

Now the expected net gain from sample information may be expressed as

$$\text{ENGSI}(n) = Cv_{pr} - E(v_{po}) - kn$$

$$= C\,\frac{n}{n_{pr} + n}\, v_{pr} - kn$$

Taking the derivative with respect to n and setting it equal to zero gives

$$(n_o + n_{pr})^2 = \frac{Cv_{pr}n_{pr}}{k}$$

$$n_o = \sqrt{\frac{Cv_{pr}n_{pr}}{k}} - n_{pr}$$

where n_o = optimal sample size.

From this expression one may confirm immediately that

a. The greater the cost of sampling, k, the smaller the optimal sample size.

b. The smaller the variance of the prior distribution, the smaller the optimal sample size; that is, the more certain one is about p in advance of obtaining additional information, the less additional data are desired.

c. The greater the cost of error, as measured by C, the greater the optimal sample size.

d. The expression for n_o may turn out to be negative, suggesting that the best thing to do is to act immediately without obtaining any additional information.

Sequential Sampling

Most of the discussion until this point has dealt with data-collection programs designed by selecting in advance an appropriate sample size. These fixed-sample-size programs clearly ignore that, as the data begin to come in, the early information obtained may be sufficiently conclusive as to permit one to make up one's mind. Thus it would be unnecessary to go to the expense of obtaining the remaining data in the previously planned sample. The obvious extension of this idea leads to the policy of sequential sampling. After each item of information is obtained, a posterior is computed. Based on that posterior, one decides to act or to obtain one additional item of information. In the latter case, the previous posterior (now in the position of a prior) is again transformed into a new posterior and one considers whether to act or continue sampling. This plan, where it is possible, clearly makes the best use of the currently available information, and will, on the average, result in the smallest reasonable data-collection programs.

In considering sequential sampling, one turns from essentially single, isolated decisions to sequences of decisions. If the assumption about quadratic cost structures is continued, it is relatively easy to see how one would undertake a sequential sampling program. Suppose that at any particular stage in the program the decision maker's uncertainty about p is characterized by a beta distribution with parameters r and n. Note that, from the viewpoint of the information already obtained, this is a posterior distribution, but with respect to the decision at hand it is a prior distribution. Let $v(r, n)$ stand for the variance of the beta distribution of p when the decision maker's knowledge is characterized by r and n. If he decides to stop and act at this point, the cost associated with the best action is

$$Cv(r, n)$$

Now define

$E(r, n)$ = the expected cost if the decision maker's knowledge is characterized by r and n *and if he follows the best possible policy at all times.*

At this point he may either stop and act, or go ahead to obtain one additional observation. $E(r, n)$ will thus be the minimum of

$$E(\text{stop}) = Cv(r, n)$$

$$E(\text{go}) = k + \frac{r}{n} E(r + 1, n + 1) + \left(1 - \frac{r}{n}\right) E(r, n + 1)$$

Thus the minimum expected cost at any stage can be determined only if it is known for all future stages.

One way out of this problem is to truncate the program by deciding in advance that sampling will stop when n reaches some specified value, n_m, if some action has not been previously taken. This truncation point might be determined by the requirement of making a decision before some deadline or carrying out the data gathering within some given budget limitation. Consider what action one would take if n had the value n_m for each possible value of r. One could then work backwards to the stage characterized by $n_m - 1$, and so on.

Even if the program is not truncated in this way, one can be sure that, unless information is costless, one will stop and act after some finite number of additional samples. Indeed, one can suppose there is some value n_m beyond which no additional samples would be taken, no matter what the value of r happened to be at that point. That is, there is an n_m such that, for all r

$$Cv(r, n_m) \leq k + \frac{r}{n_m} E(r + 1, n_m + 1) + \left(1 - \frac{r}{n_m}\right) E(r, n_m + 1)$$

Recalling that

$$v(r, n) = \frac{r(n - r)}{n^2(n + 1)}$$

and taking

$$E(r + 1, n_m + 1) = Cv(r + 1, n_m + 1)$$

$$E(r, n_m + 1) = Cv(r, n_m + 1)$$

substitute these into the foregoing expression. Considering the equality sign only and solving for n_m leads to the result

$$n_m = \frac{1}{2}\sqrt{\frac{C}{k}} - 1$$

This is the value of n beyond which no sampling would ever be undertaken.

One may illustrate this by means of a very simple example in which the cost of a sample is assumed to be $k = \$1$ and $C = \$100$. With these values, one has

$$n_m = \frac{1}{2}\sqrt{\frac{100}{1}} - 1 = 4$$

Figure 10-2 summarizes the computations involved. The reader may wish to confirm that continuing beyond $n = 4$ can only increase (or at least not decrease) the expected cost.

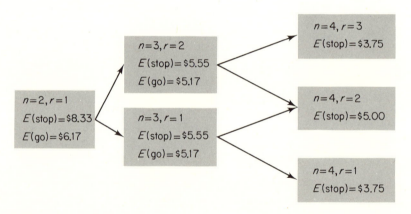

FIGURE 10-2

Management Control Systems

We turn how to some basic decision problems faced by a manager who wishes to establish a system for controlling the operations which are his responsibility. The fundamental problems are similar in structure, whether he wishes to control the quality of the output of a production machine or the profitability of a major division of his firm. In general there is an operating system whose performance may be assessed after each unit of output or at various points in time. Further, suppose that the manager distinguishes between acceptable and unacceptable performance. The whole process of management is pervaded by setting tolerances, standards of acceptability, sales quotas, budgets, and so on, which are simply determinations of what is or is not acceptable performance. Indeed, the firmly established tradition of "management by exception" involves the routine assessment of a system's performance, but a manager is informed only if the performance is not acceptable.

The design of a complete control system involves

    a. Setting standards of acceptable performance.

    b. Determining how frequently the actual performance is to be observed and compared with the standards.

    c. Discovering the causes of unacceptable performance.

    d. Suggesting the nature and timing of corrective action.

Design problems b and d are of especial concern since they are most usefully discussed in general terms.

Informally stated these problems are

    1. Whether to expend the effort to observe the performance of the system frequently, and thus be able to initiate control action as soon as required, or to save money by observing it less frequently, running the risk that if it may be some time before trouble is discovered if it should develop.

    2. When information indicates that something may possibly be wrong, the manager must decide whether to undertake the expense of immediate control action (which may be unnecessary) before things get really bad, or to wait until the condition of the system is less uncertain. While waiting of course, a good deal of unsatisfactory performance may occur.

To illustrate how these issues may be made explicit, we examine a process control problem.

Controlling the Output of a Production Process

Consider a machine turning out items, any one of which might be inspected to determine whether it is acceptable or unacceptable. The basic parameters in the design of the control system may be defined as the number of items inspected, say, n, out of every L units of production. One may think of n as the sample size and L as the "sampling interval." The basic problem is that of controlling the proportion of defective units produced by the process. Consider the process immediately following the exercise of control action which results in an adjustment of the system. Knowledge of the proportion of defectives, p, may be characterized by a beta distribution with parameters r_{pr} and n_{pr}. After such an adjustment (which may include some testing to confirm the effectiveness of the control action), there may be little or no uncertainty about p.

As production continues, there are more and more opportunities for things to happen to the process and for it to "wander" from the state in which it was set by previous control action. Thus as production goes on, uncertainty about the system grows. Generally speaking, after L units have been produced, uncertainty about p might be expressed by a beta distribution with parameters $r(L)$ and $n(L)$, a distribution which would typically have a larger variance than that with which the sampling interval was begun. Now take a sample of n items and count the number of defectives. The last n items produced might be sampled to give information on the current state of the system and further to simplify the problem by assuming that the process fraction defective was in fact constant during the production of the items in the sample. The information in the sample is then combined in the usual way with parameters $r(L)$ and $n(L)$ to give a revised impression of the distribution of p. One might then view p as a random variable having a beta distribution with parameters r_{po} and n_{po}. The problem of design is that of choosing n and L. Some of the issues involved may be suggested by formulating a simple situation.

Suppose that, at the end of each sampling interval, the costs of exerting control action are modest, and the system is returned to the state with which the interval began, characterized by r_{pr} and n_{pr}. This permits one sampling interval to be treated as characteristic of all others, since the process always begins an interval in the same condition. Suppose further, that in order to exert effective control action, uncertainty about p must be reduced to some acceptable level. This permits one to decide, for any sampling interval, L, what fixed sample size or sequential sampling plan will be required to assure effective control action. Generally speaking, the greater the sampling interval, L, the greater the resulting uncertainty about p, and the larger the sample size required to form a basis for effective control action. The design problem is thus reduced to that of selecting a sampling interval.

One might then undertake to find the sampling interval which would minimize the cost per unit of production in the face of a cost structure, such as the following.

1. The cost of exerting control action might contain a fixed element, as well as a dependence upon our state of knowledge, r_{po} and n_{po}.

2. The cost of sampling is some increasing function of the sample size. As L increases, the cost of the sample will increase, since its size increases, but the sampling cost per unit produced might well decrease.

3. As L increases, the quantity of bad product generated by the system is typically expected to increase. Thus as the sampling interval is increased, the cost of scrap goes up.

The designer who wishes to minimize the cost per unit produced, might typically find that, as he increased L,

The unit cost of control action decreased.

The unit cost of sampling decreased.

The unit cost of scrap increased.

His problem would then be that of selecting L so as to minimize the expected value of the sum of these costs. Introducing the assumption that the cost of control action depends on knowledge of the system and thus upon the sample size, and then considering the best value for n, the problem becomes somewhat more complex.

Multi-interval Systems

In many control systems the manager does not, as assumed earlier, exert control action which brings the system back to its original state at the end of every sampling interval. He may decide not to take any action at all after learning the results of a sample. The classical simplification is to decide under what conditions the information in the sample may be ignored, and the system assumed in fact to be in the state with which it began the interval. If this simplification is made, then the structure of the problem remains as previously suggested.

More realistically, however, one might expect a manager to examine the results of a sample, acknowledge that the system was not in the state with which it began the interval, and still decide to take no control action. Further, the control action, if taken, may not be perfectly effective. That is, it may restore the system not to its original condition but rather to some other state, which might depend on the manager's knowledge of the current value of p and the particular sort of control action he chose to take. The designer's problem is now that of selecting a sampling interval, a sample size, and an appropriate control action (which may include not taking any action at all). This design problem, taken seriously, requires one to look ahead to future sampling intervals in order to see what is best at the end of any particular interval. If no control action is taken, for example, the resulting cost depends on the current state of the system, when and what kinds of control action will be undertaken in the future, and how much scrap will thus be generated? On the other hand, if a particular control action is taken, it may have benefits which are felt throughout a number of future sampling intervals, and the value of such an action cannot be determined without examining these future intervals. The design problem thus shares with sequential sampling the necessity for considering a sequence of decisions. (The basic structure of such problems is examined in Chapter 11.)

Other Management Control Systems

Although the process control example just discussed serves well enough to illustrate some of the basic issues involved in the design of most management control systems, it is unrealistic to suppose that it illustrates all the important problems. When the system being controlled involves people as well as facilities, an entirely new dimension of difficulties appears. When management fixes budgets, targets, or quotas for sales organizations or production organizations, these definitions of acceptable performance not only form the basis for the control systems, but also serve very important incentive functions for the participants. If the target level is set so high that the probability of attaining it is very small, the participants may simply disregard it as manifestly unrealistic. If the budget is set so low that the probability of attainment is high, the participants may operate below a reasonable level of effectiveness, since acceptable performance is so easily achieved. These considerations suggest immediately that the manager may not limit himself to taking corrective action, as in the case of the process control example, but may consider altering the standards for acceptable system performance. Budgets which are easily and frequently met may require changing, as may budgets which are seldom if ever met.

There is considerable evidence that if the participants in the system have a hand in setting their own standards for acceptable performance, the standards will have a far greater effect on their behavior than will those dictated by higher-level managers. It is clearly important also for the participants to have a full understanding of how acceptable performance is defined and of how their own behavior is compared with the standards of acceptability. It may well be also that a control system which reports only failures to achieve acceptable behavior and elicits only corrective action may have a seriously depressing effect upon the relationship between manager and participants. It seems wiser to report successful attainment and provide for some recognition of it in addition to the corrective action following unsuccessful performance.

EXERCISES

10-1. Show that, in the case of a beta prior and binomial likelihood, as n approaches infinity v_{po} approaches zero.

10-2. A manufacturer is trying to decide whether to market a new product. He feels there is a fixed population of potential consumers for the product, but is uncertain what portion of this group would actually buy it. He is considering a costly test-marketing program in which a sample of n potential consumers would be studied. Outline the analysis needed to assist him in planning the best procedure at this point.

10-3. A firm buys material in lots of size L units. When a lot is received, a sample of size n may be taken from the lot and each item in the sample inspected to determine whether it is effective or defective. On the basis of this examination, the entire lot is either accepted or rejected. The firm thinks that there is a cost for each defective unit accepted, a cost for each effective unit rejected, and a cost for each item inspected. Outline the analysis required to determine the optimal sample size for the firm to use.

10-4. Suppose you must choose between two production processes which are essentially identical except for their scrap rates. You are uncertain, however, about these scrap rates. It is possible to make costly test runs of one or both of the two processes. You wish to base your choice on the principle of minimizing the expected scrap rate. Outline the tests and the analysis of their results which you would suggest.

10-5. In discussing management control systems, an example involving controlling a production process was used. Show how similar concepts might be applied to another area of management control.

10-6. In discussing multi-interval control systems, it was suggested that future intervals must be considered in the design. How could one decide how far into the future it would be important to extend this consideration?

11

Sequential
Dynamics

Sequences of Decisions

Several previous chapters have mentioned decision-learning situations which actually involve sequences of decisions. These are often interesting because they sometimes
severely challenge one's ability to deal with them intuitively. What one decides at any particular stage in a
sequence influences what one may do at subsequent
stages and is influenced by what one has done at previous
stages. A careful consideration of what is to be decided
at any stage depends upon anticipating what might happen at future stages and what response might be elected
in the face of various possible eventualities. Further,
as each stage in the process passes, additional information and experience often become available and can be
used to modify one's opinions and predictions about
the future. Problems of this sort were encountered in
examination of bidding decisions and in analysis of
management control systems, for example. Except in
the case of the sequential sampling scheme outlined in
chapter 10, analysis of these sequential decision-learning
problems has been postponed. We now turn to extend
the basic principles outlined for sequential sampling to
several other areas of management concern.

Search

A variety of activities are roughly classifiable as search
processes, in the sense that they involve a sequence of

decisions as to whether one ought to stop and accept the best of what has been obtained so far or continue searching in hope of finding something better. A firm seeking a machine to do a particular job, an opportunity to invest some capital, a new product, or a new vice president, may well be involved in search processes of this kind. As an example, consider the search for a new product which may involve research and development, market testing, and so on. Suppose the firm in question is interested in finally selecting a single new product or product line. At any stage in the search process, it is faced with the basic choice: stop search now and accept the best of the new product possibilities which have so far been discovered, or continue search in hope of finding something still better than the best it now has. The costs, both in time and effort, of discovering an additional opportunity are typically matters of uncertainty. The value or profit potential of an opportunity which has yet to be discovered is also a matter of uncertainty. Thus the decision to stop and develop the best of the new product possibilities currently under consideration may be a difficult one. The process is further complicated because each time the firm does undertake to discover a new product, it obtains additional information about the costs of such search efforts and the value of their results. This information offers a potential opportunity to build learning into the search process so that, as one gains experience, this experience is used to plan future stages.

In this description it is presumed that a new product possibility once discovered, remains available as an alternative to the firm for a reasonable period of time. The search process may be continued, without losing the chance to undertake one of the opportunities previously discovered. These will be called *persistent opportunities*. If on the other hand, one is considering investment in a stock with a fluctuating price, the investment opportunity at a given price must be taken up immediately or the price may well change. This presents the firm with opportunities which will be called *transitory*, in the sense that they cannot be accumulated for subsequent selection. We consider the problem of search with persistent opportunities before examining transitory opportunities.

Persistent Opportunities

Consider a search process involving persistent opportunities but suppress at first the possibility of learning from experience as the process continues. Let

x = profit or utility of an opportunity

$f(x)$ = probability distribution of x

X = profit or utility of the best opportunity so far discovered at any stage

c = cost of discovering an additional opportunity (we neglect for simplicity the uncertainty about this cost)

If the search process is just being initiated, the value of X may be zero, but as it continues, this value will change. First, consider the situation in which no limit is placed on the amount of search or number of opportunities which it is possible to discover. Suppose one views the decision at any stage as a choice between stopping and accepting the best available opportunity or going on until a better one is found. The probability of finding a better opportunity each time a search is undertaken is

$$\int_{x=X}^{\infty} f(x)\, dx$$

The expected number of opportunities which must be examined in order to find a better one is given by

$$\frac{1}{\int_{x=X}^{\infty} f(x)\, dx}$$

The expected profit or utility of an opportunity, given that it is a better one, is

$$\frac{\int_{x=X}^{\infty} x f(x)\, dx}{\int_{x=X}^{\infty} f(x)\, dx}$$

Using these results, one may say that if the best opportunity on hand has value X, the expected value of continuing until a better one is found is

$$E(X) = \frac{1}{\int_{x=X}^{\infty} f(x)\, dx} \left\{ \int_{x=X}^{\infty} x f(x)\, dx - c \right\}$$

The decision at any stage will then be to stop if

$$E(X) \leq X$$

but to continue otherwise. Note that if $E(X)$ is set $= X$, this implies

$$\int_{x=X}^{\infty} (x - X) f(x)\, dx = c$$

The left-hand side of this expression may be interpreted as the expected gain from continuing for one more stage, whereas the right-hand side is the cost of continuing for one stage. Thus we may formulate the simple rule

Continue search as long as the expected gain from one additional stage is greater than the expected cost.

Now modify the previous situation by assuming that limitations of time or the research and development budget dictate that at most, N additional opportunities may be discovered. If the first $N - 1$ stages had been used, producing a best opportunity with value X, the decision would be to continue search for the final of Nth stage if

$$\int_{x=X}^{\infty} (x - X) f(x)\, dx - c \geq 0$$

otherwise stop. $E_N(X)$ is now defined as the expected profit or utility if the best opportunity so far discovered has value X, if only the Nth stage remains, and if the best decision is made relative to stopping or continuing. Thus,

$$E_N(X) = X \int_{x=0}^{X} f(x)\, dx + \int_{x=X}^{\infty} x f(x)\, dx - c$$

Now "back up" one stage and suppose that both stages $N - 1$ and N remain, we may define $E_{N-1}(X)$ as the expected profit if the best opportunity so far discovered has value X and if the best possible decision is made at each remaining stage.

$$E_{N-1}(X) = \int_{x=0}^{X} \max\,(X, E_N(X)) f(x)\, dx + \int_{x=X}^{\infty} \max\,(x, E_N(x)) f(x)\, dx - c$$

More generally, for any stage n, we may write

$$E_n(X) = \int_{x=0}^{X} \max\,(X, E_{n+1}(X)) f(x)\, dx + \int_{x=X}^{\infty} \max\,(x, E_{n+1}(x)) f(x)\, dx - c$$

It is apparent, as one would expect, that the greater the number of stages which remain, the greater the expected profit or utility from an optimal policy. The reader may find it instructive to show, perhaps by means of an example, that the same decision rule applies whether search is limited or unlimited. That is, continue if the expected gain from one more stage is greater than zero, stop otherwise. Thus with this sort of formulation of the search problem, there is really very little necessity to look ahead more than a single stage.

Search with Learning

In the nonlearning search process just outlined it is assumed that the distribution of x, the value of an opportunity, remained the same at each stage. Each time an opportunity is discovered, however, additional information is obtained concerning the "opportunity environment" which may be used to revise one's expressions of uncertainty as to future opportunities. We suggest how this may be done first by means of a simple, discrete example, and then in a more general formulation.

Suppose search is limited to at most three stages or three opportunities. Let

$f(x_n) = $ prior distribution of the profit from the opportunity discovered at stage n

$f(x_3 \mid x_1, x_2) = $ posterior distribution of profit for the opportunity to be discovered at stage three, given that opportunities discovered at stages 1 and 2 had profits x_1 and x_2, respectively, $(f(x_2 \mid x_1)$, is defined in similar fashion.)

$E_3(X \mid x_1, x_2) = $ expected profit if only stage 3 remains, if the best opportunity so far discovered has profit X, if the opportunities discovered in the first two stages had profits x_1 and x_2, and if the best possible choice is made at stage 3. $(E_2(X \mid x_1)$ is again defined in similar fashion)

The system of equations which express this situation may then be written:

$$E_3(X \mid x_1, x_2) = \sum_{x_3=0}^{X} X f(x_3 \mid x_1, x_2) + \sum_{x_3=X+1}^{\infty} x_3 f(x_3 \mid x_1, x_2) - c$$

$$E_2(X \mid x_1) = \sum_{x_2=0}^{X} \max (X, E_3 (X \mid x_1, x_2)) f(x_2 \mid x_1)$$

$$+ \sum_{x_2=X+1}^{\infty} \max (x_2, E_3(x_2 \mid x_1, x_2)) f(x_2 \mid x_1) - c$$

$$E_1(X) = \sum_{x_1=0}^{X} \max (X, E_2 (X \mid x_1)) f(x_1)$$

$$+ \sum_{x_1=X+1}^{\infty} \max (x_1, E_2 (x_1 \mid x_2)) f(x_1) - c$$

Note that if the program is begun with no opportunities available, then the last equation might be written

$$E_1(0) = \sum_{x_1=0}^{\infty} \max (x_1, E_2 (x_1 \mid x_1)) f(x_1) - c$$

To illustrate some of the computational aspects of this type of problem, suppose that the x_n can take only the values 0 and 1. There are two hypotheses under consideration concerning the probability that an opportunity will have a profit of 1:

H_0: probability of an opportunity having a profit of 1 is .40

H_1: probability of an opportunity having a profit of 1 is .60

The following prior distribution is assumed to apply to all stages:

$$\text{PR}(H_0) = .50 \qquad \text{PR}(H_1) = .50$$

The posterior probabilities are

$$\text{PO}(H_0 \mid 0) = .60$$
$$\text{PO}(H_0 \mid 1) = .40$$
$$\text{PO}(H_0 \mid 0, 0) = .692$$
$$\text{PO}(H_0 \mid 0, 1) = \text{PO}(H_0 \mid 1, 0) = .50$$
$$\text{PO}(H_0 \mid 1, 1) = .308$$

Solving the system of equations then yields

$$E_3(0 \mid 0, 0) = f(1 \mid 0, 0) - c$$
$$= (.692)(.40) + (.308)(.60) - c$$
$$= .462 - c$$
$$E_2(0 \mid 0) = \max (0, E_3(0 \mid 0, 0)) f(0 \mid 0) + f(1 \mid 0) - c$$
$$= \max (0, .462 - c)(.52) + .48 - c$$
$$E_1(0) = \max (0, E_2(0 \mid 0)) f(0) + f(1) - c$$
$$= \max (0, E_2(0 \mid 0))(.50) + .50 - c$$

Now examination of these equations suggests that if c happens to be greater than .462 but less than .48, the best search policy will be to stop when

1. An opportunity with profit of 1 is obtained.

2. The second opportunity with profit 0 is discovered.

Using this policy yields an expected profit of

$$E_1(0) = (.48 - c)(.50) + .50 - c$$
$$= .74 - 1.50c$$

We compare this result with that obtained from a model in which no revisions are made on the basis of experience, and it is assumed throughout the problem that

$$f(0) = .50 \qquad f(1) = .50$$

If it is assumed that c lies in the range indicated previously, this model yields

$$E_3(0) = .50 - c$$
$$E_2(0) = \max (0, E_3(0))(.50) + .50 - c$$
$$= (.50 - c)(.50) + .50 - c$$
$$E_1(0) = \max (0, E_2(0))(.50) + .50 - c$$

Using this model, it turns out that the best policy is to stop only when an opportunity having a profit of 1 is obtained. Thus the best policy without learning is different from that which is best with learning.

We can compute the value of the process of learning from experience by computing the increase in profit that will result if the optimal policy for that model is used instead of the policy indicated by the nonlearning model. If one uses the rule "stop only when an opportunity having a profit of 1 is obtained," the expected profit may be obtained as follows:

$$E_3(0 \mid 0, 0) = .462 - c$$
$$E_2(0 \mid 0) = (.462 - c)(.52) + .48 - c$$
$$E_1(0) = E_2(0)(.50) + .50 - c$$
$$= .86 - 1.76c$$

Here it must be understood that this is not the expectation if the best possible policy is used at each stage, but rather the expectation if one stops only when a profit of 1 is obtained.

The advantage of the learning model is then

$$174 - 1.50c - (.86 - 1.76c) = .26c - .12$$

If c is in the range from .462 to .48 as assumed, this will indeed be nonnegative. It may be regarded as the increase in profit due to the revision of probabilities on the basis of experience, and thus a measure of what one could reasonably spend to set up and operate a system which did take advantage of experience in this way.

A More General Formulation

Even the trivial example just discussed presents some considerable computational load in the light of its size. In dealing with more complex problems more nearly like those encountered in actual management situations, the computational burden increases at an increasing rate. A formulation of the search problem with persistent opportunities which employs the normal theory is suggested; the problem of working out computational short cuts is ignored.

Suppose the profit from the opportunity discovered at stage n is regarded as a normally distributed random variable, x_n, with mean m and variance v. The means are taken to be uncertain and associated with each is a prior distribution, $PR(m)$. Thus there is also a prior distribution for each of the x_n. The profits from the projects obtained on stages 1 through $n - 1$ are regarded as information useful for revising the prior distribution of x_n into a posterior, which may be symbolized by

$$PO(x_n \mid x_1, \ldots, x_{n-1})$$

The interest here is in the system of equations which permit the evaluation of $E_n(X \mid x_1, \ldots, x_{n-1})$, the expected profit if the best policy is used at each of the remaining stages n through N, if the best opportunity so far obtained has profit X, and if the first $n - 1$ stages have yielded opportunities with profits $x_1, \ldots, x_{n-1}$.

The equations are of the same general form as those already examined in the example:

$$E_n(X \mid x_1, \ldots, x_{n-1})$$

$$= \int_{x_n=0}^{X} \max \{X, E_{n+1}(X \mid x_1, \ldots x_n)\} \, PO(x_n \mid x_1, \ldots, x_{n-1}) \, dx_n$$

$$+ \int_{x_n=X}^{\infty} \max \{x_n, E_{n+1}(x_n \mid x_1, \ldots, x_n)\} \, PO(x_n \mid x_1, \ldots, x_{n-1}) \, dx_n - c$$

One approach to the computational problem is to approximate the continuous random variables involved in this system of equations by discrete ones and resort to the digital computer. Later the discussion returns to simplifications which may be obtained by altering the learning process itself so that it becomes only approximately the Bayesian learning process.

Transitory Opportunities

Consider a multistage search process in which the opportunities involved are transitory in the sense that they are lost if not taken up immediately upon discovery. Opportunities obtained at any given stage may not be held over and undertaken at some future stage. One may think here of investment opportunities available for only limited periods, or of opportunities to purchase securities or commodities whose prices fluctuate in the market. To give some feel for the nature of the problem, consider an example in which the possibility of learning from experience is ignored.

Suppose a given quantity of some commodity must be bought within the next three days. The future prices of the commodity on the open market are uncertain and are thus viewed as random variables. For simplicity, assume that a price is quoted once each day and that any quantity desired may be bought at that price. Further, assume that no brokerage fees, storage charges, or quantity discounts need to be considered. It is also assumed that speculation involving buying more than is required and selling the extra amount is not permitted. Assume too that the entire quantity required is to be bought at one time at a given price. This incidentally, is the best policy if one wishes to minimize the expected cost of the procurement. It is better than, say, buying part of the quantity desired on each of several days. With this presumption, one may look for a policy which will minimize the expected unit cost of the procurement; and this will be the best policy regardless of the quantity required.

Suppose the price on each of the next three days is viewed as a uniformly distributed continuous random variable with distribution

$$f(x) = 0.05 \quad \text{for} \quad \$.90 \leq x \leq \$1.10$$

If the third day arrives with no procurement made the expected unit cost will be

$$E_3 = \int_x x f(x) \, dx = \$1.00$$

If, on the second day, no purchase has been made, the expected unit cost if the best policy is used for days 2 and 3 is

$$E_2 = \int_x \min (x, E_3) f(x) \, dx$$

$$= \int_{x=0.90}^{1.00} x f(x)\, dx + \int_{x=1.00}^{1.10} E_3 f(x)\, dx$$

$$= \$0.475 + \$0.50 = \$0.975$$

This amounts to saying that if there was no buying on the first day, the best thing to do is buy on the second day if the price quoted that day is less than $1.00. If the price quoted on the second day is greater than $1.00, then wait until the third day, when one must buy at whatever the market price may be. Going back to the first day,

$$E_1 = \int_x \min(x, E_2) f(x)\, dx$$

$$= \int_{x=0.90}^{0.975} x f(x)\, dx + \int_{x=0.975}^{1.10} E_2 f(x)\, dx$$

$$= \$0.339 + \$0.609 = \$0.948$$

This policy thus confirms the intuitive notion that the greater the number of days which remain before the deadline, the lower the expected cost of the procurement. On day 1, one buys only if the price quoted on that day is less than $0.975; on day 2, one buys only if the price is less than $1.00. Thus, as one would also expect, the greater the time remaining before the deadline, the lower the price one "holds out for."

Transitory Opportunities with Learning

Suppose now that not only are the prices quoted at various future buying opportunities uncertain, but that as one learns the price for a given day, it can be used to revise uncertainty as to future prices.

Let $\quad E_n(x_1, \ldots x_{n-1}) =$ expected unit cost if stages n through N remain, if prices quoted on the first $n - 1$ stages are $x_1, \ldots, x_{n-1}$, and if the best possible policy is followed at each remaining stage

$\mathrm{PO}(x_n \mid x_1, \ldots, x_{n-1}) =$ posterior distribution of the price on day n, given the prices for days 1 through $n - 1$

Then the required equations are of the form

$$E_n(x_1, \ldots, x_{n-1}) = \int_{x_n} \min\{x_n, E_{n+1}(x_1, \ldots, x_n)\}\, \mathrm{PO}(x_n \mid x_1, \ldots, x_{n-1})\, dx_n$$

Here again there are serious computational difficulties with complex problems. It may be useful, however, to illustrate the structure of the process by means of an extremely simple example.

Greatly simplify the situation by considering only two possible prices, "high" and "low," and for computation assign these the values 1 and 0 respectively. There are two hypotheses under consideration relative to the probability of a low price at any future buying opportunity:

H_0: probability of a low price being quoted is .40

H_1: probability of a low price is .60

A prior distribution describes uncertainty about these hypotheses and is applicable to all future opportunities up to the deadline, which is three days hence.

$$\text{PR}(H_0) = .50 \quad \text{PR}(H_1) = .50$$

The required posterior distributions are

$$\text{PO}(H_0 \mid 0) = .40$$
$$\text{PO}(H_0 \mid 1) = .60$$
$$\text{PO}(H_0 \mid 0, 0) = .308$$
$$\text{PO}(H_0 \mid 0, 1) = \text{PO}(H_0 \mid 1, 0) = .50$$
$$\text{PO}(H_0 \mid 1, 1) = .692$$

It is useful for illustration to assume that, if the procurement is made on the third day, there is an additional cost per unit of c, which reflects the necessity of "rush delivery" in order to meet the deadline. The required computations include the following:

$$E_3(1, 1) = (.60)(.692) + (.40)(.308) + c = .538 + c$$
$$E_2(1) = \min (1, .538 + c)\{(.60)(.60) + (.40)(.40)\}$$
$$= \min (1, .538 + c)(.52)$$
$$E_1 = \min (1, E_2(1))(.50)$$

Now if $c = .48$ (for illustration), the best policy will be to stop and buy whenever a price of 0 is quoted and also to stop on day 2 when the second price of 1 is quoted. That is, stop if $x_1 = 1$ and $x_2 = 1$.

This may now be compared with the policy resulting if one did not use experience to revise one's uncertainty about future price quotations. Regarding the price distribution as

$$f(0) = .50 \quad f(1) = .50$$

whatever the experience which accumulates, it may be shown that the best policy is not to stop unless a price of 0 is obtained. Thus, for $c = .48$ at least, the policy indicated by the model which suppresses learning differs from that previously computed.

Using the policy of not stopping unless a price of 0 is obtained, the expected cost may be computed as follows:

$$E_3(1, 1) = .538 + .48 = 1.018$$

$$E_2(1) = (.52)(1.018)$$
$$E_1 = (.50)(.52)(1.018) = .265$$

If on the other hand, the optimal policy determined from the learning model is used, the expected cost turns out to be

$$E_1 = .260$$

Thus through a process of revising uncertainty on the basis of experience, one may lower the expected cost of the procurement program by 0.005 per unit.

A Dynamic Inventory Problem

In previous analysis of inventory policy, we were careful to suppose that the decision to be made concerned only one period and had no consequences for future periods. That assumption may now be relaxed. Consider the situation in which stock remaining at the end of a period may be used to satisfy demands in subsequent periods. We are concerned with the case in which additions to an inventory can be made only at specified points in time, regarded as the beginnings of stocking periods. Management may, at the start of any period, order any amount of material desired to supplement the stock currently available. For simplicity, assume that material ordered at the start of any period becomes available for satisfying demands within that period. That is, there is little or no lead time between ordering and delivery.

If the commodity involved is seasonal or has a relatively short market life, then the problem has a natural planning horizon. A policy may extend to the end of the "season" or to the end of the product's anticipated period on the market. In other cases, for computation, one wants to adopt a planning horizon which bounds the future extent of policy deliberations. One may discount future revenues so that incomes very far in the future have very little influence on present plans, permitting neglect of the distant future without loss of effectiveness in current decisions. As previously noted, it is often the case that as one considers incomes or demands further and further into the future, increasing uncertainty is associated with them. Thus the risk-averse manager, whose utility function increases at a decreasing rate, will attach less value to increasingly remote and uncertain incomes. This will act, in effect, as another sort of discounting process. Thus, by whatever means, suppose that there is a planning horizon to be used for inventory decision making which considers N future time periods. One may write

$$E_{N+1}(I)$$

to stand for the disposal value of an inventory of amount I left over at the end of the final period.

To deal with a specific problem, let

I = an inventory level

x_n = demand in period $n(n = 1, \ldots, N)$

b_n = number of units which management decides to buy at the start of period n

c = cost per unit or buying price

r = revenue per unit or selling price

As the problem begins, the x_n are random variables, having for example, normal distributions, each with mean m and variance v. The variances are assumed to be known, but the means are subject to uncertainty. A prior distribution for each mean is available to reflect this uncertainty, and it may well be that the variance of this prior increases as n increases. Using the prior distribution of the mean for any period, allows one to obtain the prior distribution of demand for that period. As periods pass, the demand experienced is recorded and used as evidence upon which to base revisions of uncertainty about demands in subsequent periods. Thus at any stage one has, for the remaining periods, a set of posterior distributions

$$PO(x_n \mid x_1, \ldots, x_{n-1})$$

the posterior distribution of demand in period n, given that the demands in the previous $n - 1$ periods, were $x_1, \ldots x_{n-1}$. As in previous problems, the functions are defined

$E_n(I \mid x_1, \ldots, x_{n-1})$ = expected profit for periods n through N, if the inventory at the start of period n is I, if previous demands have been $x_1, \ldots, x_{n-1}$, and if the best possible policy is used for the remaining periods

At any stage, management has data on what previous demands have been, knows what inventory is on hand and how many periods remain, and must decide how much to buy at that point. Given the decision to buy b_n units, the total stock available becomes $I + b_n$. If demand falls short of this amount in period n, the revenue for the period will be rx_n, and a quantity $I + b_n - x_n$ will remain to form the starting inventory for the next period. If demand in period n exceeds the total stock available, revenue for the period will be $r(I + b_n)$ and no inventory is left over for period $n + 1$. The problem is to select b_n, the purchase quantity, so as to maximize expected profit over the remaining periods. Using this logic, one constructs the necessary system of equations, the general form of which will be

$E_n(I \mid x_1, \ldots, x_{n-1})$

$$= \max_{b_n} \left\{ -cb_n + \int_{x_n=0}^{I+b_n} [rx_n + E_{n+1}(I + b_n - x_n \mid x_1, \ldots, x_n)] \right.$$

$$PO(x_n \mid x_1, \ldots, x_{n-1}) \, dx_n + \int_{x_n = I + b_n}^{\infty} [r(I + b_n) + E_{n+1}(0 \mid x_1, \ldots, x_n)]$$

$$PO(x_n \mid x_1, \ldots, x_{n-1}) \, dx_n \Big\}$$

Here also there appear to be computational difficulties, but the structure of the problem can be usefully illustrated by means of an example.

An Inventory Example

Consider a situation in which demand in any period can take only the discrete values 0, 1, or 2. Suppose that there are two possible demand distributions:

$$H_0: f(0) = .50 \qquad f(1) = .25 \qquad f(2) = .25$$
$$H_1: f(0) = .25 \qquad f(1) = .25 \qquad f(2) = .50$$

Three future periods are being considered, and the prior distribution for each of these periods reflects the manager's opinion that the foregoing hypotheses are equally likely to be true. The buying and selling prices are

$$r = \$2.00$$

$$c = \$1.00$$

Material left over at the end of the third period is worthless; thus

$$E_4(I \mid x_1, x_2) = 0$$

for all values of I, x_1, and x_2. There follows a sample of the computations required in this problem.

Entering the third period with an inventory of I, having experienced demands x_1 and x_2 in the first two periods, one must decide the quantity to be purchased at that point. Recalling that material left over is worthless, one must find

$$E_3(I \cdot x_1, x_2)$$

$$= \max_{b_3} \left\{ -cb_3 + \sum_{x_3 = 0}^{I + b_3} rx_3 \, PO(x_3 \mid x_1, x_2) + \sum_{x_3 = I + b_3 + 1}^{2} r(I + x_3) \, PO(x_3 \mid x_1, x_2) \right\}$$

Suppose, for example, we consider the case

$$I = 0$$

$$x_1 = 0$$

$$x_2 = 0$$

The first step is to compute $PO(H_0 \mid 0, 0)$ which, by the usual methods, is found to be .80. Next, one requires the posterior distribution of x_3.

$$PO(0 \mid 0, 0) = (.80)(.50) + (.20)(.25) = .45$$
$$PO(1 \mid 0, 0) = .25$$
$$PO(2 \mid 0, 0) = .30$$

The best choice for b_3 may be determined by formulating the decision as follows:

		$x_3 = 0$	$x_3 = 1$	$x_3 = 2$
	0	0	0	0
b_3	1	$-\$1.00$	$\$1.00$	$\$1.00$
	2	$-\$2.00$	0	$\$2.00$

Using the posterior distribution of x_3, compute the expected profit for various values of b_3. The best choice is to take b_3 equal to 1, yielding an expected profit of $0.10. Thus

$$E_3(0 \mid 0, 0) = \$0.10$$

Similar decision problems must be solved to obtain the remaining values for this function for all combinations of I, x_1, and x_2. With this accomplished, one may return to the second period and consider the function

$$E_2(I \mid x_1) = \max_{b_2} \left\{ -cb_2 + \sum_{x_2=0}^{I+b_2} [rx_2 + E_3(I + b_2 - x_2 \mid x_1, x_2)] \, PO(x_2 \mid x_1) \right.$$
$$\left. + \sum_{x_2=I+b_2+1}^{2} [r(I + b_2) + E_3(0 \mid x_1, x_2)] \, PO(x_2 \mid x_1) \right\}$$

Again, one may illustrate by obtaining the value of $E_2(0 \mid 0)$. The posterior probability of H_0 is

$$PO(H_0 \mid 0) = .67$$

The resulting posterior for x_2 is

$$PO(0 \mid 0) = (.67)(.50) + (.33)(.25) = .42$$
$$PO(1 \mid 0) = .25$$
$$PO(2 \mid 0) = .33$$

The decision problem is then:

		$x_2 = 0$	$x_2 = 1$	$x_2 = 3$
	0	$E_3(0 \mid 0, 0)$ $= \$0.10$	$E_3(0 \mid 0, 1)$ $= \$0.17$	$E_3(0 \mid 0, 2)$ $= \$0.25$
b_2	1	$-c + E_3(1 \mid 0, 0)$ $= \$0.10$	$-c + r + E_3(0 \mid 0, 1)$ $= \$1.17$	$-c + r + E_3(0 \mid 0, 2)$ $= \$1.25$
	2	$-2c + E_3(2 \mid 0, 0)$ $= -\$0.30$	$-2c + r + E_3(1 \mid 0, 1)$ $= \$1.17$	$-2c + 2r + E_3(0 \mid 0, 2)$ $= \$2.25$

Using the posterior distribution for x_2 to compute the expected profit for the various values of b_2 shows that the best choice is $b_2 = 2$. This yields an expected profit of \$0.92; thus,

$$E_2(0 \mid 0) = \$0.92$$

Similar decision problems need to be worked out for each possible combination of I and x_1. With such results, one could examine the best policy at the first stage, seeking to maximize the function (assuming there is no inventory at the beginning of period 1)

$$E_1(0) = \max_{b_1} \left\{ -cb_1 + \sum_{x_1=0}^{b_1} [rx_1 + E_2(b_1 - x_1 \mid x_1)] \, \mathrm{PR}(x_1) \right.$$
$$\left. + \sum_{x=b_1+1}^{2} [rb_1 + E_2(0 \mid x_1)] \, \mathrm{PR}(x_1) \right\}$$

Formulating the decision problem as was done for the second and third stages suggests that the best policy is to take $b_1 = 2$, yielding an expected profit for the three-period program of \$2.09. Table 11-1 shows the buying

TABLE 11-1

Period	Experience		b_n
	x_1	x_2	
1			2
2	0		0
2	1		1
2	2		2
3	0	0	0
3	0	1	0
3	0	2	1
3	1	0	0
3	1	1	0
3	1	2	1
3	2	0	0
3	2	1	0
3	2	2	1

policies which will be best for all possible conditions of experience and inventory encountered in the problem.

Modified Learning Processes

The calculations involved in the inventory example illustrate something of the computational burden to be expected in a sequential decision process when learning from experience is incorporated. Problems may be made somewhat more manageable by adopting shorter planning horizons. As noted, discounting future incomes and the tendency for uncertainty to increase as one moves further into the future, lend some logical support to this sort of simplification. One may also abstract from variables which can take on many values by grouping their values into class intervals. Instead of considering a problem in terms of the actual values that, say, prices or demands may take, it is possible to consider only ranges and represent them in the analysis of their midpoints. Clearly, the larger the class intervals or ranges, the more gross the resulting approximation. Beyond these suggestions, one may want to deal with various modifications of the learning process itself. These are of interest, not only because they permit some reduction in computational effort, but also because they are reminiscent of what seems to have evolved naturally in many management situations.

One might for example, ignore experience until an observation occurs which falls beyond some specified distance from the mean of the prior distribution. This recalls the control-chart method of statistical quality control. Unless an observation will have some considerable impact on the prior distribution, unless it is a "surprising" result in the light of previous opinion, it is not used immediately to compute a new set of posteriors. When a value does fall outside the limits, one might (or might not) use all the observed experience since the previous revision in computing the new posteriors. Clearly, the further the limits are from the mean, or the wider the "dead band," the less frequently will revisions occur and the more imperfect the learning-decision process. One could, however, calculate the expected profit, using such an imperfect process in a test problem, and compare it with the expected profit, using the full Bayesian method, thus obtaining an estimate of the cost of the simplification achieved. The interesting question then becomes where to set the limits, or deciding how surprising information must be before revision occurs.

An alternative method might be to decide in advance that experience was not to be used immediately upon becoming available, but accumulated over several stages. One might plan a system in which observations were collected and used to make revisions every k stages or time periods. Within the k stages, the system operates essentially as a nonlearning one, but may anticipate revisions at the planned points in the future.

Finally, one might update or revise one's expressions of uncertainty as experience becomes available, but ignore that additional experience will become available in the future. This is equivalent to supposing that as data are obtained, new distributions are calculated, but the sequential decision problem for the remaining stages is simply resolved as a nonlearning problem. That is, although the distributions used reflect the experience already obtained, the analysis does not include the various possibilities for experience which may appear in the future.

EXERCISES

11-1. In the case of search without learning and persistent opportunities, show that the following rule is optimal whether search is limited or unlimited: continue if the expected gain from one more stage is greater than zero, otherwise stop.

11-2. In the case of limited search with persistent opportunities and without learning, show that as the limiting number of stages is increased, the expected profit approaches that for unlimited search.

11-3. In the purchasing example used to illustrate the problem of transitory opportunities with learning, it was suggested that it was best to buy the total amount of the commodity required on a single day. Can you show that no other policy, such as buying a portion of the requirement on each day, is better than the single-procurement policy?

11-4. Discuss the various possible meanings of perfect information in the persistent-opportunity search problem with learning from experience. In the context of the example given in Chapter 11, what would be the value of various types of perfect information?

11-5. Discuss the possibilities for including the following complicating features in the purchasing model discussed in Chapter 11.

    a. Storage charges

    b. Brokerage fees

    c. Deterioration of material stored with time

    d. Price discounts for quantity purchases

11-6. Two days are available within which to purchase a specified quantity of a commodity. For simplicity it is assumed that the market price can take only three possible values which have been scaled so that they may be stated as -1, 0, and 1. The following description of the decision maker's uncertainty applies to both days. Two probability distributions are believed to be possible for the market price, and they are regarded at the outset as equally likely. They are

$$f(-1) = \tfrac{1}{3} \qquad f(0) = \tfrac{1}{3} \qquad f(1) = \tfrac{1}{3}$$
and
$$g(-1) = \tfrac{1}{4} \qquad g(0) = \tfrac{1}{4} \qquad g(1) = \tfrac{1}{2}$$

Show that the best policy is to buy on the first day if the price quoted is -1 or 0, otherwise, continue. What is the advantage of learning in this example as opposed to a policy which does not include learning?

11-7. Formulate the multiple-opportunity bidding problem mentioned in Chapter 9 in the context provided by Chapter 11.

11-8. In the inventory example used in Chapter 11, what is the advantage of explicit learning as opposed to ignoring experience? What explanation can you give for the result?

11-9. A political opportunist is trying to decide which of two candidates to support in an upcoming election. If he supports a loser, his payoff is taken to be zero; but if he supports the winner, his payoff is greater, the earlier in the campaign he declares his support. The time between now and the election is divided into three periods, during any one of which he may take a survey of voter opinion, and at the end of which he may declare his own choice if he wishes. His payoffs are given by the accompanying table:

	Present	*Period 1*	*Period 2*	*Period 3*
Supports winner	10	9	8	7
Supports loser	0	0	0	0

The cost of each survey (in payoff units) is .25, and he views the surveys as being independent. The surveys are more likely to be correct as one gets closer to the time of the election. This is indicated by the following probabilitites:

Period during which survey is taken	1	2	3
Probability of a correct prediction	.60	.70	.90

The surveys simply provide the opportunist with the statement "Candidate X will be the winner." On the basis of his present information he believes that there is a 55 per cent chance of A being elected and a 45 per cent chance of B being elected.

Show that the following policy is best: support A if the first two surveys indicate that A will be the winner, otherwise take all three surveys.

11-10. Discuss the basic questions which arise in designing a management control system for the following production situation. A production process has been set up and a total of k units is to be produced. There is some uncertainty about the scrap rate of the process. After completion of any unit, the process may be stopped and one or more of the previously produced units may be inspected and classified as effective or defective. The process may then be allowed to continue untouched, or it may be adjusted. The effect of adjustment is to return the process to the condition with which the production run was begun. There is a cost associated with making such adjustments as well as a cost for defective units produced.

11-11. We have suggested a number of approximate learning models which might be used to simplify the calculations required in multistage decision problems. Discuss each of these, indicating how one might choose the critical parameters involved and how the effectiveness of the result might be tested in practice.

12

Some Organizational Considerations

The Organizational Context

Our basic objective is enhancing the art of planning effective systems for management decision making, including the associated data gathering and learning systems. The problem of information handling is to be examined from a systems viewpoint, considering not only the gathering and transmission of data, the establishment and maintenance of the firm's "data bank" of recorded experience, but also the decision makers for whom all this is designed. The question of designing an effective management information system is a part of the still higher-level problem of the design of the organization itself. We cannot undertake a really adequate discussion of organizational design, nor perhaps can anyone at this stage of the emergence of management science. At best one can point out a few of the basic issues and give special emphasis to their influence on planning management information systems.

Most organizations and their information systems have evolved over a considerable period of time. Only to a limited extent are they the result of deliberate designs or attempts at large-scale rationalization. From time to time in the life of the firm, a crisis may be met by means of a "reorganization." Installation of a digital computer may occasion a more or less careful look at the generation and use of information in the firm. One suspects, however, that, most often, the information-learning-decision system is an *ad hoc* adaptation to an existing organization structure and its incumbent personalities. As these change, some aspects of the information system are modified, but some may simply be perpetuated without serving any further useful function. The organizational structure itself may be altered in order to make more effective use of a given information-handling mechanism. What we mean to suggest by "design" is the deliberate consideration of information processing to support the learning and decision-making functions, as an integral part of designing or guiding the evolution of an organization. This is an ideal for which some support can be found among managers and management scientists, yet it is fruitless if allowed to remain expressed in broad generalities. It is easy to say that everything is related to everything else and that all these relationships should be considered in planning an organization. This is impossible in any serious sense, and this chapter attempts to avoid vagueness by dealing with a small number of specific ideas in the context of a particular example.

The Realist's View

Perspective is particularly important in this discussion:

1. One seldom sits down to design an organization or a management information system "from scratch." More often, one has the opportunity to consider small alterations in the structure of large organizations. The real possibilities for effectiveness lie in offering some understanding that can influence the directions in which the firm evolves.

2. To speak of *designing* a system is to consider the information-learning-decision situations which can be foreseen and thus planned for. This typically means situations which are more or less repetitive in the ongoing affairs of the firm. Design efforts are likely to be most productive in connection with decision problems which are important and frequently encountered, and thus warrant careful rationalization and routinization. In the repetitive situations, examined in previous chapters, these problems have been considered to be part of the design of *management control systems*. There has been an attempt to show the Bayesian equivalent of the systems engineer's feedback control principles. There is, of course, a broad spectrum of degrees of repetitiveness and degrees to which decisions may be anticipated. There will always be decision problems which cannot be, or are not, foreseen. These are often of great consequence to the firm, but may to a large extent remain beyond the range of any information system which might reasonably be designed.

3. Learning-decision systems have been considered in detail in several specific areas, such as capital investment, inventory, bidding, and purchasing. One must consider the expense and effort required to carry

out these analyses and apply the results in any particular management context. In many situations, the difficulties and costs of careful analysis are obviously so great as to be prohibitive. Intuition, trial and error, and casual experimentation are the preferred approaches to such problems. Similarly, there are situations which yield immediately to common sense and experience, producing directly an acceptable solution. There is little motivation here for careful and costly analysis. Thus one should not expect every aspect of the system to be the subject of the sort of deliberate and methodical study which has so far been explored. Indeed, one of the most difficult questions is often that of deciding just where to expend one's design efforts.

A Review of Principles

One may reasonably expect that the principles which have emerged from the analysis in earlier chapters will not solve all the designer's problems, but may illuminate some of the more difficult parts of his art. Perhaps the best way to make this point clear is first to review some of the basic ideas developed up to this point and then to consider the ways in which they are not fully adequate in the context of a specific set of organizational problems.

The relevant ideas from previous discussions might be summarized as follows:

1. Most significant for the design process is the possibility of calculating the value of information and thus comparing its value with the cost of the system required to provide it. Here lies the fundamental rationale for a highly reasonable design procedure. One may choose on consistent grounds among alternate sources and quantities of information, deciding what to include and what to exclude from the management information system on a marginal cost–marginal gain basis.

2. To do this, however, requires that several conditions be met.
   a. One must be able to develop for the decisions involved an explicit rendering or conceptual structure which makes clear how the information produced by the system is to be utilized.
   b. One must be able to obtain an explicit understanding of the preferences and opinions of the managers involved in the system. Making these a clearly recognized aspect of the information system design is of major importance.
   c. We must have a consistent method of computing likelihoods for the various kinds of information which may arise in the system.

3. Evaluating information is complicated because it depends upon
   a. The state of knowledge or the degree of uncertainty of the managers whom the system is to serve. Thus expenditures for information produce diminishing marginal returns.

b. The amounts of other types of information to become available and to be used in the same decision process.

Therefore, in the face of constraints on the amount of effort to be expended for producing information, these interdependencies may pose difficult allocation problems.

4. There are at least the basic outlines of methods for making explicit management opinions and preferences. This suggests
    a. The possibility of greatly improved delegation of decisions
    b. More effective transmission of information throughout the organization, avoiding the necessity for suppressing uncertainty
    c. Communicating the objectives of the firm to its subunits in more operational form

5. These methods may, of course, be applied to expert opinion in general, thus explicitly recognizing the role of the best-informed persons in various areas. The expert in any given instance may be a manager, a technical specialist, a supervisor at the operating level, or an outside consultant.
    a. The expert or source of "best opinion" can be more or less formally identified by requiring that
        i. His opinions be stable over time, unless additional relevant evidence becomes available.
        ii. His opinions change in the right direction in the face of relevant information.
        iii. His predictions have an established record of accuracy and reliability.
    b. One can compare the cost and value of opinion among various experts, as well as with other sources of information.
    c. The "best" source of information in a given situation may be a single expert, a group of experts whose opinions are given various weights, explicit data, or some combination of data and opinion.

6. The basic difficulty in developing explicit models for management decision situations is balancing the cost and benefits of more or less complex models and the information system they require. There is a possible structure for considering the appropriate degree of development for a model. (This important question will be treated further in Chapter 13.)

7. Having recognized that some combination of management experience, expert opinion, and explicit data is usually appropriate for a decision problem, one has logic for carrying out this difficult integration. There are reasonable ways of weighting and combining opinion and evidence.

8. When it is possible to obtain substantial amounts of data, it is unnecessary to spend a great deal of effort formulating a prior distribution. The resulting posterior distribution will typically be rather insensitive to the exact shape of the prior. When considerable data are available, one would expect to find rather good agreement among managers and a willingness to delegate the decision involved.

9. All data may be stored and processed by the information system in the form of likelihoods. The logic of Bayesian learning suggests

   a. Likelihoods present the decision maker with information in the form which he can immediately combine with his prior opinions.
   b. Computational assistance may be given directly if the decision maker will make his prior opinion explicit so that it may be combined with likelihoods.
   c. Use of likelihoods is the basic method of economizing in the use of the storage and transmission capabilities of the information system.
   d. Ready access to a central data bank containing likelihoods should be of value in achieving consistent delegation of decisions.

10. The basic feature of all the foregoing analysis has been establishing consistent methods by which the firm can learn from its experience or adapt to its environment. Note

   a. This is effective only within the context explicitly established by the analyst.
   b. Management must have sufficient understanding of the sort of data and analysis involved so as to be on guard for conditions which lead to unforeseen changes in its relevance.
   c. Management must, in the same spirit, have sufficient appreciation for the basis and logic of any recommendations produced by the information system so as to detect when to modify or neglect them.

One may now turn to look at some of the systems considerations which condition the application of the foregoing ideas.

Organization Planning

Assuming some notion of the objectives of the firm, the fundamental question for the organizational designer is how to divide the functions and decisions involved among the subunits of the firm. One broad design dimension is the degree of centralization which characterizes an organization. A firm is centralized to the extent that decisions are made at the higher levels by its "headquarters" management. A firm is decentralized to the extent that authority and responsibility for decision are delegated to the operating levels of management. The pattern of delegation and the sort of information system which it requires are key design issues.

Another dimension of the division of activities concerns the organization of subunits according to common processes or common products. In production activities, for example, one can form units which carry out similar processes on a variety of products, or bring together the various processes required to complete a single product. The same basic issues arise when one considers whether design and development engineers should be organized according to technical specialty or by bringing together the various specialists who contribute to a particular project. Obviously, these two principles for organization structure suggest quite different information systems.

The basic effects which the designer considers are complementarities on the one hand, and coordination requirements on the other. In grouping activities together, one tries to take advantage of possibilities for combining activities which can be done more profitably together than separately. Thus one seeks to bring together those operations which share common facilities, require similar skills, and can take advantage of similar set-up and fixed costs. These complementarities lie behind the unit which specializes in a given process, such as the secretarial pool, the mechanical engineering staff group, the heat-treating department, or the marketing department. Effort to take advantage of complementarities means increasing the number of units whose work must be coordinated in order to accomplish a particular final output. As this happens, the advantages of specialization by process tend to be outweighed by the growing difficulties associated with coordination and communication. Operating on the hypothesis that communication and coordination are more easily achieved within a unit than among organizational units, one looks toward a product-oriented organization which joins into one easily coordinated group, the various activities needed to accomplish a complete task. This in turn, brings duplication as the price of reduced communication needs. In very general terms, these appear to be the major issues which the organization designer must attempt to balance. It is perhaps most useful to examine specific manifestations of these effects in an example.

The Capital Budgeting System Example

Chapter 7 dealt with several problems connected with an information-learning-decision system for capital budgeting, in and especially with the basic issues of evaluating information and allocating information-gathering efforts. This chapter returns to capital-budgeting systems to examine briefly some of the organization design questions involved. For illustration, consider a multidivisional firm consisting of several operating divisions and a headquarters division. This shows at least the outlines of the structure found in many large "decentralized" corporations. The pattern of dividing the firm into subunits is taken as given, and we confront the problem of designing an effective capital-budgeting system to be operated within this structure. Assume, for purposes of design, that the firm could express the utility of a given investment proposal if given sufficient information. This may mean, for example, computing the expected value of the present worth of the proposal. In such cases, the objective of the capital-budgeting decision process is taken to be selecting a portfolio of proposals which will maximize expected present worth. The basic design choices involve the pattern of delegating the functions of searching for investment opportunities, evaluating those discovered, and deciding which of them are to be actually undertaken. Our discussion is, of course, especially concerned with the information systems required to support various patterns of delegation.

It will be recognized that in some firms, management does not deliberately calculate the level of effort devoted to the search for investment opportunities. A satisfactory flow of investment proposals seems to arise in "the normal course of business" and there is no desire to alter this flow. In other firms, however, the level of search effort is a matter of discretion, perhaps based on a logic roughly related to that examined in the previous chapter. Suppose this example to be a firm of the latter sort; hence search policy is a matter of management choice.

Delegation

One might consider several patterns for delegation of the actual decisions as to which investment proposals are to be funded. Suppose that the operating divisions, engaging in search activity, generate flows of proposals. The headquarters division carries out the cash management functions for the firm and thus controls the funds available for investment. Possible delegation arrangements include

1. *Complete centralization:* All proposals generated by the operating divisions are submitted to headquarters where decisions are made as to which will be undertaken.

2. *Complete decentralization:* Funds available for capital investment are divided among the operating divisions where they are invested at the discretion of divisional managers. An important question is how the division of funds is to be made.

3. *Delegation for clearly good proposals:* Headquarters may grant the operating divisions authority to invest when proposals emerge which meet some agreed standard of necessity or profitability. The difficulty here

is to define operationally what is meant by a *clearly good* or *necessary* investment opportunity.

4. *Delegation by functional areas:* In some firms, the operating divisions are authorized to make investments which maintain or replace present facilities. Investments involving expansion of capacity or new lines of activity must be submitted to headquarters.

5. *Delegation based on size:* A very common pattern is based simply on the size of the initial investment required by a proposal. Thus many firms permit division managements to decide on proposals which require an initial investment of *x* dollars or less, whereas proposals requiring more than this amount must be submitted to headquarters. A key design decision is the selection of a value for *x*. Delegation based on size of investment may be combined with a divisional budget restriction which limits the total amount invested at the discretion of the division management in a given budget period.

Systems Based on Investment Size

Because delegation based on the size of investment is found so often, this pattern is examined further. If the system permits division managers to decide on very large investments, it may be thought of as highly decentralized, with a substantial portion of the firm's available funds invested by the divisions. If, on the other hand, all but the smallest proposals must be submitted to headquarters, the system is highly centralized. This discussion attempts to indicate some of the factors which motivate the designer toward a greater or lesser degree of centralization in such a system.

1. Centralization has the basic advantage of permitting the headquarters group to select the best investment program from among all the opportunities available to the firm. The results will be better, generally speaking, than those from a decentralized plan, since no division will invest in one of its own proposals funds which could have been more profitably used to implement a proposal produced by another division. By giving the headquarters division the greatest possible "horizon of choice," a centralized plan assures the best possible program for the firm as a whole. To the degree that decision making is decentralized and funds are invested by divisions without knowledge of the opportunities available to other divisions, investment results will decline.

2. Centralization also solves directly the problem of coordination and control of divisional investment activities. The headquarters group can implement its major policy decisions which determine the general direction of the firm's development by its control of all capital investment. The headquarters group can also avoid duplication and

undesired competition in the investment decisions of the divisional managers. This consideration and the previous point explain the strong tradition of more centralization than decentralization in the capital-budgeting function.

3. One fundamental division of activity in many large firms places responsibility for long-range planning and forecasting with the headquarters group, whereas division managers take responsibility for the near-term operating problems arising out of the current affairs of the firm. Since investment decisions are, almost by definition, concerned with long time spans, it is important that they be coordinated with the planning activities at headquarters. There is little point in having the divisions individually and independently make forecasts already been made by headquarters. It generally appears easier to centralize investment decisions than to attempt to communicate the long-range plans to the divisions and assure that they are implemented.

4. In many firms, part of the funds available for capital investment in any year are the retained earnings. Since dividend policy is traditionally a function of the top management group, it is important that it have some knowledge of the flow of investment opportunities available to the firm. The volume and nature of investment opportunities may well influence the firm's plans for retaining earnings. Similarly, the centralization of the treasurer's functions of cash control and new financing lends support to the centralization of investment decisions.

5. On the other hand, some investments involving "small" amounts of money may well be delegated to the divisions without serious loss of the advantages of centralization. This limited decentralization helps to achieve the sort of work-load distribution which permits the headquarters division to be free of troublesome "minor" decisions so that it may concentrate more effectively on long-range plans and major policy problems. It helps to avoid the "rubber stamp effect" of communicating to headquarters a large number of small proposals which it will almost certainly approve in any case. Thus, some delegation of small investment decisions may be undertaken with only small loss in over-all results and with considerable advantages of other sorts.

6. Decentralization, of course, has been most extensive in those firms which serve a variety of rapidly changing markets. It permits the firm to reduce the delay between the emergence of a proposal and the decision on whether it will be funded. This opens the possibility for taking advantage of transient opportunities and responding more effectively to changes in the firm's environment. Typically, the headquarters group makes a capital budget or funds a portfolio of proposals once a year. If the divisions use the same policy of batch budgeting,

little is gained. Decentralization gives the division manager greater opportunity to respond to situations in which immediate and non-routine budgeting decisions may profitably be made.

7. The idea of centralization implies a management-information system capable of bringing to headquarters the relevant information about each proposal. It is extremely difficult to transmit in writing, as is so often required, the on-the-scene impressions of experienced and fully informed people. Difficult to communicate also, are the subtleties of expert opinion and the estimates of the risk associated with various proposals. As suggested before, the typical management information system of this sort makes little or no attempt to communicate any ideas about risk. Decentralization thus attempts to get the decision made at the level where the best judgments and information are most fully available. It attempts to avoid the necessity for basing decisions on only the data which have traditionally been transmitted by the management-information system. Here, of course, is a major area of potential application for Bayesian concepts.

8. One problem of decentralization is encouraging and making possible the sharing of specialized knowledge and data among the divisions. It is fruitless for one division to devote its efforts to obtaining data already available in another. Yet some designs place divisional managements in competition with each other in such ways that they are reluctant to share their information. Currently, there is considerable interest in establishing central data banks to which all division managements have ready access. Hopefully, such data banks will not only help avoid duplication of information-gathering efforts, but also assist in coordinating the investment programs of the divisions.

9. Still another basic aspect of decentralization requires a management information system which will identify the performance of each division, typically in the form of divisional balance sheets and profit-and-loss statements. An incentive scheme for division management is then built upon the divisional performance. This raises many problems for the designer, including, for example, the selection of transfer prices for goods and services furnished by one division to another. The attempt, however, is to create an incentive for division management by connecting results as closely as possible with decisions. To the extent that capital-budgeting decisions are centralized, this incentive aspect of the decentralized design is weakened.

10. In the same spirit, a management-information system which gauges the performance of individual divisions, together with the decentralization of the major decisions which influence this performance, permits

    a. Greater opportunity for divisional managers to gain the sort of experience which will equip them for eventual headquarters responsibilities.

    b. Headquarters to compare performance among divisions and with similar units outside of the firm.

    c. Headquarters to use divisional performance as a basis for allocating the firm's capital among the divisions.

11. Finally, as emphasized earlier, management is seen as basically an attempt to learn effectively from experience or experiment. If a manager uses the working hypothesis that the effects of his decisions may be seen in the performance of his division, he has a reasonable chance of connecting actions and their consequences. It may be most useful for him to assume that the actions of the managers of other divisions do not influence his results, although this may not be strictly true. Indeed, decentralization has the property of making experience and experiment more meaningful by restricting the scope of decisions and outcomes which the manager must try to understand. Decentralization thus serves to reduce the number of variables in his experiments or to break the firm up into more manageable units.

Delegation Patterns for Search and Evaluation

The discussion so far has dealt with some of the considerations which influence the designer in his choice of delegation patterns for capital investment decisions themselves. The designer's larger problem is to achieve some sort of compatibility among search effort, evaluation effort, available funds, and available investment proposals. It is obviously pointless to have the divisions search out and evaluate proposals which have no chance of being funded, or fail to do so when an adequate supply of capital is available at headquarters.

In a highly centralized system all budgeting might be done at headquarters and search policy designed with consideration given to headquarter's knowledge of available funds; divisional search costs; divisional opportunity environments; projects discovered to date. If the headquarters unit did indeed have good knowledge of these factors, a policy could be established which might achieve a high degree of optimality for the firm. A highly decentralized system might involve allocating a budget to the division and permitting the division to design its own search policy based upon its knowledge of its own search costs, opportunity environment, and portfolio of projects so far discovered. The division could then move toward optimizing this policy relative to its own operation and budget. Whether the budget allocation made by headquarters was good would be an important question here. Generally, one would expect such a decentralized system to perform less well than the centralized one previously suggested, given equivalent knowledge about such things as search costs and opportunity environments in each case. Between these two designs is a multitude of possible systems in which search policy is determined in greater or lesser degree in a centralized fashion.

Divisions operating under an investment size restriction only, with no total budget limitation, have little basis for determining search policy beyond balancing their own marginal gain from the discovery of additional small projects against the marginal cost of doing so. Although they may try to consider also "their share" of the large projects sent up to headquarters and ultimately funded, such divisions cannot effectively do this without knowledge of the headquarters budget, the opportunity environments of the other divisions, and the levels of search effort chosen by them. Thus there are reasons for centralizing the decision as to level of search effort.

Consider next the evaluation of those large projects which are submitted to headquarters by the divisions. The divisions have little basis for determining an evaluation policy for these projects, since, as in the case of search policy, they lack the information necessary to make a reasonable estimate of the chances that a project will be funded. (Of course, in a stable situation, they may be able to estimate this rather well on the basis of past experience.) Thus it would be difficult to delegate evaluation policy for large projects.

For the small projects funded by the division, under the assumptions made here, it is certain that such a project will be funded. Thus a division which must "pay for" evaluation efforts would come to much the same conclusion about evaluating small projects as headquarters would. Thus, this policy might reasonably be delegated.

Note here the importance of "charging" the divisions for any evaluation effort they control. In the case of small projects which they may fund, if evaluation effort is "free" to them, they may expend a great deal of it in the process of separating acceptable from unacceptable projects. Thus their investment results will, in the long run turn out to be rather good, possibly better than is justified in terms of the cost of evaluation to the firm. If the divisions are permitted to determine evaluation policy for the large projects submitted to headquarters, then they may reasonably assume that the more completely evaluated (justified or supported) a project, the greater its chances of being funded. In desire to have headquarters fund the projects submitted, each division may be led to devote more effort to evaluation than would otherwise be reasonable. Only if the division is charged for evaluation effort can the policy be reasonably delegated.

As an alternative to the divisions establishing search policy on the basis of their own budgets, suppose a division wishes to base its search policy on its own results plus its share of those achieved by headquarters. For example, suppose a division reasons that it will share in headquarters results in proportion to the relative number of projects it submits to headquarters. The important point is that a single division cannot appropriately choose such a search policy without knowing the level of search effort chosen by every other division as well as the budget available at headquarters. Thus a high degree of coordination would be required among the divisions; and this can probably be effectively achieved only through considerable centralization.

If search effort and division budgets are fixed, a given division may estimate the probability that it will be able to fund a small project and plan evaluation efforts accordingly. A similar conclusion would be arrived at by the headquarters group, and thus the decision may be decentralized. In the case of large projects, however, the divisions presumably lack knowledge of the funds available at headquarters, the opportunity environments of the other divisions, as well as their search policies. Thus a division has little basis for estimating the probability that a given large project will be funded. This decision may well be left in the control of the headquarters group.

Confirming Divisional Evaluations

In many partially or fully centralized systems, evaluations of proposals are made at the divisional level and submitted to headquarters. The headquarters group finds it necessary to check the divisional evaluations, in some cases almost duplicating the efforts of the divisions. Often, the system encourages the divisions to be biased toward optimism in their proposals in order to have a better chance of obtaining funds in the face of competition from other divisions. Division managers may feel that once they obtain funds to implement a proposal, the original estimates which it contained will be forgotten. Thus there is little motivation to take careful responsibility for the bias or reliability of the predictions made in the proposal. Headquarters, to get a reasonable view of the actual promise of a project, may well be forced to do an independent evaluation of it.

One possible alternative to this troublesome duplication is the postaudit process. This involves an ultimate comparison of the actual results from opportunities which are funded with the estimates appearing in the proposals. Presumably over a period of time, a rather clear picture of divisional bias and reliability could be established. At best, however, the postaudit process is difficult because of the wise separation in time between the estimates and the emergence of the actual results from a project. During this period, managers come and go, those responsible for making the divisional evaluations change, and the conditions prevailing at the time of the estimates may alter radically. The incentives for good evaluation may be so distant in time from the act of estimating as to have very little effect. Thus the problem of encouraging unbiasedness and reliability in divisional proposals is a most difficult one for the designer.

Effective Designs

Perhaps this brief catalog of a few of the considerations involved in designing a management information-decision system for carrying out the capital-budgeting function is sufficient to suggest the reasonableness of what is most often observed in actual organizations. Most firms evolve toward some balance among these conflicting effects in the form of an organizational design which is neither highly centralized nor highly decentralized. Experience appears to suggest that this is the region in which the most effective patterns are to be found. The task of the designer is then the particularly difficult one of trying to discover whether things will improve if the firm evolves toward slightly more centralization or toward slightly more decentralization. If one extreme or the other were best, the problem would be far easier than it appears to be in actuality.

With this summary view of a complex example we can really hope only to suggest that the problem of designing a management information system is potentially a more significant undertaking than simply setting up forms and computer programs. The sort of logic for learning and decision making examined in the foregoing chapters may be helpful to the designer, but by no means completely solves his problems. There are complex organizational considerations which provide the context within which our study of management decision-learning systems takes place.

EXERCISE: A DESIGN PROBLEM

You are asked to outline the basic elements of a design of a management-information system for a firm which rather regularly brings out new products in the consumer field. These products, if successful, achieve national distribution supported by national advertising. The evolution of a new product may be roughly understood as involving five stages:

Stage 1: The basic idea is originated by the firm's product development group. The concept is developed to the point at which rough designs, costs, and potential demand estimates are available.

Stage 2: The design is refined and a test model is built. A more careful study of readily available marketing data is made in an effort to refine demand estimates. The production engineering group is asked for a first estimate of production costs.

Stage 3: A small production run is made on a "handwork" or subcontracting basis. The product is submitted to a consumer panel test.

Stage 4: A pilot production run is made. Several market areas are chosen for initial introduction and promotion.

Stage 5: Full-scale production facilities are brought into operation and national distribution is coordinated with national promotional efforts in various media.

Recently, the firm's development group has brought about one hundred ideas each year through stage 1. An average of five of these ideas have been put into full production and national distribution. Of these five products, an average of two have been discontinued after twelve months.

Freely supplying details and assumptions from your experience, outline the main elements of a management-information system for this operation.

III

Professional
Problems
of
Management
Science

13

Modeling

Art and Intuition

Mathematical models play a central role in the work of the management scientist, but his work is by no means limited to model development. The difficulties involved in creating useful mathematical models are, however, sufficiently challenging to warrant some special attention. The process by which an experienced analyst arrives at a model of the management phenomena he is studying is probably best described as *intuitive*. Indeed, the really effective and experienced people in both management and science typically operate in a largely intuitive manner and view with impatience attempts to make their methods explicit. The following chapter deals in more detail with intuition in management; here attention is confined to intuition as it concerns the analyst's model-building efforts. The experienced management scientist may well consider questions about how he selected the variables to be included in the model, how he decided which were to be regarded as random, and so on, as so trivial that they cannot occupy his serious attention or so nontrivial that they cannot be answered. He is perhaps willing to regard the abstraction and translation of a management problem into a scientific problem as an art, in the sense that it must remain largely intuitive. Any set of rules for obtaining models could have only the most limited usefulness at best, and at worst, might seriously impede the development of the required intuition.

If one grants that modeling is and, for greatest effectiveness, probably ought to be, an intuitive process for the experienced, then the interesting question becomes how to develop this intuition. What can be done for the inexperienced person who wishes to progress as quickly as he can toward a high level of intuitive effectiveness in management science? What can be done for the experienced person whose mind "draws a blank" when seeking to model some management problem? Can we say only, "Get more experience for it is the chief source of intuitive development and the only recourse when intuition fails?" The following material seeks to verbalize the process of developing models in a very limited fashion. In attempting to make the process of modeling explicit, it may be reasonable to suppose that one is raising hypotheses about the process and that one is providing a possible target for imitation when intuition is insufficiently developed. It does not appear reasonable, however, to suppose that one could provide a general "kitchen recipe" for making models, nor that one could do very much more than modestly enhance the process of developing intuition. It may well be that intuition or artistic skill is largely the product of imitation and practice, yet this process of development must have a beginning. Experience suggests that this beginning must include more than simply a familiarity with other people's models.

Justification and Discovery

A basic distinction is that between the "context of justification" and the "context of discovery." Management science (and all science) is reported and communicated in the form of a logical reconstruction which aims to provide a justification for the inferences produced. This logical reconstruction has little if anything to do with the psychological process by which the inferences were first obtained. It is the custom in science to report a piece of work by stating the assumptions or premises which determine the model, showing the deductive steps by which the relevant consequences of the model were obtained, and then the orderly steps reporting the design and analysis of the experiment aimed at testing the hypotheses suggested by the consequences of the model. The danger is that, finding little else in the literature of their science than such justification, one may begin to assume that this is also a description of the process of discovery.

The experienced scientist knows that the psychological process is very different, but seldom attempts to verbalize it. One may wonder, however, whether even those with considerable experience do not sometimes practice a little delusion of themselves and their colleagues by tending to read *ad hoc* justifications as descriptions of the context of discovery. One often senses the implication that a writer is saying, "See how logical, how methodical, how brilliantly inevitable was our progress in this study." Since all the writing in a science is likely to be of this sort, one must conclude that experienced persons in a field are not of great help to the inexperienced, so far as the art of modeling is concerned. In fact, the inexperienced may be led seriously astray if they begin to imitate the logical process in seeking to develop their own intuitive ability.

Skill in modeling certainly involves a sensitive and selective perception of management situations. This in turn depends on the sort of conceptual structures one has available with which to bring some order out of the perceptual confusion. Models can play the role of giving structure to experience; thus, studying models is relevant for the development of the "trained observer." Yet one seldom encounters a model which is already available in fully satisfactory form for a given management situation, and the need for creative development or modification is almost universally experienced in management science.

Three Basic Hypotheses

The approach to developing model building skill might be stated in the form of three basic hypotheses. It is of some importance to regard these statements as hypotheses, since no really systematic test of their effectiveness has been made.

   I. The process of model development may be usefully viewed as a process of enrichment or elaboration. One begins with very simple models, quite distinct from reality, and attempts to move in evolutionary fashion toward more elaborate models which more nearly reflect the complexity of the actual management situation.

This seems harmless enough, yet it is of some importance to point it out explicitly to the inexperienced. The attempt to begin immediately with a rather rich model may become a serious source of frustration. Starting with a simpler model gets things moving and thus tends to relieve some of the tension. It does, however, require a certain amount of poise to back off from a complicated problem and begin with a simple conceptual structure. It requires that one deliberately omit and distort certain aspects of the situation and knowingly commit the sin of suppressing difficult considerations.

   II. Analogy or association with previously well-developed logical structures plays an important role in determining the starting point of this process of elaboration or enrichment.

Clearly, one point of studying models is to provide such well-developed logical structures which can be utilized more or less directly as starting points. It must be emphasized, however, that they typically provide only the starting points. When one asks whether a given management situation can be modeled in the framework of linear programming, or waiting-line theory, or inventory theory, what is really meant is whether one of these structures will give a head start in the evolutionary process of obtaining a useful model. Sometimes the search for analogy calls forth broad general structures, such as differential equations or probability theory, sometimes more specific and highly developed structures like waiting-line theory, and sometimes very specific models developed especially for another management problem. Although such analogies are important, this discussion deals with steps to be taken after discovery of such an association or when none appears possible. This is perhaps another way of saying that management science is an emergent science and a long way from handbook engineering which uses "off the shelf" models.

III. The process of elaboration or enrichment involves at least two sorts of looping or alternation procedures:

1. Alternation between modification of the model and confrontation by the data. As each version of the model is tested, a new version is produced which leads in turn to a subsequent test.

2. Alternation between exploration of the deductive tractability of the model and the assumptions which characterize it. If a version of the model is tractable, in the sense of permitting the attainment of the analyst's deductive objectives, he may seek further enrichment or complication of the assumptions. If the model is not tractable or cannot be "solved," he returns to purify and simplify his assumptions.

The importance of the first of these looping procedures is to make clear that a study need not be conceived as one grand test of a single model. Nor need one decide whether to develop the model first or "get the data" first.

The second of these alternations is the central concern of this discussion. Indeed, facility in modeling means to a large extent, the selection and modification of basic assumptions which characterize models. Here again, a certain poise is required in order to work with a variety of sets of assumptions, some of which are more nearly in agreement with the analyst's conception of the management problem, whereas others may be productive of models more tractable from the viewpoint of his deductive abilities. The task is to discover a set of assumptions which are both usefully descriptive of the problem and deductively tractable. Implicit in this sort of proposition is the refusal to resort to simulation until a serious attempt at analysis has been made.

Some Specific Hypotheses

Several specific suggestions might be made which must be regarded as hypotheses in the sense that no claims can really be made as to their general effectiveness. Used in situations where persons are very inexperienced, these suggestions appear to be helpful. At least they seem better than no explicit remarks whatever about procedure, since they do prevent the inexperienced from being completely at a loss about how to respond to the challenge of developing a model. These hypotheses are presented in the context of an example. It is natural to choose an example which furnishes a good illustration of the ideas, but in doing so one once again introduces something of the flavor of an *ad hoc* reconstruction. Clearly, things will not always work out as in the example and thus the suggestions cannot be rigidly interpreted or applied.

Suppose one undertakes to design a transportation system which is to serve a network of terminals on a fixed schedule. The locations of the terminals are known and some data are available or could be obtained on the time pattern or demand for transportation among the terminals. Suppose also that the criterion for a good design involves some measure of service furnished in response to the demands, combined with some measure of the cost of obtaining and operating the equipment to be used in the system. Clearly, considerable effort may be involved in bringing the study to this point of definition, and there are well-known difficulties with making operational the criterion for a good system design. These considerations are suppressed, however, in order to emphasize the model-building aspects of the study. Suppose that it becomes clear to the designer that he may determine the schedule of arrivals and departures to be specified by the timetable and the number of vehicles available for running out the timetable. He may attempt to produce directly a model which will predict the level of service, investment, and operating costs for any choice of timetable and number of vehicles. He may search for analogies to this problem among the well-developed logical structures with which he is familiar. Suppose, however, that this effort is unsuccessful, and that he seeks to factor the system design problem into simpler problems for which models may be more readily obtainable. This is the first suggestion or hypothesis.

1. *Factor the system problem into simpler problems.* In this example, the analyst might decide to consider

   a. The schedule design problem: Given a fixed fleet of vehicles, what schedule of arrivals and departures will give the highest level of service and still be within the capabilities of the available fleet?
   b. The fleet size problem: If a schedule of arrivals and departures is given, what is the minimum fleet size which can accomplish it? (We have already allowed the assumption of homogeneous vehicles to creep in.)

An ideal factoring of the system design problems would yield simpler problems which could be modeled and would subsequently permit easy combination into a system model. When factoring occurs, the result is several problems whose solutions are suboptimal or approximate from the viewpoint of the system model. For the inexperienced, this deliberate setting aside of the ultimate design objectives is often a very difficult step. Having done it, however, one may attack the simpler problems, for example, the fleet size problem.

2. *Establish a clear statement of the deductive objectives.* An essential early step would appear to be the achievement of a clear (but still tentative) statement of the deductive objective of the model. Does one want the model to predict the consequences of various policies? Does one want it to suggest an optimal policy? In the fleet size problem, suppose one takes the deductive objective to be simply the determination of the minimum fleet size which can accomplish a given schedule of arrivals and departures. Such a statement provides the criterion for determining the deductive viability or tractability of the model. Yet in establishing such an objective, one should keep open the possibility that it may prove unachievable, or that different objectives may suggest themselves as the model is developed. The final deductive objective may be foreseen in advance or it may emerge as a surprising result of the study of the model.

3. *Seek analogies.* At this stage, as well as at any other stage in the process, one should seek opportunities to make analogies between the problem at hand and some previously well-developed logical structure. Often these analogies occur as a sort of intuitive leap. Is the problem a linear-programming problem, a queueing problem, or an inventory problem? Is it usefully similar to one which has been modeled by someone else? Note that one should consider the possibility of an analogy even before the problem is very well defined, since analogies may well suggest how the problem might tentatively be made more specific. We will suppose that the fleet-size problem does not yield immediately to this search for analogies and that it becomes necessary to take further steps.

4. *Consider a specific numerical instance of the problem.* This we think is a key step for the inexperienced person. The specification of a simple instance of the problem is often difficult for the beginner, since it represents a retreat (hopefully temporary) from the generality and complexity which he ultimately seeks. The specific example has at least three purposes:

   a. To lead the analyst to make statements about the assumptions which characterize the example. These assumptions may be a useful starting point for achieving greater generality.
   b. If the numerical instance can be "solved" by inspection, then perhaps the process of solution can simply be generalized.
   c. The specific instance provides a workable starting point for establishing a symbolism and giving general expression to some of the obvious things which are noticed in the specific case.

Consider, for example, a network consisting of terminals numbered 1, 2, and 3, which is to be served according to a timetable specified here. The timetable is based on an eight-hour clock and repeats every eight hours.

Departure Times from Terminal

1:   2, 5, 8
2:   1, 3, 7
3:   1, 4, 7

The routings are given as 1 to 2, 2 to 3, 3 to 1; and the running times on these routes are 2 hours, 1 hour, and 2 hours, respectively. This permits construction of the complete timetable:

Terminal 1		*Terminal 2*		*Terminal 3*	
Arrivals	*Departures*	*Arrivals*	*Departures*	*Arrivals*	*Departures*
1	2	2	1	2	1
3	5	4	3	4	4
6	8	7	7	8	7

At this point one might discover by "inspection" or by "trial and error" that this timetable can be run out with a minimum of four vehicles. Perhaps by asking how such a result was obtained and then generalizing, one may find the key to a workable model for the problem. If this fails, however, the example provides a basis for making some explicit statements about the assumptions which it implies:

a. The schedule must be met: No deviations from the specified departure times are permitted.

b. The running times are inclusive, in the sense that they include the times for a vehicle to load and unload.

c. The running times are invariant: The possibility of breakdowns or delays is suppressed, and no uncertainty is explicitly considered.

d. The number of arrivals and departures at each terminal will be equal during each scheduling period.

There may be other assumptions, but these begin to define the sort of problem which has been established. If we fail to achieve the desired result with these assumptions, we can return and modify or relax some of them for another try. In this sense, the assumptions that an analyst states first in his report were probably actually discovered last as he did the work. The task is to discover a set of assumptions which lead to a tractable model, and to do this typically requires a number of attempts.

5. *Establish some symbols.* Perhaps the next step might be to translate the numerical example into symbolic terms. For some reason, this is often a difficult step. One wants to choose symbols which are suggestive of their interpretations and to give careful definitions of each. The beginner often fails here, and carelessness at this point has serious consequences later.

Suppose, for example, we elect the rather conventional double subscript notation. Let

a_{ij} = time of the ith arrival at terminal j
d_{ij} = time of the ith departure from terminal j

Now we are at a crucial point. What to do next? We suggest that, in the absence of any useful insights, one simply write down in symbolic terms some of the obvious things which can be seen in the numerical example. Our hypothesis is that giving expression to the obvious will be highly suggestive in terms of further steps in developing the model.

6. *Write down the obvious.* We have in mind such things as conservation laws, input-output relations, ideas expressed in the assumptions, or the consequences of trivially simple policies. In the fleet-size example, we might simply try to express the basic conservation law which states that the vehicles provided will spend their time either in making runs between terminals or sitting idle while waiting to depart. If we have a fleet of k vehicles available each scheduling period, we provide an input of kT vehicle hours, where T is the length of the period. These vehicle-hours will be devoted to either idleness (let I = total vehicle-hours of idleness) or running (let R = the total vehicle-hours of running). Thus the conservation law is

$$kT = I + R$$

Hopefully, such a simple statement will be suggestive. Perhaps in this case, we notice that R is fixed by the specification of the timetable, and that to minimize k one must minimize I. What can one do to influence the amount of idle time? Since idle time is generated when a vehicle waits at a terminal for its scheduled departure, it must be that the way in which arriving vehicles are assigned to departures will influence idle time. At terminal 1, we might make the following matching of arrivals and departure times

Vehicle arriving at	Departs at	Idle time
1	2	1
3	5	2
6	8	2

This matching generates a total of 5 vehicle-hours of idle time.

Before proceeding, it is worthwhile to notice a very important property of this system. So long as departure times are met, nothing done at one terminal can influence the idle time at the other terminals. This means the system can be "cut," in the sense that we can minimize idle time terminal by terminal, rather than having to consider the entire system at once. In symbolic terms, the idle time at terminal j, I_j, is independent of the idle time at terminal k, I_k, and the idle time for the system is given by

$$I = I_1 + I_2 + I_3$$

The real objective of systems analysis is not simply to study larger and larger problems, but to find ways of "cutting" large problems into small ones, so that the solutions of the small ones can be combined in some easy way to yield solutions for the large ones.

Using the numerical example, one might try some other matchings of arrivals with departures. We notice that, if at any time more departures have been scheduled than there have been arrivals, the excess departures must be made by vehicles kept over from the previous scheduling period. One can easily write out all the possible matchings and note that a matching which keeps no vehicles over from the previous period generates 5 vehicle-hours of idle time, one which keeps 1 vehicle over generates 13 vehicle-hours of idle time, one which keeps 2 over generates 21 vehicle-hours of idle time, and so on. Thus keeping down idle time seems to be associated with keeping down the number of vehicles kept over from the previous period.

Now this same insight can be expressed symbolically:

$$I_j = \sum_i d_{ij} - \sum_i a_{ij} + A_j T$$

Here A_j is the number of vehicles kept over from one scheduling period to the next at terminal j. At this point, the problem is "solved," in the sense that the minimum fleet size will result when the A_j have been minimized. Further examination of the numerical example may suggest that the A_j will be minimized when arriving vehicles are assigned to departures on a first-in-first-out basis. (There may be other policies which are as good, but there are none better than FIFO.)

All that remains is to compute the minimum fleet size. We may again return to the numerical example in order to compute the running time generated by the schedule. Then, using our symbolism, we might express this computation as

$$R = \sum_i \sum_j a_{ij} - \sum_i \sum_j d_{ij} + BT$$

thus

$$k = \sum_j A_j + B$$

Thus we can suggest: "Find the minimum number of vehicles which must be kept over at each terminal using a FIFO assignment policy. Add to the sum of these minima the number of vehicles which are on route at the end of a scheduling period, and the result will be the minimum fleet size."

If we had not been successful, then perhaps the next step would have been to return to the numerical example or to the assumptions, looking for ways to simplify and try again. As it is, we might wish to go on toward enriching or complicating the model.

7. *If a tractable model is obtained, enrich it. Otherwise, simplify.* One might, in our example, wish to consider different types of vehicles, running times which are random variables, schedules which change from period to period, breakdown and maintenance time for the vehicles, and so on.

Generally speaking, one may simplify by

> making variables into constants
> eliminating variables
> using linear relations
> adding stronger assumptions and restrictions
> suppressing randomness

Enrichment may involve just the opposite sort of modification.

Other Sources of Modeling Skill

Sensitivity to certain other ideas also appears to be associated with achieving facility in modeling. For example, it is obviously important to feel ease with mathematics. One reason for studying the advanced mathematics that will probably not be "useful," is to achieve a more comfortable and relaxed grasp of the less advanced mathematics which is likely to be used. Some appreciation of the various purposes which models may serve is helpful. Illustrating uses of models—to give quantitative predictions, to give qualitative predictions, as data collection plans, as research plans, as perceptual sensitizers, as devices for structuring knowledge, and so on—tends to broaden one's view of the sorts of models which are worth developing and the different directions their development might take.

Similarly, attempts to develop a consciousness of some of the characteristics of models appears helpful. Beyond the rough description of a model as "simple" or "complex," one might usefully consider:

> a. Relatedness: How many previously known theorems or results does the model bring to bear upon the problem?

> b. Transparency: How obvious is the interpretation of the model? How immediate is its intuitive confirmation?

> c. Robustness: How sensitive is the model to changes in the assumptions which characterize it?

d. Fertility: How rich is the variety of deductive consequences which the model produces?

e. Ease of enrichment: What difficulties are presented by attempts to enrich and elaborate the model in various directions?

The test of such hypotheses as these is, of course, whether they appear to enhance one's model-building skills. In trying them out, however, it is important to undertake model-building efforts outside any context which prejudices the result in an obvious way. Problems presented at the end of an extended discussion of some particular logical structure do not offer the same kind of challenge as problems encountered outside any such context. Similarly, exercises requiring one to substitute numbers in previously developed models may help to bring familiarity with the models, but they do not help to develop model-creating ability. One must look at actual management situations which do not have these unrealistic aspects.

14

Intuition
in Management
and Science

Explicitness in Management

Our proposals for making opinions and preferences explicit may be met by the insistent criticism that all of this is unrealistic. People, some critics will assert, are not given to such precise thought nor do they develop and discipline their conceptions sufficiently to have such clear preferences and opinions. This kind of objection may be extended in the form of claims that management is not "scientific" and cannot become so. This chapter seeks some insight into these objections so that, by understanding them, we may avoid some of the antagonisms to which they may possibly contribute.

It is often difficult to see clearly what people mean when they reject the role of science in management in this way. An experienced and successful manager might admit in moments of candor that his rejection could be expressed somewhat differently: "I find it impossible," he might say, "to verbalize the mental processes I use in reaching a decision." He might be willing to describe his thought processes as judgmental, implicit, artistic, subconscious, or intuitive.

Management scientists on the other hand, giving great attention to explicitness and operationality of expression, seem to be saying to the manager, "This inability to verbalize is a matter about which no one can be proud." Indeed, the management scientist seems to attack the unverbalized decision process with a confidence that he will soon replace all or part of it and, in doing so, clearly demonstrate its ineffectiveness.

If we describe the manager's decision process, which he finds great difficulty in verbalizing, as intuitive, then we might guess that the intelligent and experienced manager finds intuition:

1. Trustworthy: His intuitions have been developed and tested over a considerable period of experience and generally seem to give good results.

2. Habitual: He has had little else on which to rely and thus has come to regard his intuition as a primary asset.

3. Satisfying: It seems to utilize his unique sensitivity to the decision situation. It is private, mysterious, and a distinction won through long experience.

4. Well adapted to the context of affairs: It permits quick decisions in the face of limited information. It can be made to meet the constraints of time, cost, and knowledge imposed by his environment.

The manager may well see the explicitness sought by the management scientist as untrustworthy, ill adapted to the context of affairs, impossible in view of what he knows of the end products of science, and perhaps most importantly, unnecessary.

For his part, the management scientist emphasizes the explicit, logical end results of his craft. He may suppress the role of intuition in what he does, since;

1. The function of intuition and its development may have been seriously neglected in his education.

2. Lacking the manager's intuitive skill in management problems, he emphasizes other approaches to them.

3. The tradition of scientific communication limits it to the justification of conclusions rather than their discovery.

These somewhat overdrawn stereotypes may serve to dramatize the problem of the relevance of management science for management. We seek here some clarification of the notion of intuition, its development, and its role in this problem of relevance.

Defining Intuitive Behavior

The difficulty of achieving a useful definition of intuition is that of passing from an introspective to a behavioral definition. By *intuitive thinking*, one may mean that kind of thinking which the subject cannot verbalize. Intuition suggests the immediate leap to a decision rather than a process involving careful, well-defined, conscious steps. The intuitive thinker cannot report what aspects of the situation his perceptual processes have selected, what portion of the contents of his memory he is using, nor what inferential methods lead him from these inputs to a decision. He responds somehow to a total conception of the problem, his thoughts moving in seemingly illogical fashion through all kinds of short cuts to a decision. The mode of thought is obscure, inarticulate, and scarcely formulated. However satisfying this way of expressing the idea of intuition may be, it is subject to some familiar difficulties in application.

Applied to management, this introspective view of intuition suggests the following concerns:

1. Inability to verbalize may be a matter of inadequate language. How, for example, can the manager express his feelings of uncertainty? This leads one to the problem of the relation between thought and language. Does language determine thought or does it only express thought?

2. Is inability to verbalize largely a matter of a manager's characteristic dislike of introspection, his tendency to concentrate on future actions rather than past thoughts, and a distrust of explicitness which suggests to him the inflexibility of fixed rules for decision making?

3. Being unable to verbalize is clearly different from being unwilling to do so. In application, the manager may choose not to verbalize. Indeed, he may more or less consciously make pseudo verbalizations which serve his own purposes in the organizational context. He may offer socially approved reconstructions of his decision process: ("See how logical I am.") He may choose verbalizations designed to influence those who must accept and participate in the consequences of his decision.

Perhaps a more useful and interesting way to define intuition would be in terms of some observable behavior on the part of the manager. In an attempt to do this, we consider the key transaction of delegation and propose the following:

A decision maker's behavior is said to be *nonintuitive* with respect to a particular decision if there exists a verbalization, *x*, which he is willing to use as the basis for delegating the decision to a recipient, *y*.

The concept of *verbalization* is taken here to include not only verbal descriptions of whatever completeness and operationality, but also mathematical models, computer programs, and so on. Many sorts of recipients might be envisioned, from experienced executives to clerks and computers. The definition does not require the verbalization to have been produced by the decision maker's own introspective reports. It may well have been suggested by another manager or result from the work of the management science staff. Nonintuitivity is defined relative to *x*, *y* pairs and thus very much relative to the organizational context in which the decision maker finds himself. There may be several x, y pairs for which he is willing to delegate. For a given verbalization, x, some recipients will be satisfactory to the decision maker, and some will not, and so on.

Willingness implies that, given a choice to delegate or not, the decision maker would choose the former. If the decision as to whether A will delegate a certain decision is made by B, then the fact of delegation is not definitive of A's behavior. In such a case, we can inquire only what A would do in the face of a given x, y pair if he had a choice. If the verbalization, x, is empty, consisting of no verbalization at all, then the only acceptable recipient may well be the decision maker himself or someone whose intuitive abilities he finds extremely trustworthy. In the latter case, the decision maker's behavior is nonintuitive, in the sense that, when asked to verbalize his decision process, he says simply, "I ask the recipient whom I trust fully." If there exists a verbalization which a decision maker is willing to use as a basis of delegating the decision to himself, and the verbalization is not empty, then we may think of him as modifying his own modes of thought, or learning.

The more common situation perhaps, is, the delegation of parts of a decision, such as collecting some of the input data or computing some phases of the inferential process. Clearly, the definition may be applied to these cases, indicating aspects of the decision which are nonintuitive and those which remain intuitive.

From this viewpoint, the task of the management scientist is to discover x, y pairs for which the decision maker is willing to delegate, such that delegation will result in a net gain for the organization. The delegation (or implementation) decision itself may, of course, be considered from the viewpoint of the definition. If a verbalization has been produced by the management scientist, the decision maker will typically prefer to keep intuitive the choice between willingness or unwillingness to accept it as a basis for delegation. The management scientist would find the task of implementation somewhat easier if there existed a verbalization of the delegation decision which made it at least partly nonintuitive. Thus he tries to offer verbalizations, such as, "Delegation will take place for any x, y pair which appears to result in an increase in profit for the firm," hoping that the manager will accept this verbalization of the delegation decision. The manager, for his part replies, "The way in which you predict profit increases yields a useful input to my delegation decision, but there is more to it than that." Thus the delegation decision remains at least partly intuitive.

It may be worth emphasizing that, in looking for x, y pairs which will result in delegations yielding a net gain for the firm, one is not simply looking for better decisions than the manager himself may be making intuitively. Indeed, many efforts seem to result in verbalizations which in conjunction with a given recipient, result in poorer decisions. If, however, the recipient can produce these poorer decisions at a cost sufficiently low to offset the decline in the effectiveness of the decisions themselves, then, of course, a net gain results.

In computing the net gain one also wishes to consider the effects of delegation upon the decision maker himself. Does the delegation permit him more time for the intuitive decisions which he must continue to make? Does the delegation permit him to become the recipient of other decisions which he is able to carry out at a net gain, and so on? In other words, the task of discovering x, y pairs is not one of "beating the manager at his own game," but requires some estimate of the organizational or system-wide implications of the proposed delegation. Obviously, managers will seek opportunities to delegate, or to make their behavior nonintuitive. Not only do they typically share in the rewards which result from the improved performance in the decisions which they determine, but they also increase their own credibility as recipients for other delegations and thus promotions. Management science is clearly only one source of acceptable x, y pairs. The job of a manager is essentially that of a teacher, attempting to produce acceptable verbalizations for the available recipients or attempting to mold potential recipients toward acceptability in the light of available verbalizations. The latter case in which the available verbalizations are appropriate only for recipients who themselves have considerable intuitive skill is an interesting one. It confronts the teacher-manager with the old and difficult problem of how to develop the intuition of his student-recipients. To this problem we shall shortly return.

Using this definition, we may speak of a given manager's method of handling a given decision intuitive or not, relative to a specified x, y pair. Although it is now difficult to attach interesting meanings to generalizations, such as "Management is highly intuitive," it is clear that developing effective intuitive modes of thought is important in the development of managers. Our definition of intuitive behavior applies equally to scientists who reach conclusions by intuitive leaps. They find it difficult to verbalize about the process of discovery, but their training is designed to make them skillful at justifying their conclusions. The justification becomes acceptable to the scientist when it meets his criteria of operationality, logical consistency, and so on. For the scientist, *delegation* is the attempt to give a verbalization which will permit other scientists to replicate and confirm his conclusions. Thus in both management and science considerable importance attaches to effective intuitive behavior. It is a part of "good management" and a part of "good science."

Relevance

The basic concern of the management scientist is making his contribution relevant, in the sense of having some useful impact on the way his firm is managed. Chapter 15 deals with some hypotheses about the problem of implementing this contribution in an organizational context. Here we consider the problem of relevance and its relation to the intuitive content of a manager's decision process. For ease of discussion the term *analysis* is used to refer to the sort of explicit, logical verbalization produced by management science. We take the following to be a key hypothesis.

> The willingness of a manager to accept an analytic verbalization as a basis for delegation is enhanced if he understands that the roles of analysis and intuition are the same in science as in management.

We first attempt to suggest the sort of experiment which might be used to operationalize the concept of understanding in this hypothesis and then offer some speculations about why one might expect it to be confirmed.

As suggested in earlier chapters, the role of analysis is twofold:

1. Analysis is used to check the logical consistency and empirical validity of decisions reached by intuitive means.

2. In situations where intuition fails, analysis extends the range of thought.

These are, in admittedly oversimplified terms, the functions of analysis for the scientist. The problem is, however, to convince the manager with a well-developed intuitive style that analysis may serve him in the same ways. To do this, we might imagine involving the manager in a series of experiments. Whether these experiments would deliberately and methodically be carried out in a given situation may be doubtful, but they may indicate a broad strategy for approaching the sort of understanding we have in mind.

Perhaps the first type of experiment would concern relatively simple decision situations in which it was possible to obtain an analytic verbalization and in which he had intuitions which had been well developed and tested by experience. The experiment would aim to demonstrate that analysis and intuition both led to the same decision. The point would be to suggest that analysis can be "trusted" in cases where the manager is in a position to judge its validity, without any implied criticism of the effectiveness of intuition.

The next set of experiments might move to situations where again analysis was possible, but the manager was less confident of his intuitive decisions. In some such situations, the analysis might serve to confirm and strengthen his intuitions; in others, it might challenge and correct them. Finally, one might progress to situations in which intuition fails at the outset, but in which analytic verbalizations are possible. Hopefully, the verbalizations could be made sufficiently transparent as to lead the manager toward an ultimate intuitive confirmation of the analytic results. The aim of all this is to create a climate of trust and acceptance for the results of analysis in situations where intuitive confirmation is extremely difficult, if not possible, for the person who does not go through the detailed steps of the analysis.

During such a series of experiments, it would be important to seek ways of sensitizing the manager to some of the possible interpretations of what is happening. For example,

1. When analysis and intuition disagree, the first hypothesis may well be that the analysis is imperfect. The manager should get some feeling of the tentative and open nature of a management scientist's verbalizations.

2. When analysis does suggest modifications of intuition, some reflection on the general shortcomings of human thought may serve both to depersonalize the corrections and to place the manager on his guard against some of the common difficulties. For example, there are the problems of the perceptual and cognitive distortion introduced by need-determined thinking and socially shared errors. The capacity of the mind is limited, rationality is bounded, distractions interfere, critical incidents are overweighted, and so on.

3. When intuition fails to lead to an acceptable decision, one may resort to rules of thumb. ("It is our policy to spend x per cent of our net on R and D.") Analysis, however, has certain advantages over such rules. The failure of intuition may be the result of the complexity of the decision, of the uncertainties involved, or of the value conflicts which it presents. Analysis has a therapeutic function of permitting the manager to express uncertainty, suggesting how much uncertainty might reasonably be tolerated, making the value conflicts explicit, and bringing acceptance of the necessity of sacrificing some ends in order to gain others. The therapeutic effects of analysis in reducing conflict and anxiety are seldom emphasized but may well be of considerable importance in understanding the relevance of management science.

Developing Intuition

Delegation aims at freeing the manager to deal intuitively with decisions which are difficult to verbalize, yet little is known about how the manager can increase his ability to respond to this opportunity. The effective management scientist must, like the manager, be able to deal intuitively with management problems. Unlike the manager, however, the management scientist must *also* have an intuitive grasp of his own tools of analysis. His craft requires him to deal intuitively with solving an equation, raising hypotheses out of the data, or producing the beginnings of a model. For both, however, effective intuition is synonymous with "art." There is, of course, the problem of selecting people who can rapidly develop effective intuitive skills. Does good intuitive performance on one class of decisions correlate with good performance on another? Does the ability to verbalize extensively indicate latent intuitive abilities? We will consider, however, the educational form of the problem; that is, how to enhance the intuitive behavior that is important in both management and management science. There are several basic educational hypotheses regarding intuitive skill.

1. The "School of Hard Knocks" Hypothesis:

The objective of education is primarily to enhance delegation. Its function is to provide the language, the methods of structuring decisions, and the verbalizations which offer possible bases for delegation. Effective intuition is the result of experience and practice, tested in the context of affairs. It is not possible to do very much to develop it in a formal educational environment.

2. The "Simulated Experience" Hypothesis:

Effective intuitive behavior can be developed through experience, practice, and imitation. Further, this can be begun in the educational process. For management decisions, such things as cases, simulations, or games may be used as opportunities which encourage the emergence of intuitive skill. An interesting question is whether verbalizations following these simulated experiences do provide the sort of feedback which enhances the development of intuition. There are two hypotheses of interest here:

a. Those who have or are developing good intuitive skills should not be forced to verbalize very much. Verbalization leads to a degradation in intuitive effectiveness. This is a concern that pervades much of management science. Is there a danger of destroying some of the intuitive effectiveness of the experienced decision maker by encouraging him to verbalize?

b. Verbalizations, including the analytical ones of management science, do to some degree become internalized and thus improve intuitive performance. This leads to a third hypothesis.

3. The "Reason Improves Intuition" Hypothesis:

Verbalizations themselves somehow lead to intuitive skills, and thus, teaching them is really a way of developing intuition. Discussing reasonable solutions to management problems and logical solutions to scientific problems leads ultimately to the internalization of these methods. In this view, studying the analytical aspects of management science is a means of improving the intuitive performance of both managers and management scientists.

4. The "Associated Variable" Hypothesis:

Effective intuitive behavior is most often found among persons who are self-confident, tolerant of ambiguity, relaxed in the face of pressures, and so on. These people see themselves as being free of conventional rules, explicit policies, or theories. They function most effectively in situations where intuitive behavior is socially acceptable and they are not frequently challenged to produce supporting verbalizations. The function of education is to encourage the development of whatever personal characteristics and organizational conditions are associated with the flourishing of intuitive skill.

These hypotheses are neither exclusive nor exhaustive. There may well be some truth in each of them. They appear difficult to test and we cannot wait until they are tested. They are of some use, however, if they emphasize the points that intuition and analysis both must be developed in order to achieve effective management and effective management science. A balanced view is essential if management scientists are to have any significant impact on the way in which management decisions are made.

15

Implementation

Strategies for Change

Translating the work of the management scientist into
action implies change in the firm's management methods,
and change provokes resistance on the part of those
touched by it. The problem of implementing management science results thus deserves some careful attention
if improvements in the firm's operations are actually to
be realized. It is easy to dispatch the subject by saying
that recommendations must be "sold" to management
and that the way this is done depends largely on the
personalities of those involved. We attempt in this chapter to go somewhat beyond this, looking for some useful
generalizations which will further sensitize the management scientist to his role in the ongoing affairs of the
firm. The more or less informal evidence available on
the problem of implementation suggests that many managements will readily and intelligently accept the kind of
assistance that management science offers. One would
expect this to occur even more frequently in the future.
As more managers appear who are trained in science or
engineering, as management science becomes a widely
established aspect of management education, and as firms
become aware of the accumulating record of accomplish-
ment in this field, the climate of intelligent utilization
will continue to improve. In a significant number of large
firms, this kind of undertaking is firmly established and
the contributions of management science are routinely
sought. Our attention, however, must be directed to
those situations in which such favorable conditions have
not yet developed. One may expect difficulties where

there have been frustrating experiences with the analysis of management problems, where managers have little appreciation for what can realistically be expected from management science, and where people feel particularly threatened by the possible results of such efforts. How can the management scientist be more effective under such conditions? We offer first the hypothesis that "selling" in the usual sense is perhaps not a useful strategy.

Selling

The casual analogy which suggests that management science ought to be "sold" in the tradition of the hard sell is an unfortunate one. The high-pressure "pitch" is designed to point out to the customer, not the qualities of the product that would help him to evaluate it himself, but rather what the product will do for him. It focuses on how much better off the potential consumer would be and attempts to take its force from the fluency and seeming authority of the "salesman." In the management science context, this may mean making advance promises about the results of research, suppressing the considerable uncertainty about what sort of a contribution will result, and rousing more or less unrealistic expectations in the minds of managers.

The salesman may try to create the impression that he is an "expert," knowing what needs to be done in the firm, and possessed of mysterious specialized knowledge which makes him uniquely qualified to "straighten things out." Frequent use of technical jargon and casual references to the omnipotence of science are supposed to support this image. The implication is clear that the problems of management will be "masterminded" and the results are to be accepted unquestioningly like a doctor's prescription.

Clearly this approach involves little attempt to understand and utilize the management experience available to the firm. It disregards the facts: evolutionary changes in people's thinking are far easier to bring about than revolutionary ones. The hard sell appears often to create more resistance than acceptance. It does not allow time for managers to absorb new ideas. It provokes efforts to "shoot down" the final recommendations instead of efforts to contribute constructively to them. It assumes that managers can be sold, when in fact they must decide to buy. It challenges the competence of managers in their own profession and leads to an immediate rejection of the management scientist as an "expert" who can advise them in this area. If one accepts these hypotheses about selling, one must look elsewhere for effective strategies.

Involvement

We offer as an alternative hypothesis, a strategy which is far more difficult for the manager and for the analyst, yet the indications of its success appear to justify the additional effort. This strategy suggests that managers no longer occupy the role of simple users of the results of management science, but rather become directly involved in its efforts. This broad kind of strategy, we call *involvement*. Involvement of the manager in the work of the management science staff should ideally begin very early in any study and continue right through to the adoption of its results. If the manager can be persuaded to devote sufficient time to making his experience available to the staff and is shown that this then becomes a significant element of the study, there should be little need for "selling" when the final results emerge. The essence of involvement is management participation and understanding on a continuous basis throughout the progress of a study. It does not require managers to become contributors to the work of mathematical analysis, data collection, or computer programming. It does mean, however, that management cultivate a sufficient understanding of the uses and limitations of such things, so that they become intelligent evaluators of the end products.

Before any set of recommendations can be actually launched into the experimental stage, many persons in the firm must come to accept them. As many of these people as possible ought ideally to become involved with the staff work as it progresses. Each one then, having contributed something to the work, feels a familiarity and an identification with the results that greatly reduces the difficulty of ultimate implementation. All this is clearly not easy. Many managers will expect the staff to relieve them of problems which they are too busy to consider. The work of the staff must compete with many other matters for the manager's attention. The greater the pressure of immediate problems, the greater his tendency to postpone lengthy staff conferences, whose results are likely to appear only in the somewhat distant future. Yet there are indications that some considerable effort is justified to establish such a relationship. Experience suggests that the following effects support the strategy of involvement:

1. The relationship between the staff and management is not typically that of doctor and patient. A manager is unlikely to accept recommendations in his area of professional competence unless they agree with his intuition, contain his own reasoning, and utilize his past experience. Unquestioning acceptance of advice is not to be expected.

2. It is important early in the evolution of a staff effort to create realistic expectations on the part of managers as to what may be the results. One must begin as soon as possible to develop a readiness for the final recommendations. The manager must be clear about the intentions of the staff and the cost of their efforts. As the work begins, it may be well to suggest what may be expected in very conservative terms, permitting the manager to discover for himself the full range of possibilities about what may be accomplished.

3. To use management science intelligently, managers must understand the meaning of consistent decision and the ways in which their own opinions and preferences imply the results of any analysis. They must know when to modify and when to ignore the outputs of the management-information system. Involvement appears to be a particularly effective way for them to achieve these ends.

4. Managers should have some appreciation for the view that management and science are both experimental processes. They should be clear, as they begin to implement the results of a study, that these results are based upon abstractions. Assumptions and simplifications are involved; thus there is a residue of uncertainty surrounding even the most highly developed predictions of policy consequences. Implementation is best regarded as an experiment, not a vindication of one or another point of view.

5. The long-run aim of management science is gradually to sensitize managers to the nature of their organizations, to contribute a little at a time to making problems explicit, and to guide the evolution from casual experience toward careful experiment. In an important sense the role of the staff is educational more than it is one of problem solving. Involvement may well be the most effective means of achieving such long-term objectives.

6. Nothing seems more wasteful than analysis of a management problem which neglects the long experience and rich insights which managers themselves might bring to bear on it. The staff may well suppress their own opinions and exhibit some genuine humility in order to tap this most valuable resource.

7. Involvement suggests considerable communication between staff and management. The staff will thus come to rely primarily on informal sorts of communications. Formal proposals and reports may occur rather infrequently.

8. As work on a particular problem moves along, informal reports may be used effectively to keep up interest. All those who may ultimately be touched by the results may be given opportunities to learn what is going on. The gradual assimilation of the work of the staff is far more effective than sudden revelations. If the outcomes are quite surprising, it may be well to proceed more slowly than would otherwise be the case. Keeping everyone informed as data and analysis become available, allows them to foresee and verbalize the conclusions for themselves. This is likely to be far more effective than conclusions drawn and announced by the staff.

9. In this spirit, the staff may well let management make its own interpretation of the data which emerge. It is well to give managers time

to turn the information over in their minds, exploring its possible meanings, rather than supplying an interpretation on a take-it-or-leave-it basis.

10. Involvement means that, to some extent, the staff must be willing to relinquish credit for its work, freely acknowledging the contributions of many members of the organization. This in itself may promote a significant measure of acceptance. For the staff, there is often some conflict between doing an effective job and getting public recognition for it.

11. Resistance to staff work is nearly always present and will come out sooner or later. It is useful to get it out early, face it frankly, and then get on with the job.

12. The staff will need the support and authority of top management to obtain access to certain kinds of data and the cooperation of various people. This formal authority should be used as little as possible, since it is often a source of antagonism. Involvement may provide the sorts of relationships which will make the overt use of formal authority unnecessary.

However important one believes involvement to be, it is often difficult to achieve. As we have noted several times, a fundamental task of management science is to show the manager what might be expected if he did invest the time and effort to become involved.

Management's Criteria

For the management scientist to work effectively within an organization, a sensitivity to his impact on others in the organization may be most useful. To achieve anything like the sort of involvement of management just suggested, a special awareness of how managers evaluate staff work and the uses they may make of it, appears to be important. We turn now to these matters and are careful to insist that what can be said is in the form of *hypotheses*. Universal truths about how managers judge the recommendations made by their staffs are simply not available. Hypotheses, however, are valuable in that they alert us to what may possibly be found in any given situation.

It is certainly a platitude that management will evaluate any suggestion made by the staff in the light of common sense and intuition. If managers can be convinced that a trial implementation of any management-information system design is warranted, then the system will certainly be judged by its results. We hypothesize, however, that in addition to these obvious criteria (and sometimes instead of them) other bases for evaluation appear. We have insisted, for example, that uncertainty reduction is a fundamental objective of this kind of work. We may actually find, however, that a manager experiences greater, rather than less uncertainty. The mechanisms by which this occurs may well include

1. It is the very nature of management science to state as explicitly as possible all the assumptions involved in a study and all the reservations and limitations which attach to its conclusions. The manager, hoping for a simple direct guide to action, may well be disappointed.

2. As one makes management problems explicit, they appear more complex than when they were considered on an intuitive basis.

3. We hope to develop the attitude that management and science are both experimental undertakings; in doing this, we often disillusion those who have sought clear and resolute indication of the best thing to do.

4. Our analysis tends to destroy whatever illusions of certainty or "rules of thumb" a manager may have adopted to deal with a complicated problem. We raise all sorts of doubts which may previously have been suppressed.

Thus it is not especially surprising to find a manager regarding the work of the staff as excessively "theoretical," given to unnecessarily complicating his work, and likely to be more challenging than supporting of his convictions. Still other criteria seem to play more or less central roles in the reactions of managers to staff work.

1. The age, experience, and education of the staff members themselves are of some relevance. A manager may not feel competent to judge analytical work, but he does have some pride in his ability to judge people. Thus there is always some difficulty in separating the qualities of the work from the qualities of those who produce and present it.

2. The opinions of other managers, particularly those who are respected and successful, may be very influential.

3. It is common to find a manager who is highly sensitized to the kind of thing his superiors will readily accept and the sorts of actions toward which they are predisposed. Even though a manager may have full authority to act himself, there is inevitably a time when his results are examined by those above him and he must defend his decision.

4. Managers are seldom interested in being the first (or the last) to try something new. They may test the recommendations of the staff in terms of what others in their industry are doing. This is particularly true of those who judge their own effectiveness by the performance of their competitors.

5. A variety of seemingly foolish criteria may enter. For example, a study may be judged by how much it cost, how much computer time was

consumed, how many college professors were called in as consultants, and so on. Although these things may seem only indirectly related to the usefulness of the results, such considerations are often of some importance to the manager with a limited grasp of what is actually involved in the work at hand.

6. Is it possible for the manager readily to assimilate the conclusions of the staff into his own conceptualization of the situation? If one acknowledges that the work of the staff must be used reasonably and not blindly, then the ability of the manager to make it a part of his own thinking is crucial.

7. Management will be sensitive as well to the agreement between the conclusions of a staff study and positions they have taken previously. Does the study suggest the sort of thing that is "done" in the firm, in the sense of being compatible with some general philosophy of management methods which has grown up?

8. A manager, intimately acquainted with the complexities of his own firm but less so with those of other firms, finds it natural to say, "That may be fine in some other company, but of course our business is different." Thus it is not at all clear to management that techniques which have worked in one firm will work in another.

It would be most useful, of course, if the work of the staff could be the subject of an economic analysis of the sort applied to so many other things bought by the firm. The manager would like to subject the purchase of staff contributions, like the purchase of a machine, to the test of subtracting expense from income. It is difficult to do this, however, simply because it is difficult to associate directly the things that happen in the firm with the work of the staff. It is often impossible to tell exactly (or even approximately) what the impact of the particular aspect of a management-information system has been. Is it true that management does what it is doing because of the staff study, or did the study merely confirm what was intended in any case? Especially if one looks at the long-run effects of management science, economic evaluation seems almost hopeless. Thus it is rather rare that a conventional economic demonstration can give the manager his most familiar grounds for evaluating management science.

Uses of the Management Science Staff

Although the basic objective of the staff may be to design and implement a more effective management-information system, it is well to be aware of the possibility that the staff may be directly or indirectly, deliberately or accidentally, employed for other purposes. Without suggesting anything about the appropriateness of these other purposes in particular situations, we offer the following hypotheses which attempt to identify some of them.

Staff studies have a long history as "impartial arbitrators" of intraorganizational conflicts, particularly conflicts which cut across established lines of authority. Management science has played a role in many firms which permitted it to contribute to resolving decision-making conflicts among the production, sales, and finance functions. Studies have been carried out which attempted to relate the actions of all three to the over-all objectives of the firm. Obviously, to remain effective in this role, the staff must be able to detach itself from the influence of those who have special interests in the outcomes of such organizational conflicts.

Managers have sometimes used the staff as scapegoats when programs do not succeed. In some cases, this is clearly deserved; in others, the impression is that managers take the credit for successful programs while shifting responsibility for the failures to the staff. When a manager must implement a personally distasteful decision, he may well rationalize it to others by tracing the necessity for it to the work of the staff.

When a manager is subjected to strong pressures for immediate action, he may find it useful to relieve himself of some of this by transferring the problem to the staff. He may then report that he is postponing action on a problem until he receives the staff study, a plausible and sometimes legitimate explanation for the delay.

The staff may find itself being used as a tool for carrying out what are essentially supervisory functions. The manager may expect the staff to act as an additional channel of communication to keep him informed of what is going on in his organization. This sort of activity soon leads those at the operating levels to regard staff people as spies from top management, making it almost impossible for the staff to function in its intended manner. The staff may also be used to carry out the decisions made by management and may come to be regarded as having the authority of those managers to whom they are attached. Management may well condone this ascription of authority as long as it suits their purposes.

This is related to the particularly troublesome tendency of managements to make decisions first and then look to the staff to produce justifications for these decisions. The problems presented to the staff may be limited to finding methods of carrying out decisions previously made or trying to rescue the organization from previous commitments made without staff assistance.

Fortunately, these and other similar uses of staff efforts seem to occur rather infrequently. When they do arise, however, they are likely to present the staff with something of a dilemma, for they must often chose between effective work toward their basic objective and satisfying management demands to perform these other functions. Most important is a sensitivity to these possibilities so that they can be met when they first emerge and before the position and reputation of management science in the firm is seriously impaired.

Linear Normal Loss Integrals

If x is a normally distributed random variable, then the expression

$$L(k) = \int_{x=k}^{\infty} (x - k) f_N(x)\, dx$$

is called a linear normal loss integral. We define the standard normal variable z as

$$z = \frac{x - E(x)}{SD(x)}$$

or $x = z\, SD(x) + E(x)$. Substituting in the expression for $L(k)$ leads to

$$L(k) = SD(x) \int_{z=(k-E(x))/SD(x)}^{\infty} \left(z - \frac{k - E(x)}{SD(x)}\right) f_N(z)\, dz$$

This may be written simply as

$$L(k) = SD(x)\, L\left(\frac{k - E(x)}{SD(x)}\right)$$

The quantity

$$L\left(\frac{k - E(x)}{SD(x)}\right) = L_N(z_k)$$

is called the *unit normal loss integral* and is tabulated in Appendix B. The table contains only positive values of z_k, but negative values may be handled using the relation

$$L_N(-z_k) = z_k + L_N(z_k)$$

Ordinary tables of the unit normal distribution may be used to compute the unit normal loss integral by utilizing the expression

$$L_N(z_k) = f_N(z_k) - z_k(1 - F_N(z_k))$$

where $f_N(z_k)$ = unit normal probability distribution

$F_N(z_k)$ = cumulative unit normal distribution

For example, if $z_k = 1.0$

$$L_N(1.0) = .0833 = (f_N(1.0) = .2420) - (1.0)(1 - F_N(1.0) = .1587)$$

We also need the value of the integral

$$L'_N(z_k) = -\int_{z=-\infty}^{-z_k} (z - z_k) f_N(z) \, dz = \int_{z=-\infty}^{z_k} (z_k - z) f_N(z) \, dz = L_N(z_k)$$

Thus we may use the table in this case as well.

As an example of these methods, consider the case of the manager who will undertake a business venture if its expected profit is positive. Taking the profit from the venture to be the basic random variable, suppose the manager to be uncertain about the expected profit, but willing to behave as if the variance of profit were known. Based on his prior opinion, his expected profit will be

$$\max (m_{pr}, 0)$$

If additional information is obtainable, then one may be interested in computing

$$\text{EVSI} = \int_{m_{po}=0}^{\infty} m_{po} \, \text{PR}(m_{po}) \, dm_{po} - \max (m_{pr}, 0)$$

If the prior expected profit is negative, then the second term becomes 0 and.

$$\text{EVSI} = \text{SD}(m_{po}) \, L_N(z_0)$$

where
$$z_0 = \frac{0 - E(m_{po})}{\text{SD}(m_{po})} = \frac{|m_{pr}|}{\text{SD}(m_{po})}$$

If, however, the prior expected profit is positive, we have

$$\text{EVSI} = \int_{m_{po}=0}^{\infty} m_{po} \, \text{PR}(m_{po}) \, dm_{po} - m_{pr}$$

Recalling that $m_{pr} = E(m_{po})$, we obtain

$$\text{EVSI} = \int_{m_{po}=0}^{\infty} m_{po} \, \text{PR}(m_{po}) \, dm_{po} - \int_{m_{po}=-\infty}^{\infty} m_{po} \, \text{PR}(m_{po}) \, dm_{po}$$

$$= -\int_{m_{po}=-\infty}^{0} m_{po} \, \text{PR}(m_{po}) \, dm_{po} = \text{SD}(m_{po}) \, L'_N(z_0) = \text{SD}(m_{po}) \, L_N(z_0)$$

Thus we have the same expression for EVSI whether the prior expected profit is positive or negative.

Table
of the Linear
Normal Loss Integral

z_k	.00	.01	.02	.03	.04	.05	.06	.07	.08	.09
.0	.3989	.3940	.3890	.3841	.3793	.3744	.3697	.3649	.3602	.3556
.1	.3509	.3464	.3418	.3373	.3328	.3284	.3240	.3197	.3154	.3111
.2	.3069	.3027	.2986	.2944	.2904	.2863	.2824	.2784	.2745	.2706
.3	.2668	.2630	.2592	.2555	.2518	.2481	.2445	.2409	.2374	.2339
.4	.2304	.2270	.2236	.2203	.2169	.2137	.2104	.2072	.2040	.2009
.5	.1978	.1947	.1917	.1887	.1857	.1828	.1799	.1771	.1742	.1714
.6	.1687	.1659	.1633	.1606	.1580	.1554	.1528	.1503	.1478	.1453
.7	.1429	.1405	.1381	.1358	.1334	.1312	.1289	.1267	.1245	.1223
.8	.1202	.1181	.1160	.1140	.1120	.1100	.1080	.1061	.1042	.1023
.9	.1004	.09860	.09680	.09503	.09328	.09156	.08986	.08819	.08654	.08491
1.0	.08332	.08174	.08019	.07866	.07716	.07568	.07422	.07279	.07138	.06999
1.1	.06862	.06727	.06595	.06465	.06336	.06210	.06086	.05964	.05844	.05726
1.2	.05610	.05496	.05384	.05274	.05165	.05059	.04954	.04851	.04750	.04650
1.3	.04553	.04457	.04363	.04270	.04179	.04090	.04002	.03916	.03831	.03748
1.4	.03667	.03587	.03508	.03431	.03356	.03281	.03208	.03137	.03067	.02998
1.5	.02931	.02865	.02800	.02736	.02674	.02612	.02552	.02494	.02436	.02380
1.6	.02324	.02270	.02217	.02165	.02114	.02064	.02015	.01967	.01920	.01874
1.7	.01829	.01785	.01742	.01699	.01658	.01617	.01578	.01539	.01501	.01464
1.8	.01428	.01392	.01357	.01323	.01290	.01257	.01226	.01195	.01164	.01134
1.9	.01105	.01077	.01049	.01022	$.0^29957$	$.0^29698$	$.0^29445$	$.0^29198$	$.0^28957$	$.0^28721$
2.0	$.0^28491$	$.0^28266$	$.0^28046$	$.0^27832$	$.0^27623$	$.0^27418$	$.0^27219$	$.0^27024$	$.0^26835$	$.0^26649$
2.1	$.0^26468$	$.0^26292$	$.0^26120$	$.0^25952$	$.0^25788$	$.0^25628$	$.0^25472$	$.0^25320$	$.0^25172$	$.0^25028$
2.2	$.0^24887$	$.0^24750$	$.0^24616$	$.0^24486$	$.0^24358$	$.0^24235$	$.0^24114$	$.0^23996$	$.0^23882$	$.0^23770$
2.3	$.0^23662$	$.0^23556$	$.0^23453$	$.0^23352$	$.0^23255$	$.0^23159$	$.0^23067$	$.0^22977$	$.0^22889$	$.0^22804$
2.4	$.0^22720$	$.0^22640$	$.0^22561$	$.0^22484$	$.0^22410$	$.0^22337$	$.0^22267$	$.0^22199$	$.0^22132$	$.0^22067$
2.5	$.0^22004$	$.0^21943$	$.0^21883$	$.0^21826$	$.0^21769$	$.0^21715$	$.0^21662$	$.0^21610$	$.0^21560$	$.0^21511$
2.6	$.0^21464$	$.0^21418$	$.0^21373$	$.0^21330$	$.0^21288$	$.0^21247$	$.0^21207$	$.0^21169$	$.0^21132$	$.0^21095$
2.7	$.0^21060$	$.0^21026$	$.0^39928$	$.0^39607$	$.0^39295$	$.0^38992$	$.0^38699$	$.0^38414$	$.0^38138$	$.0^37870$
2.8	$.0^37611$	$.0^37359$	$.0^37115$	$.0^36879$	$.0^36650$	$.0^36428$	$.0^36213$	$.0^36004$	$.0^35802$	$.0^35606$
2.9	$.0^35417$	$.0^35233$	$.0^35055$	$.0^34883$	$.0^34716$	$.0^34555$	$.0^34398$	$.0^34247$	$.0^34101$	$.0^33959$
3.0	$.0^33822$	$.0^33689$	$.0^33560$	$.0^33436$	$.0^33316$	$.0^33199$	$.0^33087$	$.0^32978$	$.0^32873$	$.0^32771$
3.1	$.0^32673$	$.0^32577$	$.0^32485$	$.0^32396$	$.0^32311$	$.0^32227$	$.0^32147$	$.0^32070$	$.0^31995$	$.0^31922$
3.2	$.0^31852$	$.0^31785$	$.0^31720$	$.0^31657$	$.0^31596$	$.0^31537$	$.0^31480$	$.0^31426$	$.0^31373$	$.0^31322$
3.3	$.0^31273$	$.0^31225$	$.0^31179$	$.0^31135$	$.0^31093$	$.0^31051$	$.0^31012$	$.0^49734$	$.0^49365$	$.0^49009$
3.4	$.0^48666$	$.0^48335$	$.0^48016$	$.0^47709$	$.0^47413$	$.0^47127$	$.0^46852$	$.0^46587$	$.0^46331$	$.0^46085$
3.5	$.0^45848$	$.0^45620$	$.0^45400$	$.0^45188$	$.0^44984$	$.0^44788$	$.0^44599$	$.0^44417$	$.0^44242$	$.0^44073$
3.6	$.0^43911$	$.0^43755$	$.0^43605$	$.0^43460$	$.0^43321$	$.0^43188$	$.0^43059$	$.0^42935$	$.0^42816$	$.0^42702$
3.7	$.0^42592$	$.0^42486$	$.0^42385$	$.0^42287$	$.0^42193$	$.0^42103$	$.0^42016$	$.0^41933$	$.0^41853$	$.0^41776$
3.8	$.0^41702$	$.0^41632$	$.0^41563$	$.0^41498$	$.0^41435$	$.0^41375$	$.0^41317$	$.0^41262$	$.0^41208$	$.0^41157$
3.9	$.0^41108$	$.0^41061$	$.0^41016$	$.0^59723$	$.0^59307$	$.0^58908$	$.0^58525$	$.0^58158$	$.0^57806$	$.0^57469$
4.0	$.0^57145$	$.0^56835$	$.0^56538$	$.0^56253$	$.0^55980$	$.0^55718$	$.0^55468$	$.0^55227$	$.0^54997$	$.0^54777$
4.1	$.0^54566$	$.0^54364$	$.0^54170$	$.0^53985$	$.0^53807$	$.0^53637$	$.0^53475$	$.0^53319$	$.0^53170$	$.0^53027$
4.2	$.0^52891$	$.0^52760$	$.0^52635$	$.0^52516$	$.0^52402$	$.0^52292$	$.0^52188$	$.0^52083$	$.0^51992$	$.0^51901$
4.3	$.0^51814$	$.0^51730$	$.0^51650$	$.0^51574$	$.0^51501$	$.0^{0}1431$	$.0^51365$	$.0^51301$	$.0^51241$	$.0^51183$
4.4	$.0^51127$	$.0^61074$	$.0^51024$	$.0^69756$	$.0^69296$	$.0^68857$	$.0^68437$	$.0^68037$	$.0^67655$	$.0^67290$
4.5	$.0^66942$	$.0^66610$	$.0^66294$	$.0^65992$	$.0^65704$	$.0^65429$	$.0^65167$	$.0^64917$	$.0^64679$	$.0^64452$
4.6	$.0^64236$	$.0^64029$	$.0^63833$	$.0^63645$	$.0^63467$	$.0^63297$	$.0^63135$	$.0^62981$	$.0^62834$	$.0^62694$
4.7	$.0^62560$	$.0^62433$	$.0^62313$	$.0^62197$	$.0^62088$	$.0^61984$	$.0^61884$	$.0^61790$	$.0^61700$	$.0^61615$
4.8	$.0^61533$	$.0^61456$	$.0^61382$	$.0^61312$	$.0^61246$	$.0^61182$	$.0^61122$	$.0^61065$	$.0^61011$	$.0^79588$
4.9	$.0^79096$	$.0^78629$	$.0^78185$	$.0^77763$	$.0^77362$	$.0^76982$	$.0^76620$	$.0^72676$	$.0^75950$	$.0^75640$

Body of table reproduced by permission from Robert Schlaifer, *Introduction to Statistics for Business Decisions*, (New York: McGraw-Hill Book Company, Inc., 1961), pp. 370–71.

Glossary
of Symbols

x = basic random variable or process output

$f(x)$ = probability distribution of x

m = mean of x

v = variance of x

x_i = an observation of x $\quad (i = 1, \ldots, n)$

m_s = a sample mean

$LK(m_s \mid m)$ = likelihood of a sample mean, m_s

$V(m_s)$ = variance of the sample mean

$E(m_s)$ = expected value of the sample mean

$PR(m)$ = prior distribution of m

m_{pr} = prior mean of m

v_{pr} = prior variance of m

c = ratio of the variance of x to the prior variance of m

$PO(m \mid m_s)$ = posterior distribution of m, given a sample mean m_s

m_{po} = posterior mean of m

v_{po} = posterior variance of m

$PR(m_{po})$ = prior distribution of the posterior mean of m

$E(m_{po})$ = prior expected value of the posterior mean of m

$V(m_{po})$ = prior variance of the posterior mean of m

Index